MW00439820

JUST

GET

OUT

THERE

JUST GET OUT THERE

**Achieving Abundance,
Self-Empowerment
and Professional Success
as an Artist Entrepreneur**

By

GILLI MOON

Warrior Girl Music Enterprises
Los Angeles, California
www.warriorgirlmusic.com

JUST GET OUT THERE

Achieving Abundance, Self-Empowerment and Professional Success as an Artist Entrepreneur

Author Gilli Moon

Published by Warrior Girl Music Enterprises
North Hollywood, CA, U.S.A
Wyong, NSW, Australia
e: info@warriorgirlmusic.com
www.warriorgirlmusic.com

Edited by Anders R. Jermstad
Cover design by Gilli Moon
Front picture of Gilli Moon by Jeff Walker

This book is available at quantity discounts for bulk purchases, for information contact the publisher above.
Printed in the United States of America

10 9 8 7 6 5 4 3 2 1
ISBN: 978-0-9579906-1-6
Library of Congress Cataloging-in-Publication Data # TXu 1-655-099

Gilli Moon
    Just Get Out There

File under
Music Business / Music Marketing
/ Music – Vocational Guidance
/ Performing Arts-Business Aspects /
Self-New Age (Self Help)
/ Leadership / Inspiration

To my darling Jeff. Thank you for giving me the courage to stay in tinsel town... and for your hand and heart... 'cause there's no point in doing it alone. To my mum and dad, who have set me off with wings and sails and lofty dreams to be the person I want to be and become.

This book is also dedicated to my Aboriginal friend Percy Duncan, who took flight before his time, and lived his life with paper bark in one hand, a paintbrush in the other, and who had a lot to say: the true Artist.

Though he should conquer a
thousand men in the battlefield a
thousand times, yet he, indeed,
who would conquer himself is the
noblest victor.
- Buddha

What they say...

I commend you for your intention to produce a work that empowers the individual. It's not just anyone who will take the time, invest the creative energy, and actually follow through on the plan for such an endeavor. I hope you take pride in what you have already accomplished... live with passion
- **Anthony J. Robbins**, motivational speaker and author

Word after word, line after line, paragraph after paragraph. Your words regarding the music industry spoke the truth. Your book is the blueprint to this industry. And it goes further. To the essence of one's own life. Every Artist. In fact every human no matter from what walk of life can learn from this.
- **Miles Patrick Yohnke**, 5 Star Productions

So, you wanna be a big rock star? Read *Just Get Out There* by Gilli Moon! *Just Get Out There* shows you, step by step, how to navigate the complexities of a music industry that has undergone an unprecedented revolution brought on by the Internet and the Information Age. Opportunities for the independent artist have never been better and as the "warrior girl", Moon was out there in the trenches as an "Indie" long before that term became popular. But what is far more important is that Gilli Moon teaches us a lesson even more valuable than all the fame and fortune, and that is how to achieve a creative lifetime of happiness and self-fulfillment by learning to define success on your own terms. Just *Get Out There* should be read not only by those yearning for artistic achievement, but by ANYONE who wishes to live life at its fullest potential.
   Anders R. Jermstad, independent editor and musician

Author Gilli Moon gives down-to-earth, hard-news-type advice with no promises of success unless you are willing to get down and dirty. Along with sage advice, however, Moon prefaces her get-tough, get-working advice with all things encouraging.
- **Marilyn Dalrymple**, Antelope Valley Art News, California

i

Gilli's motivational book is based on her life and her growing as a human being, as an Artist, and also as a businesswoman who wants to succeed so that she can give back to others. Her writing is 'emotional soul food' that many times is needed on our bookshelves, so that we can always come back and get the needed energy from every single word that Gilli Moon is offering us from her own experience as an Artist who found her identity and didn't lose it.
- **Suzi Z. Brathwaite**, Musicdish.com

Gilli Moon enlightens us on how to become a well-rounded creative person of many talents who can deal with the nitty gritty of promotion and marketing
- **Vijaya Schartz**, Talk show host of Authors'Secrets Radio

Success according to Gilli Moon is all about desire to go beyond the given and to reach a place of personal fulfillment. This is not only a 'feel good' book about personal affirmation but also about how to succeed in what is often a cut- throat industry.
- **Monica O'Brien**, music publisher, Willow Publishing Ltd, Sydney, Australia

One of the best ways creative people can discover a blueprint for prosperity is to absorb and emulate the strategies of successful Artists. Gilli Moon is one of those Artists. In her book, she bares her soul and shares the attitudes and actions it takes to make a true impact as a professional Artist. Highly recommended! Gilli is an entrepreneurial dynamo: a successful indie musician, performance Artist, actor, visual Artist and author. This compact paperback book reveals lessons, tips and healthy philosophies that anyone going into a creative field needs to hear. Written in a conversational style, the book makes you feel like you're sitting across the table from Gilli in a cafe as she spills her guts about passion, creativity, independence, optimism, opportunity, diversification, promotion, success and more.
- **Bob Baker**, author and indie music marketing expert.

From Artists Gilli has coached:

During our work together, Gilli consistently helped me believe in my dreams while, at the same time, helped me focus on practical steps for realizing those dreams.

Gilli helped me to organize my thoughts, goals and direction, and to find out what my truth was... what was success to me?

Gilli is professional, knowledgeable, passionate and full of blissfully positive energy. She had helped me tremendously with my Artistry and music, how to set goals, how to manage time, how to express creativity through music, and showed me how to be a professional Artist. Gilli is an inspiration and the best coach I've ever met.

Gilli helps you to develop a practical and comprehensive logistical plan to marketing your music. However her real power lies in delving into your attitudes, belief systems and ultimate dreams in life which will ultimately decide the success or failure of your efforts. While I am often overwhelmed by the obstacles of this business, each coaching session with Gilli renews my positive attitude and empowers me to continue to move forward. Gilli makes it possible for me to find my sense of purpose again and feel the joy in the process of making and marketing my music.

Gilli is the consummate Artist's coach. An Artist herself, she understands the creative life and what it takes. But more than just an Artist, Gilli is skilled at coaching other Artists to help realize their vision. Gilli's sessions are tailored to what you want to accomplish, and she has developed tools that help you focus and keep you on track while recognizing your accomplishments. Working with Gilli over the course of six months I created a solid plan for releasing an EP of my songs, and I started performing again, after a two-year hiatus.

Gilli helped me to define my goals and showed me how to develop them to devise a business plan that enabled me to start down the road to making my goals and dreams a 'do-able' reality. When you have a mentoring session with Gilli, you feel positive, motivated and empowered. You want to put your plan into action and feel proud to take responsibility for all work that you do to put it into motion and keep it going.

I needed something, or someone that could help me build my vision, carve out my path, and set forth in achieving my goals and dreams in a clear and directed way. Gilli is that person.

More at www.Artistdevelopmentcoach.com

"I AM A Professional Artist
– the Key to Survival and Success in the World of the Arts"

Gilli Moon's first book offers Artists who've chosen the professional path, practical steps in harnessing one's creative abilities to succeed and survive in the Arts *and* enjoy your Artistry at the same time. For Artists of all genres, this book will certainly change the thinking of any professional Artist who may doubt themselves or their Art, who may feel pressured by the industry, or may feel the hardship of the roller coaster ride. Read it as an accompaniment to JUST GET OUT THERE.

Readers of Gilli's first book say...

I just finished reading your book *I Am a Professional Artist* and I absolutely loved it! A lot of what you wrote really struck a chord with me, and I was actually going through a 2-week Anthony Robbins program at the same time, so it was a great combination

Gilli's book helped me define my goals and what success and dreams and visions mean to me as well as Art and business. I love and enjoy making mine and others dreams come true! An encourager of faith and dreams is what I will continue to strive for! Dream the IMPOSSIBLE!

You have a wonderful and inspiring message peppered with little gems throughout, and it was a pleasure to read! I am definitely inspired

This couldn't have come at a better time in my creative growth. I'm experiencing some serious writer's block and your generosity of spirit is truly appreciated.

Excellent book! I read this book from cover to cover the day it arrived. It is very informative and motivational. Gilli Moon is an excellent example to follow when it comes to being an independent Artist. I would highly recommend this book to anyone interested in a professional career in the Arts.

** ORDER IT ONLINE at www.gillimoon.com/thebook

Contents

Music, on the air's edge, rides alone,
Plumed like empastured Caesars of the sky
With a god's helmet; now, in the gold dye
Of sunlight, the iron cloak, the Tuscan stone,
Melt to enchanted flesh – a voice is blown
Down from the windy pit, like a star falling.
Men think it is a lost eagle calling,
But the fool and the lover know it for Music's cry.

He is running with the Valkyrs on a road of manes,
Darkness draws back its fur, the stars course by,
Fighting the wind beaks of hurricanes
To keep their stations in the sky –
Away, away! The little earth-light wanes,
The moon has drowned herself, cold music rings,
The battering of a thousand horsemen fly
Belly to air, away! Now Music sings
Harshly, like horns of Tartars blown on high.

- Kenneth Slessor

 Act

Risk! Risk Anything!
Care no more
for the opinions
of others,
for those voices.
Do the hardest
thing on earth for you.
Act for yourself.
- *Katherine Mansfield*

PART 1: THE INNER WARRIOR

Getting real with who you are and what you want

The ultimate ingredient of an Artist, and a professional Artist.. is Passion. This is your fire and you should never deny it because your passion is the way to self realization.

1. The lessons I've learned

1. Learn from others, work with others, but "own" your Art.
Don't give yourself or your Art away.

2. Before you put your Art out there, ask yourself "why?"

Know why you want to exhibit, perform, broadcast, publish...expose.

3. Create a plan. Take one step at a time. Be careful not to do step 5 before you have even conquered step 1.

4. Don't fear anything. Be courageous. Opportunity is yours for the taking if you really want it.

5. If people tell you that you need them, count to ten and walk away. You need yourself most of all.

6. Being a professional Artist is not about the race to the end but the process of living it. Remember that for, in the end, it's the creative process and your creative way of life as you've chosen it that will give you more satisfaction than any award, number one hit or box office winner.

7. Be creative with a business sense

8. Learn my three Os:
Optimism
+ Organized
= Opportunity

9. Be passionate about what you do.

Just getting out there means
being able to take a risk
even if the way isn't always clear
because it becomes less foggy as
you move forward.
It also means going within,
finding who you are,
what you want
...and what inspires you:
in order to
LIVE YOUR DREAM.
- gilli moon

2. Let's get started

I have come to realize that we, as human beings, want two things: love, and a purpose. We want to know that we are loved and that our love will be received, and that we have some kind of path for us in this world; some kind of purpose or plan. We want to know where we are going and even better, how to get there.

Artists are divinely creative and unique human beings. We have the innate ability to be the eye to our souls, and shine a light on the deepest secrets we often keep to ourselves, illuminating them so we can grow, and be better human beings, hopefully, for ourselves and to those around us. Artists are like voyeurs, with a gift to see into the souls of our common human experiences and deliver to us, through their Art, a reflection on a silver platter. We hear our own heart ache through songwriters' songs; we see our pain on the canvas, and we feel our joy through the dancer's flight.

But although Artists have this gift, and so much more, many don't see this ability to value themselves as professionals, who provide a service to humanity. Instead, they can feel worthless, disempowered, financially stricken, and powerless and in a 'struggle'. In conjunction, they often think that someone else is supposed to come along and give them the "ticket to ride", so to speak; that someone else has the power to decide if their Art/music is worthy of the world, and they wait for someone else to put value on their talent. Since no one has told them how to "get there", they just sit in struggle, waiting.

Or, if they aren't waiting for someone else to validate them, then they may just not know the "way" to get there. Artists like direction. They want some kind of *plan* that shows them the steps. If they don't have it, they often don't move forward. So this causes many Artists to stay in limbo,... waiting. Let's consider the early pioneers of America, or even the settlers of Australia (two countries I know a lot about, being a dual citizen of both nations). These people came to a harsh land, and knew nothing about where to settle, what to do, or how to do it. In fact many had never built a house or farmed before, having grown up in the industrial city of London, or various European cities. They just HAD to survive in the new land, and so they just made a go of it. They went through many hardships, sickness, disease, weather, and sometimes wars and disharmony. But they just stuck it through and put one foot after the other, to finally make a home for themselves in a strange land.

They took a leap of faith because they wanted so badly to have the freedom and new opportunities that the country could provide them.

What would happen if you just took a leap of faith in your Artistry, and just got out there anyway (even if you don't know every step to take)? Are you ready to take risks in order to achieve your dreams? Are you ready to build a plan for yourself that at least allows you to START?

In the world as we know it, success comes from the ability to take risks. In the Arts business (music, entertainment, films, Art, etc.), to risk is as common as breathing. It's a business that encourages innovation, thinking outside the box, and just being brave. Successful risk-taking comes from just taking the step, whether you feel ready or not. By just getting out there, you are taking one step towards realizing your dreams. Eventually, confidence will catch up to your actions, *but to act is the important step.*

I see life as a choice. I can either choose to wait, or choose to do. In so doing, we could be faced with what can seem a torrent of obstacles, hurdles, criticism and lack of opportunities.

So will this stop you?

In this day and age, Artists need to be business savvy, and self-driven. I write about this in my books and speak about it to Artists in my workshops and seminars. What's crucial to know is that you can do many things on your own as an Artist, without thinking someone else has to be the one to come along and make it happen for you (make you famous). **Fame is an illusion** in this new world. It's created, *bought* and lasts for moments.

What you want to focus on is **being a consummate Artist** *your whole life* and that takes diligence, **integrity**, *talent*, perseverance and a **go get 'em** mentality.

Fame is an illusion in this new world. It's created, bought and lasts for moments.

But we can't do it all alone. It's important to have people you trust around you that you can share your ideas, get some advice and who can help you plan your attack. Surround yourself with encouraging, positive people who support your desires, and let go of those who want to deflate you.

Some Artists look for managers to be that special person. Some managers work with celebrity Artists and don't have much time to also develop an unknown. Other managers are too green around the ears to really offer you real advice and opportunities, even if they are enthusiastic.

I believe in **being the warrior** *in life*, and for me that means being my own Artist **entrepreneur** and being in charge of my own **destiny**; pursuing creative freedom, and at the same time being very disciplined and diligent in my pursuit of excellence in everything I do. I will detail more about my *warrior*-ship later in this book.

I've combined all my teachings and coachings into this book so you can basically coach yourself to greatness. You have an invisible coach working with you, through this book, guiding you, asking you questions, giving you exercises, and making you think and act the way a strong, business savvy Artist should, leading you to the Artist you ultimately want to become.

But let it be said that there is no replacement for the real thing: someone who acts as your advisor, mirror or confidante, and who keeps you accountable for the actions you set out to accomplish; someone who lets you dream as big as you want, and make you feel safe in the journey of the big wide world of the business of the Arts. You may call that person a manager, or an agent, or your best friend. For several years, entwined through my own Artistic journey and self-discovery, I have been coaching Artists on their journeys. They come to me for advice, consultancy and development. I don't know what prompted other Artists to seek counsel in me, for I set myself up to be an Artist and not a teacher. But after too many cups of coffee, and lunches dishing out free advice to Artists who always wanted to know my secret ingredient to how I got to where I am (wherever that is!), I turned it into a coaching business where we both win. Besides, there is something really exciting about sharing your secrets. I believe that if you give to others, you receive so much. Call it Karma, or just plain cross-sharing fun, I certainly enjoy helping other Artists as well as helping myself. There is no greater satisfaction than sharing achievement, especially when the path can be so lonely otherwise.

I find that coaches are a really great support for Artists, while allowing the Artist to be in control of their own destiny.

Of course, at any time you want the real thing, contact me to set up a real live, in person or by phone session. Go to www.Artistdevelopmentcoach.com to check out more about these sessions.

When I set out to write this book three years previously, my main intention was to offer practical tips and resources about getting out there, including marketing, promotion, touring, the Internet, and many other aspects. While I have definitely delved into all these arenas, I realized, after building the coaching arm of my company, that what Artists really needed was *inspiration,* a sense of *hope* and *assurance* that they were on the right path. It didn't matter so much that they *had* reached all their goals, but that they were also, and importantly, *enjoying the journey* to get there, with enough information about the stepping stones to hop along. And so, my book took an inward turn, which indeed my own head was going anyway, and I began to write many chapters and online blogs (which I have printed within this book) that ***inspire Artists along their Artistic journey, that allow Artists to become masters of their own destiny and provide ways to pursue their dreams with full integrity.***

Part of my journey is writing about my life, and what I know, and sharing it with others. Whilst I cannot give anyone the short cut to what's at the end of the yellow brick road (because each of our pots of gold are all different), I can talk about the **yellow** in

It's the road itself that is the most exciting, revealing and empowering

the road. It's the road itself that is the most exciting, revealing and empowering.

I also want to say that all of my writings are based on my own experiences as an Artist. I am a singer-songwriter, recording Artist and music producer, and I have done pretty much everything there can be done as an indie (independent Artist) in the music business. I set up my own record label, Warrior Girl Music, over 9 years ago and have toured the world performing my songs, and recording 6 albums. So I know what it means to take risks, and to have to think outside the box to get a look-in at radio play or any type of opportunity. This book combines my experiences, understandings and lessons I've learned about *getting out there* as an Artist. It includes excerpts from my online blogs capturing many road tours and Artistic memories, as well as motivational messages and tips for Artists. **At the end of most chapters are exercises** on how you can coach yourself to Artistic greatness, which is particularly useful as it will help you summarize everything you've learned along the way, and inspire you to enact your dreams.

My purpose is to tangibly embrace many thoughts and inspirations I have written in my travels, as well as new ones, and combine them in this book, to educate, nourish and inspire any musician, singer-songwriter or indeed ANY ARTIST who has chosen creativity as their professional passion. Though since I know the music business the most, this is the business I illustrate the most in this book. However, all Artists across all genres and disciplines can benefit from the readings and inspirations.

For the music Artists, there are practical chapters for you on how to get out there, just like you would imagine: promotional ideas, where to tour, how to deal with venues, how to work on your image; loads of tips and tools that compliment **my first book** *I AM A Professional Artist – the Key to Survival and Success in The World of the Arts.* I encourage you to grab a copy of that book as a companion guide to this one as I will refer to it a lot and don't wish to repeat a lot of the good juice in that one. For the context of this new book, I will refer to my first book, *I AM A Professional Artist* as **"my first book"** throughout these upcoming pages.

I also include, in the writing of this book, many personal stories and anecdotes, including some childhood memories, so you can see how I arrived at where I am today.

There will also be some quotes and lyrics, and tour blog excerpts (stories of my touring and travels) that build the tapestry of the chapters. Some of these blogs come with readers' feedback which they would e-mail me when I posted a new blog online.

Ultimately, this is easy to read for your bedside table or coffee table filled with hearty (from the heart) advice.

This book is not only spiritual nourishment, but a practical guide on the dos and don'ts of the entertainment business. This is no ordinary handbook and it's not a text book. I can only write from a personal place – autobiographical and real experiences.

Let's get started

I believe that my book, the outward and inward journey, is a reflection of where we are at in the entertainment business and where Artists MUST go in order to achieve their success. We live in a new era of independence when it comes to doing business as Artists, and we cannot afford to place our dreams in someone else's hands anymore. So, knowing everything about yourself, is EVERYTHING to being successful.

This book is about my journey, which hopefully will inspire your *journey*. It is a handbook, a guide, a blog, a reality check, a heartfelt song spilled onto 300 pages which I hope motivates you to live your *dream*, find the *inspiration within*, and just get out there.

I hope you enjoy the ride as you take control of your dreams and turn them into reality.

gilli moon

It's not how you
achieve your dreams, it's how you live your
life. If you live your life the right way, the karma
will take care of itself. The dreams will come to
you.

– Randy Pausch

3. Finding the joy in the journey

Inspiration

I see humanity in a conundrum. Many of us are living split lives. We compartmentalize our passions and enjoyments in one area, and our work and responsibilities in another. We go to work, come home, and become new people with our families, and then we go off to work and become something else, for better or for worse. We work hard, because we think we have to, and we live for the weekends. This is the conundrum of the Western world. Our work life has become the most important aspect of ourselves, and only somewhat enjoy, yet we look forward to that time off, where we truly live, and be happy. So we sit in limbo, working hard, waiting to go home to be happy, and then when we are home, we think we should be working, to be happy and successful. It's also a conundrum that many creative Artists face because, for starters, they are encouraged, from an early age, not to be Artists, but to get a real job and work. So they feel like they are never able to truly just follow their path as Artists, with a sense of guilt that they should be doing a real job. And those in real jobs, often fantasize about not having to have a real job, and to go off and be Artists, or some philanthropic activity.

Why are we splitting ourselves? Surely, if we pursue a passion, whatever that is, from the start, we would enjoy the journey every day, whether we are "working" or playing".

But many people are still searching for their passion. They sit in limbo at a desk job wondering what their passion is and not quite reaching that place of perfect joy because they think it's somewhere out there in the ether, unattainable to them. **They live in the mundane.**

I have always seen my working life as play. It's a hard concept to wrap one's head around, but basically, I will only accept projects and activities that inspire me. If it doesn't inspire me, I will not be happy. Inspiration is everything. If I have to do something that does not exactly follow my passion, I take on the perspective that it is a means by which to gain a greater goal and I see it as a short term thing. Everything is a journey, to take me to a new place. If we are inspired by a purpose, to do the things we do, no matter what they are, then we can enjoy the journey, no matter what we have to do to fulfill our purpose.

I am an Artist, an expressionist of many creative forms, focused, enthusiastic, abundant, confident and happy. I live my life on a day to day basis, enjoying my journey, with a strong ambition and a deep well of passion. I can do this because I see everything that I do as part of my higher purpose.

It has taken me decades to come to this realization. I wasn't always like this. I came from a world of naïve adolescence and just a big dream to "make it" as an Artist, without any sense of how, what, or who I would become. But with the modicum of self-created successes, the adventures I've had and the journey I have taken, I am not a victim of the commercial world's definitions of success, but rather, an Artist on **a very personal, creative journey** in this world.

> If we are inspired by a purpose, then we can enjoy the journey, no matter what we have to do to fulfill our purpose.

The journey of doing it

My Artistry is focused on writing songs, recording music, touring the world performing, writing and creating interesting concepts and projects. When I was younger, I wanted to be a rock n' roll star, and a famous actor. Who knows, it may happen, or maybe I am already that. **It's all about *perspective*.** I have many people come up to me and go, *"gosh Gilli, I've heard so much about you and your accomplishments"*, and then I think, well, maybe I am making a difference... I have toured the United States 4 times over, plus Canada, Europe and Australia. I have released 6 albums, produced other Artists' albums, set up my own record label and I am president of the largest international non-profit songwriters' organization (Songsalive!) with chapters worldwide. I have produced festivals (the Los Angeles Women's Music Festival) and music conferences (The Songsalive! Expo), toured with famous Artists including Eric Idle of Monty Python fame, written a previous book to this one, and get invited to speak at many music conferences about the state of the music industry and how to get out there as an independent Artist. I have a list of music awards, credits and reviews from the world's critics including a write up in Newsweek Magazine. My music gets played on the radio, in TV shows and films, and my videos have not just graced YouTube, but MTV and VH1. I have been on every online music site since the beginning of the Internet, starting with mp3.com (when it used to pay for downloads), leading up to now with all the MySpace, Facebook, Twitter and other sites. I was there first in all of them, in their previous online social network/internet site reincarnations.

I've been so *out* there, that my middle name is Gilli "Just Get Out There" Moon. When someone wants to know about getting out there, they turn to me. I've been there, done that. I've played the game, and I've won it. I know what it is to be a successful independent music Artist.

So what's next? Is that it? Is this what I'm supposed to be? What more is there for me to do?

There is something about having "done it all", now, which makes me think about something quite profound. Perhaps, having done it all, and seemingly knowing it all, **I may know very *little*.** And what does "done it all" mean anyway? Is it my opinion or others'? Maybe I've done very little with regards to what I really want.

All of my life's work to date did not happen overnight. It has been two decades of rollercoaster rides and challenging experiences to become the road warrior that I am. What I have learned the most is that **while I waited** for some kind of transformation or manifestation on the outside (***tokens of success*** that include number one hits, industry recognition, awards or great reviews), of which I have worked so hard for, I noticed that SO MUCH MORE happened **inside**, and that was way more empowering than commercial recognition.

I began to realize that much of my "getting out there" as an Artist depended on my internal joy, inspiration, strength and growth. The more I focused on what was going on inside, the STRONGER the outside became, and still continues to become ('cause it ain't over yet!)

I came to realize that none of it: the accolades, the websites, the albums, the tours, the released products, the reviews, MEANS ANYTHING. It's all just "stuff". The *lesson*, is that EVERYTHING is about the **journey of DOING it**, not the end result. The process of creating, learning, adventuring, relationship building, working, playing, reading, living….. *is* the joy.

I learned this because I found out that **even after all the accolades, reviews, and "status" that I attained, it doesn't make one difference to my personal joy.** Only my inner state of mind will influence my joy. Only I can create and control my joy barometers. NOTHING else. So, I could be picking fruit in the Himalayas, or cruising the Mediterranean, or working at a bank, or performing at Madison Square Garden, and it makes not one iota if I don't create my own joy,… which comes from feeling INSPIRED.

To be inspired, I must be doing "it" – I can't stagnate, I need to be moving, constantly. This is what I term "Just Get Out There" – the act of doing, of being out in the world. **Following your dream and travelling life's road IS the INSPIRING part, which in turn CREATES JOY.** Without the ***doing*** part, I would feel frustrated. This is the state of many young Artists because they don't think they have the *confidence* or resources or people to help them get out there. So they stay stuck in a mindset that everything will happen in the future, and meanwhile, they are not happy with their current life.

Being inspired, dreaming big, and enjoying the journey: now that's a good *start*.

Just Get Out There,
just do it!

"Inch by inch,
anything is a cinch"
- Robert Schuller

4. The master your own destiny

It's all business... or is it?

Not a day goes by when I don't get an e-mail, a phone call or a question in person by an Artist asking me what the secret to success in the music business is. I scratch my head most of the time wondering how to give them the answer they are looking for. Actually, I wonder first, why are they asking *me*?

In my first book, I was pretty obvious with my take on the definition of "success" – that is, reaching success in this new paradigm is not necessarily about "commercial" success, or any notions of fame and fortune and what you read in glossy magazines. Rather it is a personal definition that you make, like your own personal contract with yourself, that includes what makes you happy, what provides you a sense of accomplishment, and about enjoying the journey – and NOT so much about those tokens of commercial success like fame, fortune, Grammy awards and number one hits (though if they come, that's cool, but they are fleeting in the bigger picture of life). Also, if you never achieve those, you may think you've failed, and I don't believe in the word 'failure'. I believe in life, in living, in enjoying the journey, and that means that every travail, every adventure, every learning curve, and every feat whether small or large, is success in and of itself.

I have a secret to tell you, but before I tell you my little secret I want to start out by saying that defining your notions of success – what you want to achieve – is very, very important, and has to be the first thing you do before embarking on your wonderful journey. Why so? Because if you don't know what you want, and how far you want to go with it, you will just end up in a fog of never achieving what you want, and never being satisfied with what you actually get.

Too many Artists set their sights on ambitions filled with high expectations and dreams that riddle them with fears and anxieties in trying to attain them, simply because they are way too unrealistic. What we read in glossy magazines doesn't necessarily add up to a life fulfilled, nor a successful career. The glamour of fame is simply that, just glamour. The hard work is never truly noticed when you see a music video on MTV (or all your hard work in the music studio squashed into a compressed mp3) - and the realities of *what Artists have to do to get heard are never truly understood by the common fan and listener*. What that means for Artists trying to "make it" in the biz is that they are expected to live up to that kind of glamorous world to be approved by their fans, friends and family, who only see the illusion (this final end result). But REALLY what should be appreciated is ALL THE HARD WORK ARTISTS DO TO GET THERE.

What really happens is that a very small handful of Artists actually get to be on the Top 40 radio, get their videos played on TV, or more to the point, get a major record deal. What is even more enlightening is that most record deals are created around an inner circle of producers, A&R executives, publishers and media who actually "create" the career of the Artist. Talent helps, but it doesn't guarantee success.

If an Artist does, by random chance, land a major record deal that is worth any salt (and quite frankly they are few and far between these days), it is about becoming majorly famous, not majorly wealthy, and even "fame" is a misconception at most times. In the U.S alone you have to sell $500,000 CDs to go Gold. (Let alone now that CDs just don't sell like they used to, as the Internet has shifted the value of music.) Some of the most famous Artists that we all listen to and love on the radio are still in debt to their label, have not recouped the amazing amount of expenses their label has expended, and in the end are STILL not happy. **A record deal does NOT guarantee happiness** and certainly doesn't give you complete creative freedom. But does a typical fan really know all that?

I grew up in my teens wanting a major record deal. That was my dream. I thought, if I get a deal, then everything will be sweet. I would be "discovered", developed, recorded, promoted and voila,... fame. Mostly, I wanted someone else to "make it happen for me", to give me the opportunity where I could record all my songs and get them out to the big wide world. I thought having someone else with all the money and opportunities in the world would be the ticket for me to have the same, as well as creative freedom. I just wanted to write, record and perform all day long, every day of my life, and let someone else take care of the rest.

Well guess what... I learned soon enough that the reality of the music business was that the business people didn't give a rat's a...s about nurturing the Artist's creative freedom and their craft. **The music business is about business** – money and advertising, and fashion (yeah, I sometimes say it's a "fashion" business). It's not so much about ART. In fact, in the experiences I've had with labels and knowing Artists signed to labels, it's not much about freedom either.

The entertainment business is tough! You need money, lots of it, to compete with that "inner circle" of labels, execs, media, film and major opportunities. You will discover a lot of people will try to zap your energy; there are incredible hurdles to climb; you'll face a lot of criticism, even when you think you're doing the right thing; you'll face a lot of ignorant people who have no clue as to what it really takes to get things done; you'll discover that opportunity is limited and prejudiced; and the worst bit is we will be our own worst enemies with our own negative thoughts (what I call Torments of the Mind).

So, if you think about how rough it can be, it can thwart any Artist to start, right? **Wrong!**

So here's my little secret: Look within to the well-spring of what you know and who you know – *dream big* – put out what you want – AND GO FOR IT. **JUST DO IT**. Don't wait around for someone else, the label or anybody. This is your life and your journey. **Just Get Out There**, little steps, large steps, any step. You may not know how to get there, but the road will reveal itself as you start taking the steps. The rest will follow.

Self-empowerment

Discovering you **are already the creative, magical, prolific, talented and successful Artist that you are**, opens up the largest of doors. This is very much an inward empowerment. "Know" it, "feel" it, "be" it, and it will be realized on the outside.

Listen again: the music business, any Arts business, is about... business. So much of it has nothing to do with the Art of music, songwriting or performing. It's about making money and most people who are "in control" of the industry have no idea about creativity. DON'T BE FRIGHTENED. DON'T GET FREAKED OUT. It's time for change – it's time to revolutionize the music business. WELCOME TO THE RENAISSANCE OF THE NEW MILLENNIUM.

> You may not know how to get there, but the road will reveal itself as you start taking the steps

So many independent Artists are now starting to achieve success because they are standing up to the old, tired 'norm' and creating their own niche markets. They are paving their own roads because they have become SELF-EMPOWERED.

The music business is a *business business business*. It can be tough, and you need money. A lot of money. (I'll talk more later on how to get it!) *If* you want to survive and succeed in the music industry, the first thing to realize is that you have to be two people: An Artist, and a Business person. I coined the phrase:

The three Os:
Optimism + *Organized*
= Opportunity

I wrote a whole chapter about this in my first book. You need to be organized, and you need to be optimistic. You also need: **Drive**,

Commitment, **Focus**, Energy and above all: PQSSioN.

Seek no one else's approval

Success needs to be defined on your own terms, and not by what others think are notions of success. It's a daily journey of creating and realizing. Everything about true success is about enjoying the process, and not so dependent on the end result.

Are you an end result type Artist or a process Artist? Do you equate success as an Artist by making a living from it, receiving an award, or, completing projects off your to-do list?

Who are you an Artist for?

Being an Artist is not for others, it's for you. If you are looking for validation to be an Artist, I wouldn't be surprised if you feel stuck creating. Needing to seek others' approval to feel successful is a myth and can lead to unhappiness. But if you create for yourself, and you enjoy the process of creating (the journey, the moment), you will find greater satisfaction, and a fluid stream of creative

consciousness, time and freedom to do it. Live by your own rules!

True happiness happens without you pushing hard, without you knocking on doors, or getting tired. It happens when you focus on your Artistry, believe in yourself, keep inspired, and be business savvy. Making each step forward is all it takes.

Remember my saying:
Seek no one else's approval but your own.

Along the way, you'll have a lot of people telling you what you should do or shouldn't do. Sometimes it's good to listen to advice, counsel and gain feedback. But at the end of the day, YOU are the one to make the decision as to what is right for you.

Exercise: What is your Artistic purpose?

Write down five (5) reasons why you are an Artist.

Ask yourself, is it for you, or for someone else? Is your success as an Artist defined by **outer** commercial definitions (tokens, awards, financial, some kind of recognition), or **inner**, personal definitions (excellence, joy, creative freedom, etc.).

Think about it long and hard, and spend a good page writing the answer to this question.

1.

2.

3.

4.

5.

WHEN YOU STOP DREAMING YOU STOP LIVING

If you want to enlarge your life, you must first enlarge your thought of it and yourself.

Hold the image of yourself as you long to be, the image of what you long to attain, the image of health, efficiency and success. You can lift yourself by your thoughts. Your vision will help you surmount the highest obstacles.

High achievement always takes place in the framework of high expectation. What you see is what you get.

You'll become as small as your controlling desire, or as great as your dominant aspiration.

The courage to follow your dreams is your first step toward destiny.

You can live your dreams.

©by Max Steingart

5. My story: letting go of the past

I am writing this chapter from my parents' property in Australia where I spent most of my childhood. I remember that most of my childhood was spent dreaming. Dreaming that one day I would be able to do whatever I wanted to do in life, achieve many goals and aspire to some kind of greatness. My childhood dreaming lasted 'till I was thirty years old. I don't think I truly began to realize my dreams until then. One of the reasons is because I spent most of my focus on some future destination, rather than living in the moment and taking hold of the opportunities that were around me. I was always thinking ahead, never satisfied with the present, or with who or what was in my hands at that time. For starters, I didn't think I was old enough or wise enough to know what to do. I didn't have the confidence to listen to my own ideas, and everything seemed to happen too slowly. I couldn't see any results, because I wasn't out there pursuing it. I was just dreaming it. I have always been ambitious, and my notions of success were based on other people's ideas of what that meant, for example, success to me at that time was getting a number one radio hit, or a best selling CD or being famous on television. I equated success to such things, and therefore felt that I was not successful because I didn't have those things yet.

Being confident that I am, I never questioned that it wouldn't come in some time. I just wasn't truly appreciating who I was or what I had done, in *that* current moment. I also lived in a state of scarcity, where I didn't feel like I had enough to be who I wanted to be. So I felt like I constantly lived in a stalemate, which caused frustration and inner turmoil. My inner state of consciousness was not happy. I lived too much in the future and just didn't appreciate where I was. I also didn't believe in myself. I thought I did, but now I realize that I really didn't. I was always in awe of others who had done well with their careers, and I kept on dreaming that my time would come one day in the future.

Perhaps, by reading thus far, you have felt similar things in your life?

In this trip down-under, I became fully aware that my thirty year childhood was like this. When I hit thirty, I had a massive wakeup call which made me think that life wasn't endless and that I better do something about pursuing my dreams. It came from getting sick and having to go to hospital for a while. My health all of a sudden became my utmost priority and I realized that life was fleeting. This "call" allowed me the opportunity to *wake* up and get on with it. For now, let me be a little nostalgic and invite you into my childhood, the way I reflected on it today.

Writing this chapter, I am staying with Mum and Dad in the main house which is gracefully situated on top of a rugged mountain overlooking acres of forest. But when I lived full time in Australia 10 years ago, I lived on my own in a cabin they built up behind the main house. This cabin is a symbol of my early twenties, my major growing up era, and the time when I dreamed of being the Artist I am today. I decided to go visit it.

The old cabin on top of the hill was unlocked. I gently wrestled with the latch, slightly rusted up, to open the door. It finally gave. I had forgotten how small the place was. It was almost empty. No one had lived in it for some time. But it seemed clean. Still furnished with minimal furniture, I walked past the desk, the open planned kitchen, past the wood burning pot belly fireplace, down into the second level bedroom area. It overlooked a magnificent view of the rugged bush.

My abstract painting of the ocean, which I painted with acrylics on canvas, was still on the wall. I loved that painting, filled with deep blues and flowing lines. It's a melancholy painting, with much emotion. My kitchen pots, plates and cups were still on the wooden shelves. My presence was still here, barely. But I felt my past here strongly. It brought tears to my eyes. I became emotional. This simple, rustic, small cabin represented a deep part of my past. A decade or more from my teens to my mid twenties of struggle, frustration, unrealized desires. I remember living in this cabin with everything that I owned, up here on the mountain, deep in the forest, far from civilization, with a dream for a glamorous life that I yearned for so much, away from here.

I can't imagine any other person having experienced their thirty year long childhood like I did. Rather unique really. At this moment, looking around the little cabin, I soak in the good and the bad. Right now I feel the isolation, the ruggedness of how it was living in this place, on this mountain. The Aussie bush is not beautiful per se. Majestic to a certain extent. *Awe*-some in appearance, but it represents a harshness fit for only the strongest. I grew up without modern conveniences, microwave ovens, hair dryers or dish washers. Water was hard to come by. Life was lived a day at a time, thinking about food, shelter, warmth. This was my childhood. Safe, great, loving, but isolated and surrounded by the depths of the forest.

I realize now that I had some repressed feelings about my youth. It wasn't an easy upbringing, out here in the bush. We did it hard. We came here from the city when I was fourteen, to nothing but an old dam and unruly terrain. My parents built the main house out of second hand off-cuts, wood from the forest and rocks. We lived on solar power and caught water in rainwater tanks. We never had a new car or new clothes—always second hand. I caught a school bus every day that took half an hour, mostly on a dirt road, to drive to the bus stop and another hour to get to school. It was a long day for me, every day, which started at 6.30am and I arrived home at 6pm. Homework was done only by candle light and 12 volt solar powered lights. Left over food in the pantry was attractive to field mice, and if they didn't get it, the heat did.

No wonder I went on to live my twenties in scarcity. Everything in my teens was based around saving and protecting every little morsel we had, from food, to clothes, to money.

But I know I had fortunate life. I had, and still have, loving and nurturing parents, and the place which we built to live in was really magical and beautiful. It really was! We were surrounded by the beauty of the Australian bushland, untouched and ours. This was our piece of heaven. I am also VERY lucky to have experienced such a magical childhood on the mountain.

At eighteen, I traveled a bit and then moved to Sydney to study. But I kept coming back to the property. It's when I was about 24 that I actually moved "back home" and into this little cabin Mum and Dad had built somewhere along the line. They were always building something. Still are!

In this cabin I began to dream big. This is where I'd write songs and record them on my four track'till 3 in the morning, singing freely at the top of my lungs because no one could hear me for miles. This is where I painted some of my best paintings. This is where I planned my music career, where I wrote the concept for Songsalive!, the songwriters organization that has crossed 4 continents now. This is where I came back and wrote my first book when I turned 30 (that magic number). I have always kept coming back to this cabin. I'm here now too. There is something about this ol' cabin that meant everything to my soul. I created who I am in this cabin. I've since gone on and achieved so many dreams, traveled the earth, become somewhat stable and.... abundant.

I didn't feel so abundant ten-fifteen years ago. On some nights I remember feeling alone in this place, in the harshness of winter, without a light and no inside bathroom. I'd grab a bucket for my night loo and toss it on my roses in the morning. I didn't want to go outside in the dead of night, up here on the hill, alone. I would huddle under the covers and imagine there weren't any spiders or ants. I would always feel a grub or two under my sheets at night. I'd try and read under the candle light, but the moths would be fluttering around, competing with me for the light. However, that didn't stop me reading lots of books. I read all the Agatha Christie books and any espionage book I could find. My clothes tried to stay fresh in the old cupboards but there was always a woody smell to them. Things got dusty quickly. I never wore white. I didn't have an iron. I spent a lot of time on my own. I was an only child.

I remember being naïve, yet ambitious. I remember how simple the life was. It was all about making sure there was enough water, or firewood for the night. I remember feeling like "one day" my Artistic dreams would be fulfilled. I remember only living for the future. I had no idea how I would get there, but I remember being imaginative and creative, and thinking big, and having large dreams. I remember feeling like I could do anything I wanted in my life,... tomorrow. I was a quietly frustrated Artist, with big dreams, and no idea how to fulfill them.

I always had a car that broke down on the highway. I could never afford a good car. The roads leading to our place were dirt, and full of pot holes. One time, my first car, a second hand 1972 Ford Escort, caught fire from a leaky petrol lead on the highway. It burned to a crisp as I stood watching it, with all my possessions from college inside. The melted steering wheel is hanging on the outside of the cabin, a sculpture reminding me of what I have overcome.

Today, I stand in the middle of the cabin feeling my past. My eyes are teary again, feeling the anguish, yet also the beauty of my past here—such a dichotomy (a symbol of life really). I gained my inner strength here. I loved my childhood, don't get me wrong. At the time, I knew nothing else. To this day, coming here is also like coming to paradise. What I realized, though, is that as a teenager, and even in my early twenties, I felt an inner isolation, and the bush didn't help. But then, I could have felt the same growing up in the city. I was who I was. I cannot say my environment made me who I am, but then, I cannot ignore its influence.

The biggest influence would be that it taught me how to

Be self-empowered and be strong

Be able to overcome obstacles of any nature

Be able to find resources and create something from scratch – a true testament to the house my parents still live in today on the mountain.

I feel like I am a late bloomer. While other twenty year olds were out clubbing, I was up here dreaming of large stages and dancing in imaginary dance halls, in the middle of the night, to myself. It took so long for me to leave this mountain and grow up. Coming back is like a culture shock, but then... it's like I never left. I've taken the country girl, the survivor, out into the world. I've used my tenacity and strength to climb any hurdle. If you can survive the bush, you can survive anywhere.

All of a sudden I felt amazingly strong, standing in this room I once called home. I felt connected with the old green carpet and the spider webs in the corners of the wooden poles. Every inch of me was part of this place, even if I wasn't living in it anymore.

I noticed the plants were thriving outside the kitchen window sill. My roses were still alive and breathing on their own. I noticed that the termites hadn't eaten the wood in the walls. This place was a survivor of its environment, just like me.

I know now that time stands still. There is no time, past, present, future. I am who I am at 16, 26 and 36. I embody the same will and strength now that I had back then. I am my parents' daughter. I am part of this place, no matter where I roam.

I know that ever since I can remember, I had a dream. This was the first step. When I had the chance, I went off and pursued my dream, and this pursuit is what continues to inspire me on a daily basis. I now see the results of time spent pursuing, and I feel joy in enjoying my journey. It all started with the dream, and boy what a big dream have I had.

I took a deep breath standing in the room, and wiped away my tears. I have come a long way since then. But, I knew that a lot of me was still in this room, when I was struggling to break free, yet enjoying the creative freedom.

I took one last look at my painting on the wall, hanging there against the empty weatherboards like it was hung in a private, lost Art gallery. I walked out of the cabin, and closed the door on my past. I removed some weeds from around my rose bush, and headed down the hill, into my future.

I was ready for a journey.

Exercise 1: Letting go of the past

Write down a major episode that happened in your past, that you feel you still hang on to and you feel affects you moving forward. Write at least a page about it. Feel free to "journal" – let the pen wander for as long as it takes.

At the end, create an affirmation about who you are now, based on who you were. Start with "I AM….."

Keep it positive.

A little note about the Warrior Artist Path

You have to remember how you got here.

You've worked so hard to get here. It CAN be tough.

But you don't become relentless and a WARRIOR Artist Entrepreneur without having felt the mountain to climb.

Hardship often prepares an ordinary person for an extraordinary destiny.
C.S. Lewis

6. My story: living in a maverick town

I discovered the importance of the word "Journey" and not so much about the word "Destination" when I got out of my safe comfort zone in Australia and began to travel.

One day I got the gumption to get on a plane and pursue my dream. In April 1996 I traveled from Sydney in search of the Holy Grail, and arrived in Los Angeles. For me it was foreign, un-traversed soil. When I first arrived here I knew no one, except for my uncle, who knew no one in the music business. I had about $300 to last me six months. How idealistic I was! Idealism saved me though, because if I had even thought for a moment about the reality of my situation I would have been doomed. I was on a mission. I searched for the epicenter of the music industry. For me it was on Sunset Boulevard, at the National Academy of Songwriters (NAS). I met other songwriters like myself, and brushed shoulders with Lionel Ritchie, Diane Warren, Joni Mitchell, Lieber and Stoller and Artists I never even heard about, but who were famous, all within the first month of being here. The NAS for me was like the epicenter of finding out about everything.

I had put together a five song demo in Sydney that was produced by a motley of producers (all talented in their own right) that all thought they could define a sound for me. I didn't think I knew enough to listen to my own opinion, so I always sought out other people's opinions as to what would be right for me as an Artist. How could I know anything? I'm just a girl from the Aussie 'bush'.

My first attempt at securing my music career was so half hearted. After 3 months in L.A. I then went to New York, with five songs, all different in style, with no common thread except for my voice, which really wasn't showcased at its best. The music was too eclectic, from pop to R&B to dance to a ballad. There was no commonality. I'm surprised they didn't throw me out by my ear. I was determined though, and strong.

Determination was my birth name. I had grown up on a rugged mountain, I could take on anything, right? Fortunately (whether it was my Aussie accent or my assertive voice, I don't know) I was able to meet with at least six top A&R execs between the East and West Coast, in person, within a day of calling them, simply by saying I had flown all the way from down-under to meet them. Who would not let me in? I met them, barely knew what an A&R rep did, showed them my lame CD of five songs (In 1996, a burnable CD cost $50 each so I asked them to give it back to me at the end of the meeting...ha ha) and waited eagerly in front of them for their response while they listened. I figured, if I got off my butt and flew all this way, dressed right, had attitude, showed determination, then they could discover my unending talent and, well, sign me as a developing Artist to be the next big thing Right? Surely, yes? Wrong.

Each of those A&R execs, in their pleasant way, was able to swiftly cut me down to size. Perhaps they noticed the talent. Some expressed that. But the music was not right. Too eclectic, style too wishy-washy, too cross over, too... well, just not what they were looking for. I was a diamond in the rough that they were just not willing to take on.

Every single one of them asked me, *"Gilli, what is it that you want?"* I could not answer this question. I didn't know enough to give them the right response. I couldn't just say, *"I want to be famous!"* That wasn't true anyway. Fame is nice. But I just wanted to be *out there*. How do you describe that intangible ambition in words without sounding embarrassing or egotistical to a record company executive who has heard it all? But the truth is, *I didn't know what I really wanted*, then.

They were right about my music. As much as I had spent money on getting these songs produced, the problem was that none of those songs truly captured who I was... what I was about. I was on Madison Avenue in New York for God's sake! I had to be perfect, right? To make this demo, I had allowed other anonymous producers (with all due respect, very talented in their own rights) to whip up my songs in a way that was not me. I never spent enough time allowing them to discover who I was, as an Artist, and as a person. I didn't even know who I was! I felt like a complete ignoramus.

Everyone back home was proud of my expedition though. I had done a whirl-wind business trip (apart from my flight cost) on $300 (that's Australian dollars) and met everyone in town, all in 3 months. The word "networking" was just getting trendy, and I was definitely into it. I even had an e-mail address. Woo hoo. I paid $60/month through Compuserve for a 9600kb dial up connection! Not many people had e-mail back then in '96. I had already begun to feel the power of the Internet, before the Internet had power.

I went back home to Sydney at the end of October 1996 with loads of business cards... but no business. What to do? Simply... move back to Los Angeles, the "Mecca of the music business", as I was told, and stay a while. Right? So after 2 months of just having landed back in Oz, I was back on Hollywood's doorstep. Don't ask me how I organized that one! I worked my butt off in Sydney and packed everything up in the little cabin on my parents' property, and off I went again... determined.

This time, I had come back to L.A. with knowing at least 5 more people. I stayed with a family friend down on Santa Monica beach, nannying her children. I love to rollerblade, so it was a perfect spot down near the Venice Beach boardwalk. I found an immigration lawyer through an Aussie connection, started work visa proceedings and went back to the NAS (National Academy of Songwriters) to volunteer and watch. I found a manager and soon after I remember being one of only two white girls in an R&B/Hip Hop showcase for the NAS in Burbank. They clapped and cheered when I sang my song "This Life We Live" to a backing track and I did a whole four minute dance routine while performing in my full white linen suit. A small Artist-owned record company, Drama! Music, were putting together their first trip-hop electronica album "Lust" and they saw my performance and invited me to sing their song "You Belong To Me" for their album. This song went on to be my first single, and my first claim to any notion of fame outside my homeland. It hit No.1 on a Belgian radio station, apparently, for a week and I thought all my Christmases had come at once. At least it looked good on paper. I wasn't sure how all that was supposed to translate to sales and an income. Income? What was that?

Slowly, slowly I began to attract an audience who liked my music. I started performing downstairs at the old Luna Park, plus the Troubadour, the now deceased venue, The Gig, on Pico and Melrose, The Whisky on Sunset and many others. The gigs were heating up and the venues were turning over, so too were my band members. It was hard to find players who could play for free or little money, and then, you were left with the "green ones", the new L.A. arrivals who had enthusiasm but couldn't play for pits. But I was pretty fortunate. My musicians became close friends, so we all got on famously, even when we parted. To this day I often bring some musicians back for a paid studio session in thanks for that era. Some are still with me.

All of a sudden, a journalist wrote an awesome review in Music Connection on one of my Luna Park shows. I was about to leave L.A. because I was so broke and so lonely. When I opened the paper and read the review I burst out crying. All the stress of living in a foreign city, alone, being broke everyday with not even a bank account, living out of a suitcase on someone's floor or in someone's closet and trying to make a name for myself at the same time, had taken a huge emotional toll. As much as seeing my name in print was a great remedy, it wasn't the answer. I began to see that any token of fame, merit or reward doesn't fix what's going on inside. Still, it was a great review!

I had yet to record anything of merit that I liked or that anyone else proclaimed to like. I tried working with a producer or two, but never felt anything that seemed to represent who I was. My little home recorded 4 track versions gave me more solace. I could hear the passion in my own home demos that I made on those lonely nights up on the mountain. Why wasn't the same passion oozing out in the big studio?

I feared that I would only deliver again the "average" I had delivered before. What's that saying? –

The fear of not being good enough to measure up to my ambitions.

That's it. That was what I had: "The fear of not being good enough to measure up to my ambitions". I had a bad case of the jitters. My money had run out. How could I possibly get a record deal if the music I was making was crap? Let alone the very fact that I couldn't work here, so my financial stability was zero. So, with a sob and a shrug, I packed up, stored my tapes, my beat up old '82 Honda Accord that barely made it around the block, and other stuff at my manager's house, and flew home to Sydney. That was April 1997.

Sydney was... Easter time. That means bunny rabbits, delicious Cadbury chocolate I had missed so much, and a plethora of things to do in what seemed like an outback town compared to the bright lights of Hollywood. But all of a sudden I could see so much of what I could do back home. It was like a fire had been lit in my belly and I had all this amazing energy. I immediately fell back on to what I had been doing before, producing events (I paid my bills by being a corporate event producer), and helped produce the huge Light Rail (tram) launch down in the inner city of Sydney, a few car launches and some award nights. That same moment, with pen to paper, I devised the creation of Songsalive! which in a matter of months became a non-profit organization supporting, nurturing and promoting Australian songwriters, co-founding the operation with my friend Roxanne Kiely.

I was motivated to start Songsalive! when I was living in Sydney because I noticed how limited the opportunities were for original songs to be played in venues. In 1997, Australia was still a "covers scene" with pubs and clubs primarily playing Artists who would play standards and the latest hits, not original songs. It was rare to find a place where you could get paid to play your own songs. This is still the same today.

I also realized that being a songwriter can be lonely. It's a solitary experience: we write our songs mostly on our own and we go through our journey as Artists mainly on our own, trying to get the songs out there. I felt that if we had a "force", an umbrella to reach out to music organizations and become a link in the chain for songwriters, then we could provide opportunity, exposure, support and promotion. Songwriters are the least considered in the music business. This is a known fact, but never really talked about. We get the short-end of the stick when it comes to writer deals, any exposure or recognition. Yet without the song, there is no music industry. I feel it's important to recognize the songwriter and provide them support. Roxanne and I launched the small organization in Aug 97 with a handful of volunteers and a huge 20 band celebration at Sydney's Hard Rock Cafe. It is interesting to say now, that since 1997 Songsalive! has gone on to become the largest international songwriters organization in the world. We have over 20 chapters in Australia, the U.S, Europe and Canada and members worldwide. I've been pretty busy! If I died today, I would be happy due to the contribution I brought to songwriters through Songsalive! Besides, it's selfish to assume that the music industry, or any Arts industry, should be based on your own career alone. **Art is about giving and providing for others.** *(Later I'll talk about how important it is to have a mission built into your Artistic goals.)*

So, back to '97. I jumped into the Sydney recording studios once again and in months I came up with a fourteen song "business card" called "Girl in the Moon", my first CD. 'Girl' was essentially another calling card, and I didn't want to sell it as an album because even after spending months collating the masters and recording new songs, I just didn't think it was good enough. What was wrong with me??? What's that saying again? *"The fear of not being good enough to measure up to my ambitions."* I need to remind myself of that one as I write because it will be the focus of my conclusion later. So I made enough *Girl in the Moon* CDs to travel and promote with, all packed in flat cardboard sleeves. The songs were a compilation of recordings I had done pre-L.A., some from my time in L.A., and a couple of new ones I produced myself over at Velvet Studios in downtown Sydney. I learned much during that time with some musician friends about reworking songs so they would be catchy, and getting a good feel and vibe in production. But I never treated this album as a real album. It was another mish mash of ideas again, very eclectic. Only recently did I finally decide that this was a real album, worthy to be sold. Years later, after making "Girl in the Moon" I am pleased to say that I have "re-released" it and it's available on iTunes.

As much as it was nice to be back in Sydney, the challenge was still yet to come for me. With my renewed strength, fuelled by the very fact that I was able to achieve mighty things at home, I packed up once again and on the 1st of January 1998 (New Year's in the plane!) my Songsalive! co-hort, Roxanne, and I both landed in L.A. I showed her around like a pig in mud and then in January we went to Midem, Cannes, the huge international music convention in France. It was an amazing experience, wandering the booths one after the other, hocking your music to every publisher, recording company and music organization there is. This was a civilized market bazaar – pre-internet marketing age. "Come here, buy this... only fifty dollar! Last forever!" I got my bug for music conferences at Midem. Since then I went back 3 times, and have pretty much attended most conferences in the U.S, even produced one for Songsalive! called the Songsalive! Expo (02).

I went back to Los Angeles after Midem, and a quick trip to London, empty handed, saying goodbye to Roxanne as she flew back to Sydney to handle the home fires with Songsalive! So. It's February 1998. Hollywood. I was once again living in a shoe box, this time on a photographer friend's couch with even more suitcases. I had somehow begun to accumulate suitcases, now stored across town in various garages and closets. Each time I came here I was hoarding stuff for some future "I live here" purpose but always lived like a transient.

I was a little unsettled coming back to L.A. because I kind of didn't have a purpose, except that I felt I needed to be here and continue the journey. The rest of my story, my life and this book will focus a lot about the word "JOURNEY". Back at this time, however, I wasn't cognizant of the importance of this word. It was always about the DESTINATION, some future arrival of being.

I started living in a friend's closet (literally) down in Mid Wilshire and playing out as much as I could. Then I moved to another place with a friend near the 405 freeway. I got back into gig mode really quickly in Los Angeles and was surprised that even though I had been away really for about 7 months, that the clubs still remembered me. With still only 2 suitcases of belongings, I moved in to the slums of Beverly Hills, with a fellow muso room mate, whose brother was in the band 'Yes' and who had 10 adorable white cats with loads of fur, nicely covering everything I owned. I say the 'slums' because it was the south side of Pico, heading toward the

10 freeway, so it's kind of on the edge. It's actually a cool neighborhood now, and quite pricey! Also, I think the movie "Slums of Beverly Hills" must have been filmed in my street. It had the same 70s retro run down feel about it with the occasional BMW in the neighbor's driveway. I lived in a room that was about 10 feet by 10 feet, but at least I had my own bathroom. I didn't need much room, just enough for a bed and my keyboard. I was making zero money and all I could do was hug my little keyboard every night hoping things would turn out all right. But in true Gilli fashion I managed to do a hundred things at once to keep moving forward and up.

My gigs were heating up once again and reviews were even coming in from my *Girl in the Moon* album which even though was not for sale, was circulating on the Web. I began an online diary in '98. I was one of the first to start an online diary. Now it's called a blog. But it means the same thing. I was totally into the Internet back in '98 when most Internet buffs of today were still teething. I created my own webpage which was as long as something like this:

http://www.compuserve.com/mypages/~gilliwebpage.html.   You won't find that exact page on the web but it was ridiculously long. Early 1998, I got the bug to surf the Net. I joined mp3.com which was really the only official website where you could upload your songs to the Internet. They even paid you for downloads back then for a short time. Then, when they attracted thousands upon thousands of Artists, they realized they couldn't afford to pay for every single download, so the checks stopped coming. But the reviews kept on coming, and my website had lots of nice things to say about the music that didn't say much about me, but still I was happy. I think I was even number 1 for a few weeks in my alternative genre.

I attended as many songwriter open mics and showcases as possible and began to know the little promoters who ran them, thus increasing my inner circle of songwriters within the Songsalive! umbrella. It was great finding kindred spirits. What was a complete shock to me was the NAS (National Academy of Songwriters where I had volunteered) folded after twenty years, and I shed a tear in sadness for their past glories and also in happiness that I was able to be part of it, even if it was in their last phase. I had met some wonderful friends through the NAS including Marci Kenon; Alan Roy Scott, who runs Music Bridges; Brett Perkins, who served as the NAS managing director in its last year and now runs the Listening Room Retreats in Denmark; Pamela Phillips Oland, a terrific lyricist and teacher; Dan Kimpel, now a respected author in his own right, and a great journalist; and John Braheny, the author of "The Craft and Business of Songwriting", a must-have for anyone who is serious about their songwriting. I am friends with these people today. I am reminded that the *music business is all about relationships*, and even more so... great friendships.

At some stage my application for a Green Card was approved and all of a sudden, my vision opened up and I saw a bright U.S. future. My destiny was secured. My dreams would come true. More importantly I could work. I could earn money. This made my struggle, well, struggle-less.

The little things that citizens take for granted are the hugest obstacles for new people to foreign lands, way bigger than fulfilling ambitions. Getting a Social Security number, a bank account, a drivers license, learning to drive on the right side of the road, a work permit... these are the hardest hurdles. When I look at Nicole Kidman, Russell Crowe, Naomi Watts, Rachel Griffith and Toni Collette, as examples of Australian actors in America, I think about how they too have not only surpassed these "living" hurdles, but also grasped the American accent AND made a name for themselves; twice the obstacles than any other actor. It's a huge feat.

So, early '98, I started to do some office work with an Aussie friend who ran a PR firm and budding film distribution company. It was a lot of fun, and it was great to work with another Aussie who could understand my 'lingo'. (Really, let's face it, Americans and Australians speak different languages.)

I then worked for a video distribution company and soon I was working for myself designing web sites and CD Art, the beginnings of being self-employed. Throughout 1998 I was running on fire and LEARNING a lot about supplementary industries that plug into and support the music biz. While I still had little money (living on roughly $200 a week and air), with no music for release, and hence no record company connections, I was, however, writing songs like wildfire. Summer in July and August was great and my '82 Honda was still working even though I had replaced practically everything on it. The dark days were temporarily gone, and I had no reason to go home. Besides, going home meant going back in time, and I wasn't about to go back there when I could see far, far ahead.

But then again, I had no reason to stay. Or did I? The gigs around town were fun and I started putting together my press pack which included everything I had done in L.A. I didn't realize how thick it would get. I was amazed at what I had really achieved without looking. I had performed a lot. One night we did this really cool show downstairs at Luna Park to a packed audience with Matt Lattanzi (Olivia Newton John's ex) on didgeridoo. Loads of fun. We hit the news in Sydney. That's all I could think about... "I wonder if people back home know what I'm doing now!" Australia's media king, Molly Meldrum wrote a short piece and Who (People) Magazine caught the Luna Park gig with a photo. I was happy. I guess you could say that there was a buzz. And I had created it. MTV television contacted me to be part of a new contest, so I appeared on "The Cut "/MTV singing an R&B type ballad, with my long beaded braids I got made by 4 gorgeous sisters who lived in the heart of Compton. I had certainly developed an interesting look. I had been grocery shopping one day and I asked one of the check out girls if she braided hair (she was a beautiful African American with long braids). She said "oh, of course, my sisters and I do it all the time!" So one day I drove down to Compton in what seemed like the scariest part of the universe with not one white person in the area. I looked so out of place, and I got so many stares and even some snarls. The helicopters were always hovering. But I found the house, quite quaint really with a neatly mowed lawn by its inhabitants, and stepped into the warmest house I'd ever been in. Four sisters were waiting and ready, with combs, hair extensions and elastic bands in hand. They spent six hours braiding my hair which, when complete, fell down to my waste. It was a lot of fun, and certainly one of those days where I learned to never judge a book by its cover.

I started Songsalive! in L.A. Why not? Seemed to be a good way to share with like-minded songwriters and I discovered that people began to knock on my doors instead of me constantly hoping a door would open elsewhere. I began by hosting songwriting workshops which started in my 10 x 10 room in the shared house and eventually we moved to the Musicians Institute in Hollywood. We would each share a song and the rest of us would provide positive critique and feedback on the song, hoping to elevate the song's writing and provide inspiration. This is still the meat and potatoes of Songsalive! today, these songwriting workshops, only bigger and global.

As timing would have it, a record company came along, offering me a deal, which is ALL that I wanted (or at least thought that's what I wanted). It was September 1998. They were an independent label, who signed me to a non-exclusive one record deal. **All I had wanted was a record deal.** My whole life. THIS WAS IT. Finally, someone legit had come along to make all my dreams come true.

No matter what, I couldn't go home or visit home without a record deal. That was the promise to myself. **Getting a deal would solve everything,** I thought. It had become a symbol of my determination and ambition.

All I could think about was recording my music. I had been a frustrated Artist all my life, wanting so much to record my music right. I was eager to start recording the album with a record company. The first reality call came when I realized I wasn't on the top of the list for getting into the studio. Being signed means also realizing there is an Artist roster, with other Artists also in the line of production... and I had to wait my turn. I had to wait. Again.

Getting a (record) deal would solve everything, I thought. It had become a symbol of my determination and ambition.

I moved to the dusty, desert town of Palmdale in February '99 where the studio was, and ended up living there for a year. Palmdale is about an hour north-east from L.A., up in the high desert. Everyone kept saying, "why are you moving up there? It's so far away!" Well, for me it was a lot closer to things than Sydney was. I had a different perspective I guess.

By May '99 we had put some players together for a new band called Jessica Christ, and we started quietly in the coffee houses in the Valley to get us ready again for Hollywood. I worked hard developing the new band. I brought some of my old musicians, and the record company brought some new ones in to create a dynamic live band. Meanwhile, I had still not been able to get into the studio to record my own record but I agreed to be part of the Jessica Christ album which featured various songs and Artists.

Recording what was to be the quintessential solo record for me, took a back seat while the Jessica Christ band came to life. All of a sudden I realized that my dream of being "signed' was an illusion. Not that it was a bad experience. It was quite creative. I will always honor and thank them for giving me this experience and teaching me so much about music and the business of music. But it wasn't *my* experience. Also, at the time, I had allowed the label to make all the decisions for me, because that's what I thought was supposed to happen, and I lost sight of my own inner dream, and my inner strength.

Living and working in Palmdale was an interesting experience, sometimes fulfilling, but mostly emotionally draining. I was still creatively frustrated. I had been this way before signing the deal, and I was still under contract, very frustrated as I had yet to really put my music, my creativity, out to the world. I was also living alone in a lonely small town. I felt like I was back up in the cabin on the mountain, isolated, frustrated. This was not the label's fault. But the very fact that I felt isolated caused frustration, and this created a domino effect which this book doesn't have enough pages for me to write about.

By the end of the year, I had not yet recorded a solo album. All my life I had felt like I had to be patient, that one day "my turn would come". I had yet to realize my own potential as an Artist, and as much as I had believers in me, I never really got to do it the way I wanted to do it. I was always waiting. I felt terribly frustrated, and very alone. It's no one's fault. I place no blame. As stated before, I had been living in a childhood dream for thirty years. Most of my perfect world was in my own imagination. I still had no money (flat broke), lived in scarcity, did not enjoy the moment at all (was dreaming of some future hope of joy, fame and fortune), and I did not believe in myself. I had a very poor concept about myself by now. My esteem was at the lowest it had ever been my whole life.

Unfortunately, or fortunately, my childhood dreaming ended at the turn of the century. I have to say that when I turned thirty, I came to a dead stop. This is where my old life ended and my new life began, through what you might call a major shift in consciousness.

I went home to Sydney upset, drained, tired and wondering if my dreams of a record deal, or living and working in America, was all worth it. I had worked hard thus far, and conquered many hurdles, to find that I still hadn't achieved this undetermined goal to success. I had BIG EXPECTATIONS on what I needed as an Artist, to be creatively fulfilled.

But my internal self-doubt discussions were discarded when I had a much bigger issue to deal with. I discovered through a routine check up (the day before I was supposed to go back to L.A.) that I had to go into hospital for emergency surgery on my right ovary, which had developed a dermoid cyst the size of a football. They say cysts are symbols of creative frustration, and of anger. I mulled over that for ages. I didn't even know it was there! How could I have overlooked a football in my abdomen? My doctor could not tell me if it was cancerous until they operated.

I had to wait ten days until the operation. Ten days is a long time when you don't know if you are terminally ill or just a quick fix with the knife. I had what you would call a "spiritual awakening." I discovered my mortality and realized that nothing was more important than my health and my family.

My mind played games with me. Imagine, right there on the operating table, dying with my intestines on the metal table, looking up to the heavens without an album released and an unfulfilled recording contract.

It was only after the operation that my doctor (the best surgeon in the world as far as I care) told me it wasn't cancerous, but if it had been, having opened me up, that would have been the end of me. He asked me if I wanted to see the tumor. I said "um, no thanks. I'd rather not be reminded of my past." In that moment, *I let go of the past*, of all my frustrations, of any lost ideal, and began a new life.

While in hospital, flat on my back for 10 days, and then recuperating on my parents' farm for four weeks, yep back in the cabin which had become my energizing spring for recuperation, I asked myself those empirical questions like *"what is my purpose?", "how long will I do this until I feel my dreams are fulfilled?", "what is my dream?", "is my goal intangible, too unrealistic?", "am I happy? What do I really want?"* and so forth. Many people on this planet have had these awakenings and often over a life and death situation. I am lucky that I had it relatively young.

I read "Conversations with God" Books 1, 2 and 3, by Neale Donald Walshe, I re-read the "Celestine Prophecy", a few other books that empowered my spirit, and then I began writing my first book, "I AM A Professional Artist", up in my little cabin on the hill. I cannot tell you what a glorious month of reading and writing it was. It was magic. All my motivational writings, my new warrior visions, my new dreams were all born on top of the mountain in this month, lying in bed barely walking and breathing, but so, so much alive.

My career was momentarily put on hold while I regained my strength and learned to love myself again. You see, what I had realized was that not only had I been physically sick, but emotionally sick as well. I had placed myself under immense strain in order to take on the record deal experience, the Los Angeles experience, and overall, my ambition. All these years of pushing and proving myself, convincing others to believe in me, and doing this alone, lacking any real INNER JOY, had placed a toll on my health.

I made a full recovery, and I was very lucky. When I returned to L.A., late December '99, I knew that I could not live in Palmdale or be involved in someone else's dream anymore. I had come to learn what was meaningful to me, and what was not. I was either going to follow my dream or go home. So by January 2000 I had moved to Sherman Oaks, in the Valley outside Hollywood, to start my music career on my own terms.

I was starting all over again. I sat in my new apartment, with boxes around me, with no money, no plan, no idea on how to achieve anything. But... I was onto something.

I now:
1. **believed in myself.**
2. **knew that all that was important was the journey.**
3. **felt abundant.**

I realized for the first time that *I no longer needed approval by anyone except myself.*
I didn't need a record producer. I didn't need a manager. I didn't need a record company and some A&R exec telling me what would be good for me. I didn't even need a boyfriend. I just needed myself. **I needed to really listen to myself.** Listen to my heart, and feel the inspiration come from within.

That was January 1, 2000. The year was not just the new millennium, but my personal new life. Early 2000 I began recording my first officially released album, "temperamental angel", with my friend, Evan Beigel, at his North Hollywood studio, Seasound (now Jo Jo Ocean music). I registered my business, Warrior Girl Music, with the local newspaper and set up a bank account. Nothing was in the bank account, but I opened up the vessel for the money to come. I designed my own website and just started GETTING OUT THERE on my own, truly for the first time, ever, **without needing anyone else to make it happen for me.**

Let's take a moment to let that sink in.

Ten months later, I wrote this on my online blog (Aug 2000):
"Having gone through my huge personal growth in the past ten months since my hospital experience, I have discovered the truth behind my mission. My journey here is not about catching the industry's attention to become a star or to be famous. A record deal will not fill the voids. I'm here because, firstly, I have had to learn about myself and who I really wanted to become. I am an Artist. And I am an expressionist. I have nothing to prove except to create and to share with you my messages, my emotions and my heart-felt creations through my expression of music, writing and performing. My destination is to create better, more enriching, vehicles to express myself to you in hope that it enriches your lives. I am much calmer these days. Not so much in a rush. Still determined. Still strong, I am a warrior girl, yet a spiritual warrior and a silent warrior working diligently, with determination, on my quest. I am finally recording my music. I have waited so long to do this. And it was me, really, who put the road blocks up. I gave myself so many distractions and gave away the power to others to make the decisions for me. I thank each and everyone who has inspired and influenced my creative growth. They will always remain special in my heart. Now, I am truly growing, because I am bringing my Art alive. I am over the fear. For the fear of death is far worse than the fear of not being able to measure up to ambitions. And the fear of being alone is scarier than aloneness itself, for being alone is important. It's where we find our true selves. For the first time ever I have tapped into who I am musically and Artistically. I have found my sound, and I have found it alone. I am working consciously, almost methodically in the creation of my music, music that's

mine, and a vision that's mine. You might like it. You may think it sucks. I don't care. What will be, will be."

Since then, I have released 5 more albums, *"temperamental angel"* (2001), *"Woman"* (2003) , *"extraOrdinary life"* (2005), *"Skillz"* (2008) with J.Walker, and my latest solo album *"the stillness"* (2010). I've produced ten albums for other Artists, created a compilation album series for female Artists called *"Females On Fire"* and a male one *"Art of Men"*; co-produced the inaugural Los Angeles Women's Music Festival; expanded Songsalive! across the world; won many songwriting and performing awards; toured the U.S. more than 4 times; received mountains of reviews, garnering high praise from the most jaded of critics; and worked with legends in the business. But none of my accolades thrill me. In fact, if I didn't want to make a point writing this book, I wouldn't mention my accolades. They are merely a barometer of what most Artists think they want to read about when reading a book written by an Artist, and they are a reminder for me that once upon a time, I had nothing.

When once upon a time I yearned for recognition, for some notion of fame, for people to believe in me, for me to prove to people my worth, I now seek none of that. What excites me is what I do on a daily basis - my journey; the process of living my dream.

I am in love with my life, my path and my creativity. I began my career looking for someone else... *"them, they, the others"* to come along and make it happen for me. Most young Artists live in this illusion. I thought "ok, I have talent, they will come along and help me." I was a frustrated, unhappy person because I could not follow my true creative path and what my soul was telling me to be and do. I was looking for others to give me permission. The reality is, **we can't wait around for others to make it happen for us.** It was only when I took responsibility of my life and dreams, trusting my own musical instincts and my own heart, that it has proven to be the right choice. The only choice.

Enjoy your own journey.
GIVE YOURSELF THE PERMISSION TO SHINE.

Exercise: Self Discovery

Courtesy of Fowler Wainwright International. See Bibliography at end for details of this marvelous Coaching organization that I'm accredited through.

Answer these questions in depth. Take the time to reflect before you write. Preferably, have a notebook to write in, and under each question, provide several answers (eg 1., 2., 3., up to 10):

1. List my positive attributes

2. List of areas I need to improve

3. What's holding me back from experiencing success? (List thoughts, feelings, emotions, limiting beliefs, old paradigms, and resentments)

4. What can I change? What actions can I take to have new and rewarding experiences?

5. What resentments am I ready to let go of? Who am I ready to forgive? What habits am I ready to eliminate? What lifestyle am I ready for?

6. What new rich experiences, beliefs and lifestyle conditions do I want to have today?

We live in a time
where
entrepreneurial
excellence is
paramount. It's
time for Artists to
take control of
their own
destiny...

7. The little voice called fear

The voice of the fallen angel is so loud, sometimes we can't hear the other voice that is silent, the truth. Inside us, we have a voice that never believes you are good enough, telling you why you don't deserve success, why you can't trust, why you are not perfect. That voice is lying, and the only power it has is the power you give it.

I tell you my story up 'till now based on a perspective I had about myself. It was written, as it was felt then, with that little voice inside me speaking. I believed in that voice that told me lies about myself. But it's only a story. The truth is, I have lived a perfect life.

The only suffering, or scarcity, or frustration I ever felt was due to me believing in that voice's story. To be honest, I have always had everything I needed. I have been loved and nurtured. I have had many opportunities that most would only dream of having.

Much of my disgruntlement was based on *fear*. I was living a thirty year long childhood, and when I hit thirty, I stood face to face with myself. I looked into the eyes of truth. It's all about perspective.

The truth sets us free. This doesn't mean that all of you who are reading this have to wait 'till you're thirty, or fifty, or some age figure, to have this revelation. I hope not. If you can catch that little voice early, you can thwart any frustrations and hesitations you may encounter as an Artist.

In retrospect, I should have stood behind my first album, "Girl in the Moon", and released it officially back then, instead of shelving it because of some industry exec's criticism of it. It was and is a blueprint of who I was then, immortalized in a 13 song album. I could have set up my record company back then and just put it out there, but I was afraid to do it on my own. I thought I needed someone else's record company, or other people who knew better than I, to put my music out to the world. So I didn't release it, and I didn't stand behind it. I apologized for it, made excuses as to why it wasn't good enough, and listened to TOO many people who judged it.

I reiterate: **Seek no one else's approval but your own.**

No matter where we are, no matter what our circumstances are, or who we are surrounded by... it's up to us to make the best of our situation... to put on that smile and to see the beauty of the glorious opportunities life brings to us.

These opportunities come in ways we least expect, and may take us to destinations we never expected or thought possible, and yet will be wondrous and full of adventure if we can see the positive side of that.

We all have trials and tribulations. We all have time constraints. We all have responsibilities. We can go through hardships such as financial, personal, career-wise, circumstantial. Yes, many things can thwart us, detour us, scare us... just freak us out.

Sometimes what we may go through as a hardship may be an unrealized dream. It's about realizing that what we have in our hands quite possibly could be the best thing that's ever happened to us.

In thinking all this, I have to admit that I am truly blissful and thankful for what I have and where I am at in my life.

Live with No Fear

In my first book, I wrote in depth about Fear and the word "Failure".

Remember my story at the beginning of this book? The saying was this: the fear of not being good enough to **measure up to our ambitions**. A few years ago, it was me really, who put the road blocks up for myself. Fear can stop us in our tracks. I had not released any of my music for years for fear of not being good enough to measure up to my ambitions. Sometimes we just have to say "heck, let's do it anyway", for by doing, we grow.

I gave myself so many distractions and gave away the power to others to make the decisions for me. All of a sudden, for the first time in a long time, I had tapped into who I was musically and Artistically. But I had to *will* myself to take full responsibility for my creativity and not allow others' perceptions to cloud my vision, and my mission.

Art can illuminate the darkness and bring it to light.

Artists are gifted human beings with that ability. If we are able to go to the edge of that extreme, the only thing that stops us from really shining in our potential is the fear of what people think. Realizing that we have a gift can give us strength to deliver that gift to others and relinquish the fear. Why try to be perfect before we express our Art? If we try to be perfect in everything we do, we will never attain anything.

The working actor represents 3% of the acting population. Just that knowledge alone can make us very scared that we will never realize our dreams. But everyone lives with fear in their daily life. It's a common, shared experience. So if you know this as fact, then embrace your goals and dreams for you are not alone in the dark.

Perseverance in this fickle industry will win. Don't give up on something if you really desire it. That dream is yours so don't let anyone take it away from you. In athletics, you either win or lose. You win the race or you don't. **You cannot succeed unless you're willing to fail.**

You cannot succeed unless you're willing to fail.

But failure is inaccurate as a description of not succeeding. For in truth there is no failure, only a varying degree of success. If you don't win the race, winning second or third is still a sense of winning. Just running in the race is a great accomplishment because most of us are too lazy to get off our butt and be motivated. One person may get first place in the race but twenty ran. Those nineteen that didn't get first place must enjoy the very fact that they competed because they are motivating themselves and winning little victories in their own heads (maybe a personal best).

Once again, this is a reminder that the **process** must be more enjoyable than the result: the journey. I know someone who is 62 and who has been retrenched from three jobs three times. He needs to work another three years before he gets his pension and since he hasn't been able to keep his job, he feels like he is a *failure*. "I'm a failure!" he proclaims out loud to anybody who will listen. But he isn't remembering all the times he has succeeded.

His first job lasted twenty years, his second and third jobs were five years each - longer than most are able to keep one job. He has seen the world and experienced life. He has four healthy children and a wonderful marriage. But he forgets these victories. He just sees what he doesn't have and labels them as failures. Perhaps the one failure he does have is in learning how to have a positive attitude. **Attitude is everything.**

What if we are able to write that novel, produce that album or that film, only for it to "flop" by industry standards? Only 1000 sales of CDs instead of 100,000. A number 40 hit not number 1? A box office 'failure'. That's commercialism for you and it is really, really important to know the difference between what society and commercialism deems as a failure, and what you feel you have failed yourself as an Artist. Don't buy into the myths, for if you begin to believe the stories, you will feel like the industry has rejected you. In truth, you are the only person who can evaluate your sense of failure. **I personally have chosen to remove the word 'failure' from my inner dictionary.** Try substituting the word 'opportunity' every time you want to say this 'f' word and see what happens instead!

What may look like a failure in comparison to another is, for me, just a different path, a different experience and a unique outcome that only I alone can truly appreciate. Everywhere around you are dozens of "average" people enticing you to see life in a negative way. I encourage you to see life in a positive, optimistic way, a strong sense of self, with leadership qualities and a value system that you alone determine whether you have succeeded or failed in the goals you are setting.

Commence-aphobia

You have to want it bad enough to get up out of bed.

Many authors have made tons of money writing books about creative motivation. Artists go to class just to stay motivated, well-oiled and disciplined. What we often term as 'writers block', or just plain 'unmotivated' is a natural phenomenon in our society. Some wait for divine inspiration, others force themselves to sit, often for hours, at their writing or creative tables until they start.

We manage to find way more important things to do, take care of or concentrate on before we create. We manage to complain about having no time, no money, no resources, no opportunities, in order to create. I think we use all of our wonderful excuses as a crutch.

You have the tools within you to start. There is no need to wait for life to come around and give it to you. It's all up to you.

For some reason, and even I am to blame also, Artists procrastinate. They want to record a CD, or act in a play, or get head shots done, or write that book, or start auditioning for roles... but they don't. They think about it more than do it. It's terribly frustrating.

Much of our procrastination comes from fear of rejection, fear of leaving our safe home 'nest', fear of talking to the outside world, or fear that it or they won't be good enough.

So how do you rid *commence-aphobia*? (This is a term that was made up by our neighbor Bill Bottomley, you won't find it in the dictionary ☺) My mother, when she first started her chain of twenty games retail shops, simply began with this: "Hold your nose, shut your eyes and JUMP!"

It's so important to be self-motivated when it comes to Artistry. Only *you* can make that first step. Take the initiative.

Be a self-starter! Jump in with both feet! Later, I will provide ideas on how to manage yourself to achieve your goals.

Let your talent flow

GIVE YOURSELF PERMISSION to be the Artist you've always wanted to be. ALLOW yourself to just be the conduit of your talent.

Be the conduit, not the block

Live in the moment and surrender to the amazing opportunities that the universe is bursting to deliver us. The only way you can do that is to GIVE YOURSELF PERMISSION to be the Artist you've always wanted to be.

ALLOW yourself to just be the conduit of your talent. Most of us are too busy thinking we're 'not good enough' or 'not talented enough', that we are really *in the way* of just letting our talent flow and be whatever it's going to be. If we could just step outside of ourselves for once, and get out of our own way, then perhaps the flow would come so much more easily. I call that 'being the conduit' of your talent, rather than being the block. When I'm in the studio recording as a producer, I see myself merely as a slave to the song that is speaking to me. I become a conduit to let the best production of that song come through. If I start putting my **fears,** insecurities, and even my own judgments to the process, I would only sabotage the act of creation. So being a conduit means to help the creativity come through, but not hinder it with negative self-sabotage.

We get so many little voices whispering in our heads saying "no no no", that you just have to turn them off sometimes and shout out "yes!", even if you're unsure of the direction you're going. Just by saying "yes" and giving it a go will help eliminate all the doubts, and your confidence will grow just by doing.

YOU ARE WORTHY OF YOUR SUCCESS. Why?
BECAUSE YOU LOVE WHAT YOU DO.
That's all the answer you need.

No matter where you are, manifest the positives and the joy. Be passionate about what you do, because passion is everything. Be ambitious and go for what you truly want. Dream your dreams - because dreams can come true. We are just at the beginning and there is so much for all of us.

Believe.

Exercise: Torments of the mind

Every single one of us - be he (she) a ruler or warrior, be he (she) rich, middle class or poor, is subject to all sorts of physical and mental suffering, i.e. "torments of the mind".

1.   Draft columns on a full length sheet of paper and draw the lines and write the headings as per the picture below.

Torments of the Mind	Affirmations

2.   Write your *Torments* in the left column (those demons that sometimes wrestle with your consciousness and thoughts at night, making you unable to sleep). Think about what are some of the issues, roadblocks and worries you are facing in your life, whether it be professional, creative or personal. Some examples could be, 'not enough money' or 'not enough time'. Or it could be something specific like, 'don't know anyone to help me get my record out'. It could be something personal like 'I am not skinny enough to be famous'. Spend some time writing at least 10 *Torments* with several lines of space in between the next one.

3. Underneath each *Torment* on the left column, write how it makes you feel. This is usually an inner emotion such as fear, anger, sadness, worry, or you can be more general like 'left out', 'unheard'. Etc.

Torments of the Mind	Affirmations
e.g. **Not enough money** - I feel frustrated, sad, angry at myself	I AM wealthy I HAVE enough money I live in abundance I AM capable of making money

4. In the right column, opposite each *Torment*, write affirmations that turn the negative *Torment* around to a positive statement. An affirmation can sometimes be a white lie, where you are saying something positive to help heal/change the *Torment*. For example, "Not enough money" could be affirmed with "I live in abundance".

Do as many of these as you want, and then CIRCLE your affirmations, write them down, stick them to your walls, and know that this is called

self-empowerment 101!

So many people are looking for wisdom from other people thinking they're going to make it happen, you think you need a manager, you need an agent, you need a record company; you don't. You need yourself. The rest will come if it's necessary.

- gilli moon

8. Who are you... really?

Being there

Did you ever see Peter Sellers in the movie *"Being There"*? I strongly recommend watching this quirky yet introspective flick. It really masters the topic about Endowing your life – being the person YOU want to be, no matter what other people think.

It's confusing sometimes to know how we are supposed to get out there. Is there a road map to follow? Many of us search for the answers, or the stepping stones to take. We ask others, we search within ourselves, looking for the road map. (Surely the universe has a plan for me?)

But there is no plan we can all follow that is the same. There is no true road map that can be one blueprint for all, because we are all different and unique, *and* the business is always changing, so we can't just follow what was done before. Not anymore.

Most of us feel we can only proclaim to be anything if we are earning a living from it. If we can make money from our music then we are so-called professional Artists. Until then we sit in our little cubicles at work earning an income we resent because it's not from a job we are passionate about, and procrastinate about doing what we prefer to do.

But nothing is done unless you **endow it first**. You BE it. That means that if you are a songwriter and you want to earn money from your songwriting, then you have to write songs first. Even working a part time job, or full time, you can still find time to write songs, even record them. Heck, put the CD out there too. The job might be able to fund it if you're good at saving.

You have **to BE the person before you can DO anything**. Just by being that person you will begin to think in the right way, and your intentions will manifest to action and immense creativity, which then brings opportunity and an amazing adventure. I talk about "endowing success" a lot in my first book "I AM A Professional Artist".

> We do not attract what we want, we attract who we are. And that is a culmination of our belief systems and everything that is about us. And we can change who we are at any time.
> – Wayne Dyer

Who are you... really?

There are no cosmic lessons to learn by sticking to a mundane life and only dreaming. You need to enact!

No reason to rationalize the why-nots.

Be courageous and be self-defining, before people define you.

It all starts with these two questions:

Who are you?

and   What Do You Want?

When you've been able to answer these, as an Artist, you have pretty much worked out most of how to get it, because by really investigating the answers, knowing it, and writing it down, begins the magical journey of achieving your dreams.

Let's start with **Who You Are**:

The "I Am" Statement

> "What you must dare is to be yourself."
> - Dag Hammarskjold

How would you describe who you are and what you do to someone in the street, at a party, at a meeting, in an elevator? The WORDS you use are very important. *If I were to ask you, upon first meeting, who you are, would you be able to answer it in one clean, easy sentence?* And if you were to do that, how accurate would you be? In the workshops and one-on-one mentoring that I've conducted, I've discovered that 90% of Artists are unable to describe their true selves in one sentence, off the cuff. They stumble over the concept of

a) having to explain who they are.

b) saying it in a realistic, yet *positive* way.

Most end up describing themselves with all their personal frustrations and negativity, and put their dreams so far in the future that their statements aren't about who they are right now, but a figment of their intangible imagination. Their introduction is filled with their inner critic's self-sabotaging, doubting words.

'Who you are' is not what you do, what you think and what people think of you.

It's a higher awareness: all things are possible. So who you are means what you feel is possible for you.

Here are some examples of Artist introductions, or what I call an **I AM Statement**, when I meet them:

"Hi, I'm Bill. I'm trying to be a better songwriter and working hard at practicing my music. One day I'd like to be a professional musician with my own band, but already I feel I'm too old and I just don't know if I'll get there what with all the learning I have to do."

"Hi, I'm Elaine. I want to be a professional songwriter one day and tour if I can. I just don't know how to get there yet. I just need to find the right people, maybe a manager or an agent. I don't know."

"Hi, my name is Tom and I am a guitarist, songwriter and producer. I run my own production house and am creating new projects on a weekly basis, building my credits and writing songs with a strong global mission of unity and human consciousness. I'm very excited by my journey and am discovering new opportunities on a daily basis."

What is different about the first two introductions compared to the third?

How we perceive ourselves, including self-worth and self-discovery, and how we express it to others, indicates why we create success in our lives or not. Clearly, Bill and Elaine are not quite in touch with the law of attraction yet, compared to Tom. Bill is "trying" to be a songwriter and looks into the future as to when he will truly come into his own. He also has issues about his age and feels he doesn't know enough to consciously acknowledge his talent nor his status as an Artist. Same for Elaine... desiring to be professional, but feels she doesn't know the way to get there, and feels she needs other people to make it happen for her.

These are introductions from Artists I get ALL THE TIME. Ninety percent of the Artists I come across introduce themselves with language like this, not realizing that it sabotages their goals and dreams in coming true. Here's the crux of it:

whatever you put out there, even just thinking or visualizing it, is what you'll get. If you are not clear with what you want, then what you want may take a long time because it's fuzzy. If you are clear, you get clarity. This is the essence of the law of attraction. So let's take a look at some of these self-thoughts, and how to overcome some negative patterns, in order to create positive results:

Let's work on an Artist's I AM Statement. I'll call her Jennifer: Hi, my name is Jennifer and I'm trying to be a songwriter (well I'm doing my best but it's hard), and I write inspiring love songs, well that is most of them, and I'm looking to become a better Artist and maybe get out there.

Firstly this I AM Statement is filled with lots of "maybes" and "trying" and negative thoughts that the rest of us now have to hear, and that totally camouflages the *real* Jennifer.

Who are you... really?

My suggestion would be to

a)   remove all the "maybes" and "tryings" and "wanna bes", and turn it around with positive affirmations of I AM, I CAN, I WILLs.
b)   describe yourself more: we want to know what type of Artist you are, what music you play and how you play it.
c)   perhaps add a "worldly" on the end: something that takes it from the "me, me, me" to the "what I can do for the world". A higher purpose/mission.

So, let's revise Jennifer's statement:
"Hi my name is Jennifer and I am a professional singer, songwriter and pianist, who performs original R&B songs about relationships, my experiences and observations in the world, and I look to inspire people to look into their own self-doubts and fears by singing songs that are uplifting and hopeful."

Not the perfect, quintessential I AM Statement, but it's so much better, and now I know a little more about Jennifer, her style of music, what she plays, and who she's playing for, with a higher purpose in mind. I also see she's positive and confident in herself – which leads me to the second part of why we write these **affirmations**:

People will believe in you when you believe in yourself.

So, it's really important to SHOW your self-belief and confidence in yourself the first moment you introduce yourself to someone. If you fill it with maybes and negativities, people will feel that and won't believe in you: simple as that.

When writing your I AM Statement, be bold and dream big. It doesn't have to be exactly where you are right now but more of an idealized version of yourself as to who you want to become. Don't be egotistical and arrogant, assuming that you *are* already inspiring or amazing. Just be real. So many Artists tell me they write "inspiring, soulful and life-changing songs". Or they tell me "I am talented". How arrogant of an Artist to say they are talented or are inspiring. It comes across as egotistical. Let reviewers write verbose words about you instead. Just sing your songs, and we'll either feel it, or we won't. **Your "I Am" Statements need to be sincere and a little humility goes a long way.**

Include your mission statement, so that your statement becomes larger than you, and more about your contribution to the world. (See the next chapter about adding a mission to your "big dream".) *When you can get outside of the "me me me", we will all join in your cause, support you and love you.*

Once you begin to narrow down Who You Are and What You Want, the next step is to work out WHY YOU WANT IT. It can all be for naught if you don't.

* * *

"If you wish to know the mind of a man,
listen to his words."
-- Chinese Proverb

* * *

Exercise: Who Am I?

See if you can write down one sentence that describes who you are as an Artist, as if you were to introduce yourself to someone who is interested in your Artistry. Try and avoid negative words or phrases like "trying to be", "one day I'll be", "kind of". Be convinced, positive and affirmative. Consider elaborating on what kind of Artist you are and getting specific with genres. Don't flatter yourself too much. Stay humble. Oh, and if you have a mission (like something global or make change) add that too! Feel free to e-mail me your "I AM Statement" through the contact page at www.warriorgirlmusic.com.

I'll respond and comment.

Exercise 2: Who am I, who am I, no... who am I really?

Answer each of these questions honestly and feel free to write on another page (beyond the area I have provided here).

1. What do I like?

2. What don't I like?

3. What are my favorite things in life (to do, to have, to see)?

4. Why am I an Artist?

5. **Write down one (1) sentence that describes who you are.** You can make this sentence long, with lots of commas, but only one sentence. Start with the words *I AM.*

I Am a ...

Be bold and dream big. It doesn't have to be exactly where you are right now but more of an idealized version of yourself as to who you want to become. Include your mission statement, so that your statement becomes larger than you, and more about your contribution to the world.

Once you have edited it, and felt it to be who you are, right now, in this moment, type it up on a piece of paper in big writing, and draw a big fat box around it, and stick it on the wall or your mirror – somewhere you'll see it every day, to remind you.

9. Dream big

What does it mean to dream big?

I believe that I am the master of my own destiny. I am imaginative and creative and I don't take 'no' for an answer. I believe I can be anything I want to be and thank God I didn't ask for the Moon, I just changed my name to suit it.

For three decades I have lived and breathed music, performing, dance, Art and writing, and with some exciting adventures in far off lands and even near at home, I managed to land on some amazing stages, playing the parts I have always wanted to play. I guess I have been living my dream. It's a nice feeling to be able to say that. Not many can say they "live their dream". But I am doing just that. It has got a lot do with three notions.

1. I believe in myself,
2. I enjoy the journey, and
3. I live with the theory of abundance.

All of these notions are created from being inspired to pursue MY DREAM. This is the essence of my joy. When I don't feel inspired about *pursuing* my dream, I don't believe, I don't enjoy and I don't feel abundant. The pursuit of my dream is what KEEPS ME inspired. And of course, seeing results along the way keeps me pursuing it. It all works together... this fine balance.

Know what you want

When you've written your I AM Statement, you are ready to focus on **what you want.**

It seems easy right? "Oh, I know exactly what I want!"

Do you? Many a seminar I have asked my Artist participants this question, putting them spontaneously on the spot to answer it. You'd think they can answer it immediately.

"Huh, oh... well... I want....um... a big.... no I want lots of.... well I want something that helps me... ahhh...."

Can you answer this question immediately in a concise, straight sentence? Have you really asked yourself why you are an Artist and doing all that you do? What is it that you truly want by doing everything you do?

Hard huh?!

Some examples of what Artists want:

- Financial freedom / to make a living playing music

- Balance my time with writing, being creative, and doing the business

- Be more motivated

- Have more time

- Work less, accomplish more

- Give back to the community

- Become a better musician

- To record a variety of music

- To finish my CD, release it, promote it and get to the next level

- Know if there is a place for me in this world as an Artist

- To be a star, shine brightly and affect the world with my music.

- To develop a business plan

- To tour the world

It means to think about your highest purpose for yourself, and to think *big*. Dreams come to us in our sleep, while we walk, while we talk, while we write, while we create. It is our inner most life map that some say has been set for us before we were even born. Whatever you believe, it's your biggest life quest. I believe that Artists need to dream big, in order to actualize even the simplest of steps. Many of us are told "we can't" from an early age, and so we don't even try to dream big. But dreaming about what you want is half way to actually achieving it. How can you have your dream, when you don't dream? Think about Kevin Costner's character in the movie "Field Of Dreams". What a classic film! This movie so eloquently explains the need to dream, and also to not believe in what everyone else says. He saw a vision, of his baseball players playing a game. He needed to build the field in order for them to come and play. No one around him believed him, but he stuck to his dream, and he persisted in building the field. They came. Then everyone believed. That movie was so much bigger than a baseball game. It teaches us to build the vessel in order for the water to be poured in. If you don't have

> **I believe it's important to dream big because this gives you inspiration to move forward**

something, then create the room for it. If you want money to come in, then open that bank account ready for it. If you want something new to happen in your life, then open up time in your life for that new thing to come. And most importantly, by dreaming, you start the ball rolling for such dreams to come true... as it's in your active consciousness.

I believe it's important to dream, and to dream big, because this gives you inspiration to move forward. Some say, "Oh, dreaming is pointless. If you just dream, all you get is dreaming, no action." I disagree. Dreaming is the first step to actualization.

Visualization

The dream is what keeps us going, is it not? But the next step to dreaming is visualizing. I think there is a strong difference between dreaming and visualizing. Visualizing is the act or process of putting ideas into visual form. It is multi-dimensional, and is based on reality. The goal? To gain a deeper understanding of a concept that might be in our head, and bring it out into visual form.

We use the word "visualizing" a lot. People use it in conversation, in yoga (*"everybody visualize you are calmly sitting on a beach, soft breeze flowing..."*). The word has been *over* used and watered down to a point that the essence is forgotten. Visualizing is really, really important. It is the difference between dreaming, and achieving that dream. Just like your words (the **I AM** Statement and how you talk), **how you THINK and VISUALIZE your dream coming true is the key to making it come true**. So what does visualizing mean? Is it putting it in visual form? Drawing our ideas? Not necessarily. Visualizing can be a mental drawing: we see it in our minds, and it becomes tangible to grasp.

So what's the difference between dreaming and visualization?

Visualizing means you are taking your dreams and seeing it in your mind. If you have an idea, and if you spend more time seeing it in your mind, mulling over the various forms of the idea and its outcomes, writing a little, drawing even, but definitely "seeing it" in your mind... that idea has more chance of coming to fruition.

vi·su·al·ize (v $\bar{I}_{zh}$ ' $\overline{oo}$ ·ə·| $\bar{I}_z$ ')
v. vi·su·al·ized, vi·su·al·iz·ing, vi·su·al·iz·es
v.tr.
1. To form a mental image of; envisage: tried to visualize the scene as it was described.
2. To make visible.
(thefreedictionary.com)

Next time you're sitting on a beach looking at the sunset, grab a stick and start drawing a plan in the sand. Or when you're next doodling on a piece of paper, start creating balloons of thought (bubbles) and write goals inside them. You never know what might happen!

Getting clearer

Do you want a record deal? What type of deal? How much money do you want to make? What kind of job do you want? Where do you want to live and who do you want to be surrounded by? Don't be vague. Ask yourself real questions about your direction and your goals. Try and visualize exactly what you are looking for in your life. Is success measured by wealth, a dollar value, commercial notoriety or personal excellence? Know it. Know what you want well. It could be a combination of various factors. The other part about **knowing what you want** is *knowing the difference between a 'want' and a 'need'.*

A NEED is something that is a necessity to your process, your life, for example... food, or shelter, or a car to go from A to B.

A WANT is a desire, something that can give pleasure or fulfillment, and is something new and different that may actually change your life. It may cause you to work harder to achieve a desire, but ultimately, knowing what you want, and believing in it, will bring it to you.

Stay positive

If you start to think negatively, then you can also attract negative wants. For example, you may not think you are good enough to achieve *that* award, or that job. Well, guess what? You won't, if you think that way. Zoning in on positive goals, with a little pep talk on your self-esteem in believing that you actually deserve them, is the way to achieve those dreams. Keep it real, but also aim high with courage and confidence. If you know what you want, you can create your own reality - your own self-fulfilling prophecy of becoming and achieving.

The power of Intention

Intention is *the* most important factor in creating change. Thoughts are powerful. By merely thinking an idea, you have set the seeds for it to come to fruition.

Dr. Wayne Dyer, brilliant author of the *"Power of Intention"*, wrote *"The use of mental imagery is one of the strongest and most effective strategies for making something happen for you."* It is my opinion that if we can appreciate our past creative results, know where we are right now, and set upon new goals based on intention, we can achieve amazing dreams and accomplishments. If we are able to write down in any form (point form, paragraphs, full pages) of what creativity we have achieved in the recent past, what we don't want, and what we do, then we can create tangible goals MENTALLY that provide fuel for our thoughts and intentions to come to life. By visualizing our past, present and future towards the end of the year, it's even better: way better than a New Year's resolution which can sound exciting on New Year's Eve to think about it, but rarely do we actually accomplish it.

I was listening to an awesome online audio seminar by iPEC Founder, Bruce D. Schneider, called "Know Your Purpose". He spoke of some key topics that I have always believed in, and I feel can translate to the Artist audience. He talks about how the world needs proactivity from positive and powerful people. Proactivity means to be very proactive. How this is achieved, is by

1. aligning your goals.
2. energizing and motivating yourself.

It means not only to be focused with our goal making, but also to do it in a way that you are taking control of your destiny (I've said these words before!).

If you don't lead, you'll follow. If you're going to wait around for someone else to change, you're waiting for others to shift instead of you shifting. That is, being at the effect, instead of being at the cause.

> # Creativity begins with intention

It takes you, as an Artist to be **energized and be able to motivate yourself to make changes in your life,** in order for anything to be accomplished. Make the changes now, and inspire others in your own change. Artists have the keen ability to inspire others just by the Art and music we make, so think about you being the change, rather than following some fashion or trend. That's just being a sheep!

Instead of being reactionary, be at the cause of your life.

Most people sit around and wait for others to guide them (that's what Schneider calls being "reactionary"), but instead take the bull by the horns (become "proactive").

When I talked about creating your life dreams, and visualizing them coming into fruition, I speak of **creating intentions**. This takes work. It means that we need to go deeper and create real intentions (not superficial goals) – looking at your core foundation, your beliefs and value systems... and that means, usually, change.

The result of the chaos of the music industry can kick start you to think outside the box and decide to take action.

What do I truly, truly, want? Set the intention to create it.

Intention is the key. It's all about energy.

Where is your energy? **In fear** - doubt - anger? That's reactive.

If you're intention is in creating a difference today, in your life and others' lives, and all your energy is behind it, then it doesn't matter about the past anymore.

Let the past go, today, and take positive action.

Inspiration, part 2

"Inspired" means: "in spirit", in the flow.

I've learned a lot about the word INSPIRATION these past few years. My father in law, Dick Schiendler, and I talk about it quite a bit. Inspiration, he says, is quite different than being "motivated". Being motivated "is to move away from something you don't want to do" (reactive). Whereas "inspiration is moving towards something you want to do" (proactive). It's one thing to be motivated, but one

The reason why people procrastinate is because they are not inspired by what they do.

should never do anything **for fear of not having the success or not achieving**. And certainly if it feels like you're swimming upstream, then it's something to consider as to 'how' one goes about being motivated. The whole point of creativity is to feel inspired by what you do. So the minute you feel uninspired, then that's telling you something. It has nothing to do with success or failure, just feelings about what you love to do.

Passion and joy... they are the objects of the game :)

You can have intentions, and dreams, and visualize all you want, but if you're NOT INSPIRED by what you want, and who you are, then it's all for naught.

The reason why people procrastinate is because they are not inspired by what they do. For example, at a sales meeting, the speaker may try and motivate you to sell a certain amount, and if you do, you get to go on a particularly special trip, or some other incentive prize. People would be motivated by that so they won't feel left behind of the other sales representatives.

On the other hand, Churchill, in WWII, inspired his troops against all odds. He didn't motivate them.

Most focus on *where they are* (and running away from where they are) and not where they want to be.

So they are focusing more on a fear of failure, instead of going towards pure joy.

Statistics tell that motivated people don't change as much as inspired people. So remember that when you think you are being motivated to do something, or whether you are inspired.

Thanks Dick, for your words of wisdom.

Exercise: Building the dream

Spend a moment for some visualization. Think about your dreams and see them in your mind. **What does it <u>feel</u> like to have these dreams realized?**

Write down the big dream you have for yourself. What is that dream for you? Don't be afraid to dream big. Just write it all down. Take a few pages (I have some handy for you at the back of the book) and let the pen scribble long, fast and wide. Every time you start thinking of negative things, like *"oh, I can't do that"* or *"no one will believe me/accept my ideas"*, stop yourself. This is a private moment with yourself to write down your dream, or dreams, without anyone, or any voice, stopping you or doubting you. As we will move forward in this book, you'll find that the only person who can stop you from doing what you want, really, is yourself and your own doubts and fears. Write it all down: your big dream.

WHAT ARE MY LIFETIME DREAMS?

1.

2.

3.

4.

5.

6.

7.

8.

9.

10.

4. Create a DREAM BOARD: Get a cork board or just plain cardboard and put it up on the wall in your room.

Cut out cool words and pictures from magazines, find photos, and draw on your dream board. Let the words find you, as you scan magazines.

They usually pop out at you because they want you to find them.

This is an example of one of mine below ☺

Food for thought...

*Where are you in your life today?
You made an appointment to be there
five years ago.*

*Where you'll be five years from now
will be determined by your actions today
and in the future.*

*The first step toward getting somewhere
is to decide that you're not going to stay where you are.*

Analyze your life in terms of your environment.

*Are the things around you helping you toward your success or
are they holding you back?*

*You're a product of your environment. So choose an
environment that will best develop you toward your goals.*

*Your world today is a living expression of how you're using
and have used your mind.*

*It's something you can change at any time. Don't remain a
captive to your environment.*

Don't say "If I could, I would," say, "If I can, I will."

You can make changes any time.

Why not start today?

The quotes above are supplied courtesy of
The Daily Guru - Higher Awareness blog
www.thedailyguru.com/higherawareness.htm

10. On a mission to somewhere

Create a mission statement

The most important part of being a professional Artist is to be sure and confident that what you want is the very best for you. As a Warrior Artist, listen to your heart and ask yourself

"Am I prepared to give my whole life to this mission?"

"Am I ready to devote my attention to this?"

I hope the answer is yes, because you are going to need every waking hour and every muscle in your body to be directly focused on this great intention of yours. See if you can come up with a **mission statement** that states WHO you are and WHAT you want, and WHERE you are going. This is something for you personally and internally and doesn't need to be mentioned to anyone else.

Also, create this mission to go beyond just "you". As soon as you remove the "me me me" out of your everyday living, and start thinking of "we", opportunities open up. More so, being willing to go beyond the call of duty to complete a project, with a pursuit of excellence, coupled with a keen desire to tap into the spiritual part of ourselves, brings forth a renewed sense of self. This calmness is based on a certain 'knowing' that you will embrace about yourself and the world around you. Live life to grow everyday and evolve as a human being, with all facets of your life in full harmony: physical, emotional, intellectual and spiritual.

Include your **mission statement** in your I AM Statement, so that your statement becomes larger than you, and more about your contribution to the world.

Adding a mission to your "big dream" takes you outside of the "me me me" and allows the rest of us to join in your cause, and we can support you and love your Artistry. A mission is our central force for why we do what we do.

A mission describes our existence, why we are who we are and where we are heading. It drives us forward and dictates how we will live our lives and, hence, express ourselves. This is very well described in Donald Clifton's book *"Soar with Your Strengths"* . Having a mission, or knowing your mission, motivates you to succeed and excel in your chosen passion... in this case, **Art**.

Beyond the me me me

Realize though, that a mission is STRONGER when it is *altruistic in purpose*. By benefiting <u>others</u> for the greater good, your purpose in Art and in business has more meaning, as it's not just about YOU, but about EVERYONE. The sooner you tailor your visions to benefiting others, you will find your dreams will come true in the truest sense. I have several missions that relate to different parts of my life. One of my most treasured missions is separate from my Artistry and that is in supporting and promoting other Artists, which I do through Songsalive! (www.songsalive.org). I never realized, in creating such an organization, supporting and promoting songwriters, how humanitarian I would have to become. Firstly, it's non-profit and, secondly, I volunteer my time, energy and finance to helping other songwriters build this global, much needed, community. I spend a lot of time coordinating and running the organization and I love to do that. Some people would prefer to devote fifteen hours a week to world peace.

Songsalive! has given me twice-fold what I expected. In fact, I expected nothing in return and, instead, I have made many friends, learned a lot from other Artists and have been provided with a wealth of knowledge, contacts and inspiring, creative times, simply by the act of my own giving. Lacking a mission, people are likely to have only materialistic goals. A mission is the right of every person interested in developing his or her strengths, and it's one of the essential ingredients of excellence.

Write what you believe you do that makes a difference to other people and to mankind. In other words, *why do you do what you do?* By writing your answers down fast, without too much emphasis on spelling, logic or grammar, the objective is that your thoughts flow intuitively. All of a sudden your mission will come to life. This is not about writing goals. Don't define actual plans, just express values and beliefs, no matter what others might think.

Goal making

Once you have narrowed down what your mission is, then you can **define your goals to get there**. Goals are changeable and evolve as you evolve. Once achieved, others replace them. They are like stepping stones in enhancing and realizing your mission. Goals are sometimes best kept far enough away yet close enough that you can reach them one day. *Goals give* *you a sense of purpose,* whether that be what you are going to do today, this week, this year or for the next five years. Your goals are what you live by.

The key is **to create and choose goals that are large enough to really make a difference not only to your life but for others, and yet humble enough to be attained.** Create <u>realistic</u> goals.

If you believe in the following misleading goals of success, it will lead you to only a short term at the top of your echelon, if at all…

Ugly goal 1. Power - climbing the ladder just to say "I got there". Power means you have domination or control over others. Not very humanitarian.

Ugly goal 2. Glamour - the excitement of the industry. Guess what… it's not all that exciting.

Ugly goal 3. Others' needs - the very notion of doing something to make your parents or your wife/husband proud. Don't allow these people to live vicariously through you. Your mission is about what you want, as long as you don't hurt anybody in the process. Without looking out for 'you', you will be unhappy.

Good goals:

1. Personal Excellence - going for the best you can be as an Artist will attract wealth, abundance and many other attributes.

2. Ultimate happiness and fulfillment - success is about getting what you need, not about getting everything. So many people who we think are successful in materialistic ways, or in the media, are still searching for that universal balance: happiness. I know several people who have gorgeous homes that are like paradises, with a pool or ocean view, all the conveniences and comfort. They are either never there to enjoy it (as they are working hard elsewhere), or they still go on holidays elsewhere thinking the grass is greener on the other side of the fence.

I suggest that the next time you sit there day-dreaming, why don't you **plot out a course of action that might work**. Yeah, a little bit of dreaming helps to build on your imagination, but seeing it in your mind and seeing it coming true, then WRITING IT DOWN will make it true. This turns your dream into a tangible goal.

Exercise: My mission and goals

What is my MISSION?

What are some global or humanitarian areas of interest you'd like to be involved in as an Artist and support? (A mission.) Write a paragraph that describes your mission. You might like to incorporate that into your original I AM Statement (re-word it), to include a broader mission. Consider then, investigating into some organizations/charities that you feel you could support, with your Artistry. Why not even contact them? Perhaps they'll give you some stickers, or a banner or giveaways for you to offer at your shows, showing your support. Perhaps your next project could be uniquely tailored to suit that organization with donations or promotion.

Working on my 10-year goals

Spend at least a page or two for each question below. Use separate paper so you can put it away in a secret place when finished. Consider pulling out that piece of paper in a year's time and see if you feel the same way.

Qu. 1 - Where are you in 10 years time? – Before you answer this question, close your eyes and visualize yourself in 10 years time. Where are you? What are you doing? Who are you surrounded by? Really visualize it and then spend at least **20 minutes** answering just this question (maybe 1-5 pages) writing about this place where you are at.

Then, when you have finished writing, and only when you've finished, answer the next questions, each in the same way, without skipping ahead.

Qu. 2 - Where are you in 5 years time? (same process as above. Be sure to give it the same amount of time)

Qu. 3 - Where are you in 2 years time?

Qu. 4 - Where are you this time next year?

Qu. 5 – How did this exercise make you feel? Did it bring you closer to your dreams? Are they now within reach?

Once you have done these exercises, you can put this away. Let it hibernate and do its work in a little drawer somewhere in your room. At some stage you can pull it out and revisit it. But the writing down part is merely a tool to help your brain focus on who you truly are and who you want to become.

11. Get your priorities straight

As a Warrior Artist Entrepreneur, it is very important to be able to cut "like a sword" things that don't serve you, and with diligence, discipline and strength, focus on what does serve you. It's a lifelong lesson to do this, as Warrior Artists are also very apt at helping others, and may put others first before they serve themselves. But it's very important to really fine-tune your priorities so that your Artistry gets the attention it deserves. Yes, it is true: we need a mission in life. We want to be able to offer something to the world. We, as Artists have a responsibility, and a keen ability, to create change through our music.

> "Don't choose the easiest road but the best. It will become easier after a while."
> - anonymous

But, as the old saying goes "if you help yourself, you can then help so many others". When the airplane is falling, the flight attendant tells us to put the oxygen mask on us first before we help others. If we can't breathe, how are we supposed to save anyone else?

Warrior Artists also learn to focus so acutely that your attention can not be diverted. It's a like a bee line to the goal.

As Artists, we are always facing tough decisions, mainly because we are running our own affairs and usually don't have a team or especially a company with advisers to tell us which moves to make.

The process of decision making can make us feel anxious, create fear, and thwart our process of creation. Making a decision usually requires a very black and white answer - will I, won't I, can I, can't I, should I, shouldn't I? Whilst some people might say that there are right and wrong decisions, I believe this to be inaccurate. There are no wrong decisions. Just make a decision, and make it the right decision.

Once you choose - and empower that choice - follow through with it, with conviction. You will surely then feel that decision work for you in a very positive way. You will grow enormously from enacting a decision.

Reflect on some of the hardest decisions you've had to make in your life... I'm sure you'll recall that as a result of following through with that decision, you would have received enormous good lessons and amazing outcomes. Trust your instincts.

TRUST YOUR INSTINCTS

Priorities are the broad elements in your life that mean a lot to you, and that you live by (lifestyle) and are your overall focus. They can be anywhere from your family, your health, or getting your album out or touring Europe. They can be about "achieving financial independence" or "being creative on a daily basis". As much as we worked on our big dreams and goals, our priorities oversee how we function on a day to day basis.

It is by fleshing out your priorities that you can then work on your time management, which we will discuss in the next chapter.

When you've written down Who You Are, and What You Want – the big dreams, the highest goals, and your short term (1-3 year goals), the next step is to refine *how* you live your life and what you give focus to. If your "to-do list" of today has at least 1 of your highest goals being nurtured, then you know you're on the right path. But if your day or week doesn't allow you to focus on your big dreams, then you know you have to make an adjustment. For, if you are not working on the things you want right now, then you'll never attain what you want. I always say that life is a journey, not a destination, and what I mean by that is, what you are doing now IS the end result. If you aren't working on your Artistry, and instead spend more time on work, the kids, other people's projects, or just spinning the wheels, then you are not living your dream.

Get the focus back to you

Start now by giving energy and time to your passion, even if that means just a little bit towards it, and a lot on "life". That's ok. Just at least make it a priority now, and make YOU a priority now.

Here's a letter I wrote to one of my Artist clients recently, who was struggling with the notion of "focusing" on herself, as well as figuring out how to find time for her Artistry. For the purpose of this book, I've changed the name of my client. Jenny was always focusing on others, and what they thought. She was spending her time running around catering to them (family, friends) and was assuming a lot about what other people thought of her, which stopped her from moving forward with her own plan to attain her goals. I wrote her this e-mail:

Dear Jenny,
I want to summarize a few things based on our conversations in hope that it will remind you where you can be, rather than where you are.

Get your priorities straight

Get your priorities straight

I want to reiterate what I first said in our session. Don't be afraid to have POWER in your life right now. "By feeling powerless". You're giving THEM and some FUTURE result, your power.

Don't forget YOU are the director of this play (your life), and that you have brought in this cast of characters for a reason. Even if they are not giving you what you want specifically right now, there for a reason.

FOCUS MORE ON YOURSELF. That's the decision you can only make. Don't worry about what OTHERS think of you. Don't worry about all their little life challenges. That's their life story, and they need to address those. You don't need to save them or fix them. Just focus on you. You have to follow your bliss. The world around you will respond to you being happier more than if you stay in "the struggle" and "the fear". If you follow your own bliss, and you ask the people around you to become responsible for THEMSELVES, It makes them become better people because they know they have to be responsible for themselves. This is the biggest lesson you can offer in their lives.

Your choosing to focus on what COULD happen NEGATIVELY; instead of positively will ONLY attract the NEGATIVE outcome. If you focus on that, that is what you get.

Make a decision on GROWTH. Don't make a decision based on FEAR. If you focus on fear, then you're not going to get the results you want. So make a decision on GROWTH.

THE GOAL for this month is to make the commitment to YOU and to give yourself permission to shine.

You, the whole person

As I wrote in my first book, it's important for Artist's to care for their souls, and that means the whole person in you. You are an Artist, but you're human. You may have a family, you may have other jobs, interests or just responsibilities. Getting clear with your priorities can help you feed all aspects of you so that nothing gets left behind.

I am writing all this at the somewhat beginning of the book, before we leap into the nitty gritty of the business end, because I've come to realize that if we start on the right footing in how we define our goals, priorities and therefore the way we USE our time, then we can really propel ourselves into the big world and be very, and I mean VERY, successful as professional Artists.

Being a professional Artist is not merely a job, it's a way of life. Think of your "life-style" and everything else will fall into place. However, life also delivers its own cards and sometimes we have to play the cards we are dealt. Yet, at the same time, it's your game of life too and remember, "thought creates action." Your *will* is your future. Think positive thoughts and you will have a healthier, happier, more successful life.

Get your priorities straight

While we strive for our goals that we set, some so high, others tangible, let us not forget that life is not just about Art, Music, Career or Business... A healthy body, healthy mind and healthy spirit is what we need to maintain and life's circumstances can wreak havoc on that balance. It is crucial to stay centered and grounded, freeing yourself from all unwanted influences. Life is about happiness and happiness is a journey, not a destination.

The minute you allow your Art, but more specifically your profession, to completely envelope you, it can begin to ruin you. It's important to keep a clear head and a healthy attitude about your profession, about business, and about your priorities as a whole person with a big dream.

Exercise 1: Organize your priorities

Jeff Davidson, author of the *"60 Second Organizer"*, has a cool exercise in getting your priorities straight. I've embellished more of it here myself. Here goes: Write down everything that is important to you, assigned to you or that you seek to achieve. Make it long and involved. I suggest at least 10 items on the list, with descriptions under each one.

Keep the wording around your lifestyle and overall desires and how you want your life to be. Make each one a great, positive affirmation, e.g. "achieve financial independence" or "build my presence and reputation in the music business".

These priorities should be standards by which you want to live by, and that are extremely important to you.

They don't just have to be your Artistic priorities. Include your personal ones. We are human, after all. E.g. "give support and love to my family on a daily basis".

Several hours later or the next day, come back to it and revise the list. Toss things out that aren't *crucial*. Combine any items that seem similar. Pare down the list. Restructure and define the list. When in doubt, toss it out.

Put the list away again for another day or two and then look at it and revise again. Go ahead and make a working list of your current priorities. Put them on the wall.

Visualize them all coming to fruition. Take the time to close your eyes and see, feel and taste each one of these priorities as if they are real and constant in your life. Remember, thought is powerful.

Exercise 2: Circle of Personal Perspective

The following exercise is used by permission and is courtesy of Fowler Wainwright International. See bibliography for more details.

I thank Berry Fowler from the Institute very much for allowing me to include this exercise in this book, as well as training me to be the best Professional Coach I can be. The Circle of Personal Perspective is an effective tool to work out how you perceive yourself in each area of your life, and then allow you to determine what areas to focus on more at any given time (an overall guide to building your priorities).

Take a look at the circle below. On a scale of 0-10, (0 being completely unsatisfactory and 10 being thoroughly satisfied), decide where you perceive yourself to be in each area of your life at the present time. Write that number in the appropriate area of the circle. (See circle on next page as an example.)

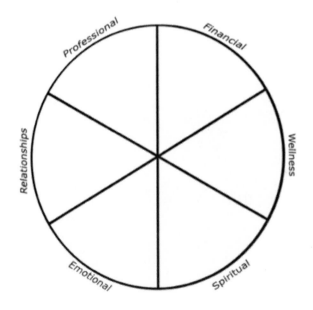

Get your priorities straight

Then, color in the areas around your numbers so it will look something like this:

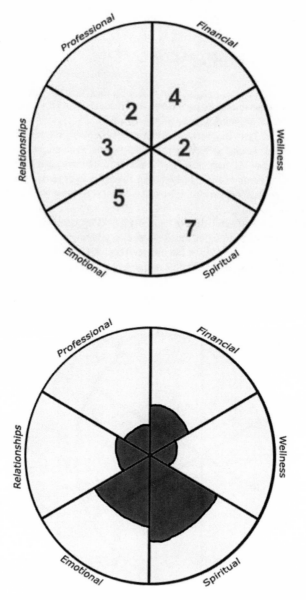

Get your priorities straight

When you've finished with your circle, you will be able to have an overview of the areas in your life, and how you see them. If you have a low number in Wellness and Professional, but a high number in Spiritual and Financial, you can see which areas you need to focus on, and you can then set goals for each area that you work towards, to build the numbers up. Most importantly, create priorities in your life, which you live by, that include ALL the areas, as well as including extra priorities for areas in which you want to increase the numbers.

Hold on to your DREAMS, GOALS and PRIORITIES lists. We will come back to these and implement them into a real and tangible PLAN for your career a little further into this book.

Once upon a time there was a thought aiming up towards the sky.

When we seek others' counsel, it sometimes is diverted, this thought, towards a perspective others feel is best for us.

And sometimes we go down that path and it turns sour, away from our original intent.

And we lay flat wondering why we tried so hard, when we feel we have failed.

So we go within, still, and regroup. It's okay to be here, for as long as necessary.

Until we once again dream big, visualize and think. Focusing our thoughts, listening to our own true heart, aiming up towards the sky.

- gilli moon

12. What's time got to do with it?

When it comes to being an Artist, the words "effort", "energy" and "time" should be irrelevant. You give attention to your Art not because it needs attention, but because it INSPIRES you.

I was at Starbucks this morning at 8am ordering my favorite Green Tea Soy Latte, when the girl behind the cash register had a problem processing my payment and caused a delay. When I had arrived, I was the only person in line, but as it took a bit to get the cash register to accept my card, the line behind me had grown. Finally as I was leaving, this lady in the line (she was third and had about 10 behind her), said out loud so everyone could hear, *"this woman has wasted 10 minutes of our time"*, to which I replied,

"Yes I have, I'm sorry."

"And so you should be", she rebutted angrily.

I didn't know what to say next because she obviously blamed me for every ounce of time she lost at that moment and wasn't going to even accept an apology, even though it wasn't actually my fault.

What is it about time with everyone? Is time so precious that we are willing to

Be rude to each other?

Blame another person for one's lack of time?

Feel it's one's duty to represent everyone's waste of time?

Moral to this little tale?

There is no need to blame someone else for your lack or waste of time. We are responsible for our own lives. If the lady had arrived 5 minutes before me, I wouldn't have "wasted" her time at all. Perhaps allowing a little longer getting her coffee before work might actually help. But instead, she chose to blame me for her schedule.

What's time got to do with it anyway? Patience is a virtue. It actually didn't take 10 minutes. It was more like 3 minutes. But hey, who's counting? Does it really matter? We've got our whole lives to drink coffee.

Learn from your past, but appreciate where you're at and leap into the future. If the lady just looked around for a moment, she would have noticed there were 10 people behind her, whereas she was only 3rd in the line until the cash register. Perhaps she could be grateful that she didn't have as long to wait as the others!

On a side note, why can't we all just get along? Just be nice to people. Treat others like you'd like to be treated. I had to hold my tongue not to bite back, because I didn't want to play her game. Instead, I bit my tongue, took my drink, and walked away.

Take responsibility for your time: don't blame others, don't believe "others" are taking away your time, or holding you back – YOU are responsible for everything in your life.

All of the above, of course, translates to every aspect of your life, including your Artistry, career, and just plain ol' living!

The victim of time

When it comes to being an Artist, the words "effort", "energy" and "time" should be irrelevant. You give attention to your Art not because it needs attention, but because it INSPIRES you. When we stop focusing on how much effort or energy we need to give it, or how much time we need to do it, and start focusing on the joy of creating (basically getting out of your own way), it is amazing to see HOW MUCH opportunity comes.

Stop spending time micro-managing your life. Every second you waste managing your seconds, you could be spending creating. In my experience working with other Artists, the number one concern Artists have, in creating success in their lives, has to do with time management.

"I can't seem to get it all done in one day, being an Artist and doing all the music business stuff."

"There's so many things to do as an Artist, and I just don't know where to start."

"I feel overwhelmed."

"I need help on getting focused, because I feel scattered."

And so forth....

A lot of Artists don't think they have the time to write songs, record, paint (do their Art/create), let alone run the business side of it all as well. It can seem very overwhelming.

Julia Cameron writes in her book, *The Right To Write*, "one of the biggest myths around writing is that in order to do it we must have great swathes of uninterrupted time." She then goes on to reveal that no one gets this kind of luxury and that getting things done is like finding the moments. I truly believe this is how it happens. We may wish we have a day, a week, a month, our life time... to completely dedicate ourselves to our music, Art and creativity, but the reality is, we don't; nor should we. For while we are Artists, we are also human beings, and we also have responsibilities based on choices we make, such as paying the bills, covering our lifestyle by bringing in money; family, social life; and so forth.

I find the best artwork I've ever done is in the spaces between my life, when I don't dedicate hours to focus on it, but rather follow the spontaneous impulse I may get in any given moment. Living in the moment helps too. I've touched on this subject so far, and finding time to do your Art is, to me, finding Art... and giving it the time. When a moment opens up to scribble down lyrics to a new song, or tinkle on the piano, or draw on a piece of paper... do it, even if you only have "a moment". That might be the most golden moment you've ever had. You can always finish it off later.

The only obstacle we have with time, is what we place on ourselves. Time for one's Artistry has often been an obstacle for many professional Artists.

The fact of the matter is that TIME is an ILLUSION. How you limit or expand your perception of time is relative to what you want to do. If you need your coffee in the morning, you could either make it at home (15 minutes including boiling the kettle), drive by Starbucks or a Café (25 minutes including driving), or pick the coffee beans, and grind them (5 hours to perhaps a change of career into the coffee industry!) It's all relative.

If we didn't have an attachment to time, then we might be able to focus more on the creativity – the doing – of what we love, without restrictions. It can be quite limiting to think you have to do everything you want in a specific amount of time.

But we live in a world that is caught up with deadlines, schedules, and outcomes. We live in a world where people judge others by what they do in a certain amount of time. We are influenced by society's need to succeed, and it all has to be done in a certain time frame, otherwise we feel we've failed. One way to avoid all this is not care what others think, and just LIVE in the MOMENT. My *Enjoy the Journey* chapter writes about this, of course. But I do understand that we all have goals that we want to achieve and that means fitting very abstract dreams into a compartmentalized framework of years, months, weeks and days. I get that. I even want to achieve something by a certain time. So I'm caught between living in a mind frame of **no time** – *non time continuum* – to scheduling my hours so I can achieve what I want to achieve.

So... *it is up to you to create that time for your Artistry*, even if that means being strict with your time management. [Now here's where it might all seem like one big oxymoron – floating in no time – to scheduling time in a very disciplined manner!]

But let me remind you about my **warrior-ship**: *Finding freedom through discipline* is one of my warrior mottos. That means that through disciplining myself with my time, my process and my choices, I can actually find amazing creative freedom, where all my Artistic goals can be fulfilled. Exciting prospect, aye?

All that being said, crossing that line from the overwhelmed, scattered, sleep deprived multi-tasking Artist, to the successful, action creating, fulfilled Artist, comes down to understanding how time can work for you. It does not mean you need to be a **victim of time**. You are an Artist... get creative with your time.

As I've discussed, we build a dream, we create a plan, and off we go. So how do we manage our time to fit all these beautiful goals and dreams in our lives? One thing is clear, Art is creative, and it can be spontaneous JOY, while the business may not be. So, I am all for managing your time to get the icky business done. That is, if you think it's icky. I personally thrive in the business side of my Art, because I see it creatively. I want to inspire you to see it the same way and here are a few tools to get you going...

Time management 101 for the biz busy-ness of you

Time management is not rocket science. There are hundreds of books about it and we all can create our own time management ourselves if we put a little time into it! The hardest concept for Artists to manage is the very notion of "managing" and "scheduling" themselves. *We are creative. Why should we fit ourselves into a routine or schedule? We get inspired at any time of the day. We must create when the Gods are speaking!*

However, like any business, Artist Entrepreneurs can think strategically in order to get it ALL done and balance the Art and Business of their lives. If you have a lot going on, a little time management won't kill your creative flow. In fact, the discipline of it might actually give you more creative results, because you've allowed time to BE creative.

It has been proven, and it's pretty obvious, that constant interruptions and demands can get in the way of our creativity. So it's important to not only remove the distractions when you want to create, but also take the time to just focus on being creative. Putting your mind to the task at hand can allow you to create mountains of creativity. It's up to you.

I think I have to be a bit of a nut to take on all the things I do in my life. But then, I'm creative. I can't help it. Getting out there takes a lot of careful strategies and a lot of organization. We just went through the gamut of building your dreams, goals and priorities. That's all part of the first step. But then, it takes discipline to see it all come to fruition. That takes planning, and the first step to planning is working out your time management. You can get lots of books about time management, and I'll point out a few cool things to help you. What I do know, is that time management is the number one complaint from Artists.

Being a multi-tasker, I think, has to be innate in you: the ability to multi-task and to be a left and right brain thinker. But time management can be mastered by all, as long as you tailor it to your nature. I compartmentalize my week, and my days, sometimes my hour. I work best when I have a to-do list in front of me with the hot/important things for the day, and then what my priorities are for the week (including any upcoming deadlines). Then, with the list in front of me, I then like to "paint" so to speak – be free in what I do. I have learned that I'm not a linear person, no matter how organized I train myself. That means I work creatively. I like to work on tidbits at a time for each task/project. A little bit of this, a little bit of that... then come back to the first one again. So in the space of an hour, I may be working on about 4 different tasks, just jumping to each whenever I get bored or frustrated or just need a change. By the end of the hour, and the day, I've accomplished them all (usually) but not one after the other... all the time. This diversity keeps me interested in what I do, and gets the job done.

But everyone is different. It's up to you to figure out your relationship with time, and how you can use it to the best advantage to achieve your goals.

Some ideas. Pick any that suit...

Get specific

Put everything else aside, and focus on the task at hand. It's easy for me to say it isn't it? What with the distractions of work, phone calls, e-mails, those terribly attractive internet social networks that lure us in to spend wasteful hours socializing... but it's true: if you have even just one task a day that you want to do, focus on what's important and discard the rest/put off 'till the next day. What's crucial is to focus on what you REALLY want. That means getting real with your big goals and your short term goals. Being specific with what you want to do is important. Putting them on top of your to do list (making them priorities in your daily life) can be hard, but necessary. But once you know what you want, just taking the steps makes it a whole lot easier to attain them.

Learn to say no

Learning to let go of the things that aren't important, can be very difficult in life. It can be tough enough to decipher what is or isn't important. Working on your priorities is a big start. One of the hardest things I've had to learn is how to say *no* without hurting anyone, and in order to save *me*. It's a lesson I'm still learning. I am quick to take things on, run things, create things and be a leader, because I know I can. But I also know that taking too much on means that things aren't always done with excellence, or they may take a long time. So I'm learning to cut my work load to a few projects that I enjoy, so I can give them my utmost attention.

Take time to make life happen

You need to **give yourself time** to develop your professional career. Don't expect it to come overnight. There is truth in the term "paying your dues" and also truth in the term "becoming an overnight sensation takes ten years".

Some people are too impatient. They want it all at once, and now. We think that all these superstars are overnight sensations and that if our career takes five years, no ten, then we are complete failures. How fickle we are! A great career in the Arts business takes t-i-m-e.

Did you know that most bands that sign big record deals have actually been together already for about 10 years? The sad fact is that by the time they've released their big CD with the label, with all the marketing money spent on them, that a lot of these bands are already burned out. But it DOES take a long time. That's called the "10 year overnight sensation". Are you ready for the long haul?

Firstly, don't think you have to win over who's already out there "making it". It's not a contest. It's about you finding value in what you alone can determine. This might take a life time. In fact, as I've mentioned before, it's a life long journey. If you were to "make it" right now, what would you do then? Give up? Die?

Sit back and enjoy the ride because the process is the best part. Take the time to discover who you want to be. Heed the sign "when the time's right, it will come". Life is about timing and sometimes we want to try and push that with our will.

Patience is a virtue, and time is of the essence. You've heard it all before, and it's all true.

Take your time, develop, study, expand your business, nurture your talent, focus on your choice, and allow the universe to deliver in good time.

The job that eats up time

Some feel that they can't take on a full time job, because then they wouldn't have time to create. But the constant focus of trying to generate income can be an even bigger obstacle because you spend more time worrying about money and not creating! Imagine if you spent the same amount of time figuring out cool ways you could make an income by diversifying your own creative talents? Perhaps you could design websites or give singing lessons? Who knows? But I do know many Artists who just worry way too much about getting a job, working in a job, or not having a job, and not enough time thinking about some cool ways to make income, or build their own business. Worry versus creativity. Which road would you take?

Having a day job demands a lot of time and attention and it's hard to give the same focus at night or weekends to pursuing your music or Arts business. But it takes fortitude and energy to do both. Some people love to work, day, night, weekends, all of it. Others don't.

On the other hand, a full time job can help a lot towards managing your creativity time. They say when you have something to get done, give it to a busy person. When I decided to take on a full time job at one point in time, I began to realize that I was still able to make the time to create. In fact, I was *more* creative than normal. The full time job gave me two opportunities.

I was able to afford the investment into my music – go into the studio, record the songs, and produce the CDs that I owned 100% because I had the money to pay for the production completely and not have to do a deal with someone else for investment.

The job put me on a schedule and a routine. I got up every morning and went to work. I did my job. I came home. I continued my schedule: I either wrote songs, recorded them, or went online and did some "business". I was productive because of the routine my day job gave me. I felt secure, and I felt empowered that I was in control of my music and product, and I was productive.

If you decide to work for yourself, and set up your own business, it can be one of the most exciting things you'll ever do. Maybe it's the thrill of letting go of the nine to five, or the notion of being your own boss. Whatever the reason, you become the master of your own destiny, and that is what this book is about!

Creating a routine and schedule

Time can eat up your whole week. You have to treat your Artistic business like any job. You get up, you go to work. Simple. But of course, the important part is combining your left side (logical business side) with the right side of the brain (creative, passionate). I have always believed that as a professional Artist, you need to be both a left and right brain thinker, and that means taking on your creativity with vigor and excellence, as well as the business side with as much flair and focus.

These days, running my own record label, music publishing and coaching company, plus writing songs, recording my new album and performing live, I treat my days with **a careful balance of business and Artistic pleasure.** I compartmentalize my days in a way that balances business efforts with creativity. I reward myself with writing, and song writing, performing and simply playing in the studio. I create a schedule that I work off on a weekly basis, and it gives me a routine. I feel that Artists need a routine in order to achieve their goals.

It begins with creating the short term goals for the week. I like to do this at the beginning of the week, either Sunday night or first thing Monday morning.

Get organized

I first take a good look at my BIG GOALS. These are the ones we created in the first few chapters of this book. I like to look at them, evaluate them, and see if I'm still on the same page, each week. I then give myself some weekly goals, based on my agenda (meetings, gigs, life stuff...). I write down what goals I want to accomplish for the week. Then I write down the goals for the day. Sometimes it's cool to write a big fat box next to each daily goal, so you can check (tick) it off when completed. This gives you a sense of accomplishment. We all want to feel the accomplishments along the way, so that's a good way of doing it.

My daily goals drive my day, but I don't want to be beholden to them. They act merely as a guide. I'm a creative person so it's natural that I want to deviate off the linear map. For example, say one of my goals is to log into LinkedIn (www.LinkedIn.com) and find a music supervisor to send songs to. LinkedIn is cool for that as you can find who you know, or within six, or three, degrees of separation. If you know someone who knows the desired contact, you can ask your friend to introduce you. It's a very cool network. ANY way... say I want to find someone there, and I end up clicking a link and go off to another website because it was interesting. My natural instinct is to delve into that new website and I get lost in a new world. But now I've learned to not go there straight away. I write down that new website as a new action item, and I continue on the original path I was on 'till I feel confident of some kind of completion.

My week is, in theory, built around a *weekly schedule* that I have on the wall. It shows the days of the week, Monday through Sunday, along the top. Down the left side is a column dedicated to the times of the day. I break them up in two-hour blocks from 8:30am to 10pm at night. I then block out parts of each day dedicated to my focus areas. Some of these, for me, include:

Online marketing, such as web updates, promoting my products online, and social networks.
Following up on e-mails and business leads.
My record label activities with Artists and current events, productions and promotions.
Going to the studio to record.
Coaching an Artist.
Volunteer projects I may be exploring at the time.
Exercise and health.
Writing songs, recording music.
Writing this book, my online blog and articles.
Time off, family and relaxation.

Take a look at the schedule at the end of this chapter and see if you can come up with something for yourself that balances your work life, creative life, play and personal.

Each of these focus areas of mine I block through the week and I even color code them in different colors, so that I can see them from a distance on the wall, and they become important "babies" that have a certain color (helps my Artistic eye). My weeks don't always go perfectly to schedule though. Meetings, trips, unscheduled mishaps have to happen. But I try and make it up where I can. What this schedule provides for me is a sense of stability and focus. It helps me not feel like I have to answer every e-mail on a subject when it comes in (I filter certain e-mails for different projects until I am ready to read them). It allows me to give my best on each project/task/priority, and not get distracted.

When I give my best on one thing at a time, it's much better than being mediocre in hundreds of things.

There is a great book out there called *60 Second Organizer* which has some great tips on how to get organized (see Bibliography at the back) and I'll pull some out and splash them on this page for you, that I feel are Artistically helpful:

Work smarter, not harder

Follow your intuition on what feels right. "If you're figuring out how to organize something, it's often okay to simply start and let your intuition guide you."

Get in the mood

"When you wait until you are 'in the mood' to get organized, you run the risk that the right mood will come at an inopportune time or even not at all." Schedule the time to create your goals. I created a goal today to complete this chapter. I didn't leave the seat 'till it was written. (I happened to be flying across the Pacific Ocean right now from Sydney to L.A. Woo hoo! That means I have only enough battery time to get it down, so I have to just get it done. What a challenge!) I wasn't really in the mood to do it, but I just disciplined myself to get it done. While you may not feel overly enthusiastic to complete a task, there is an amazing sense of accomplishment if you do complete it. That's the time to reward yourself.

Begin easily

If you don't want to dive into a huge project, work on the little ones first. Maybe you need to check your Myspace inbox, or respond to the easy e-mails in the inbox. Maybe organizing your photos from your last gig might feel good to try, before you consider updating your EPK (press kit) or designing your CD cover. Little tasks completed mean little accomplishments and that helps the reward factor throughout the day. **Tangible goals will give you more confidence that you can achieve your dream, and remove any fears of inadequacy. Take one step at a time.**

Reward yourself

When you finish them, take a little break and change your environment even for a moment (walk around the block or light a candle in another room and sit out at some view outside if you have one). Maybe you can reward yourself with a fun project you've wanted to do but it's like a guilty pleasure. Don't wait too long to reward yourself after tasks are completed. It's best straight away.

What's holding you back?

If you find it hard to start a task, there could be a valid reason why you can't start it. Maybe it's just not meant to be right now? I really believe in universal timing, and some things just aren't meant to happen at a certain time, and are supposed to happen when the time is right. Perhaps those tasks can go to the low priority list for now, and get on with what is achievable, feels right and tangible.

Schedule time to organize

Sometimes I can't do anything until my bed is made and the kitchen sink has no more dirty dishes. You might have similar needs. If you work from home, like I do, I need to have the house in order and my home office room completely tidy, before I can sit down at the desk. If the desk is full of files all over the place, I need to take time to get them in order before I can focus on the computer.

Create deadlines

Deadlines can restrict creative freedom if all you think about is the end. But they can also help you complete them. As long as you focus on each task one at a time, a deadline can be really helpful. In fact, the whole project doesn't have to be complete. Perhaps the daily deadline is to just get to a half way point. Whatever the deadline is, right it down next to your to-dos for the day.

Put today's goals up top

From all the goal oriented fodder so far in this book, I'm sure you have pages and pages written about your dreams and goals so far. But today, put your days' goals up top of your to-do list, so that they become the focus. Balance your short term goals (today, this week, this month) with your long term goals (this year, next 5 years, life) but mixing a few in to the top 5 things to do for the day. Keep the short list to 3-9 items a day so you don't get overloaded.

Create a project list

Keep your projects on the wall where you can see what are the important ones you are working on right now. Each project should have a list of strategies accompanying them. See exercise at end of chapter.

Organize Your Inbox

Have you ever felt like you didn't want to turn on your computer because you had so many e-mails to respond to? I have figured out a way to put the joy back into e-mailing. It comes down to a simple strategy on how you attend your e-mails. I used to attend to every e-mail I received as it came in. I ended up spending all day answering e-mails [because I'd get up to a thousand e-mails a day] and I would never get on to my projects or creative time. After reading David Alan's book *Getting Things Done*, I realized when to defer e-mails and when to attend to them immediately and it all came down to these few points. A.) I am not obliged to answer everyone's e-mail just because they contact me. B.) It is up to me to decide what is a priority and what isn't. C.) I am learning not to answer e-mails first thing in the morning and instead leave that time for creativity, exercise, writing, or only things that are about me and not about other people's agendas.

Alan writes that when you get an e-mail come in, if you feel you can respond to it or handle it in under two minutes, then do it then and there. But if you think it will take more than two minutes, defer it to another time when you allocate follow up time for your e-mails in your daily schedule. In order to get rid of thousands of e-mails in your inbox, the best thing to do is to set up folders in your e-mail's software, where you can drag the e-mail to. Here are some of the folder ideas that you can create, which is inspired by Alan's book.

Action Hot- these are e-mails you need to answer that very day.

Action Low- these are e-mails you need to take action on, but it is not a high priority and you can answer in your own time.

Waiting For [W/F] or Pending- these are e-mails you're waiting for someone else to take action on but you are keeping track of them so you know when to follow up.

Read/Review- these are e-mails that don't require action except for you to read and then later file or delete.

Reference/File- these are simply e-mails you want to keep and you will file at some stage when you are in your filing mode.

Agendas/Calendarize- I think I came up with the word "calendarize", and it makes sense. These are simply e-mails you need to add to your calendar agenda with specific event dates or appointments.

Calls To Make- these are e-mails that you need to follow up on with a phone call [I know we are all addicted to the internet but don't forget a phone call can be way more powerful and is still a very important part of business practice].

Data Entry- these are e-mails that had data that you need to add to your contacts, mailing list or database.

Someday/Maybe- these are e-mails that you may enact in the future at some time or they may offer an idea for a new project you may pursue. As Alan writes, this list is an "inventory of your creative imaginings".

So now you see that if you have one hundred e-mails or actions all jumbled up its hard to see what you need to focus on now. But by adopting Alan's two minute rule whereby you handle e-mails that can be done quickly or defer them, you are maximizing your internet time in a productive way and not drowning in e-mail mess.

These kinds of folders can also work for your paper to do lists and files. I like to have a notebook on hand for my Hot Action items, and I have different pages for all the other lists. I also use manila folders with legible or typed titles for paperwork and files and I have them on my desk where I can see them but filed neatly in the corner. At the end of each week, or in fact the beginning of a new week such as

Monday morning, I like to go through everything that is pending so that I have an overview of what I need to accomplish in the short term. On that note it's really important to understand that part of achieving your goals includes 1.) setting aside time to organize your lists, 2.) setting up the space where you can work and be organized, and 3.) have the tools in order to be organized such as filing supplies, labeler, etc.

What to focus on?

We often mismanage our time. Ernie Zelinski writes in his book, *The Lazy Person's Guide To Success*, that time devoted to just hard work (being busy, thinking we are accomplishing something but instead spinning our wheels), is generally a poor use of time. If we spend time on creativity and imagination, then this is more effective. *"The wise use of the assets you have - time, energy, creativity, motivation, money, patience, and courage - is what will bring you success and happiness over the long term."*

Spend your time doing what you LOVE. Minimize the time you spend on things that you don't like and that are not important. Set your priorities straight, build achievable goals, and then figure out what's important THIS week.

> *Spend your time doing what you LOVE.*
> *Minimize the time you spend on things that you don't like and that are not important.*

You CAN find the balance between work, and free time too... ultimately if you can combine creativity in all of it, you have found the key.

Do what you need to do based on WHAT *YOU* WANT, not on what you think you should do because others are doing it.

I build my day around tangible goals that I want to achieve THAT very day, reminding myself of the WEEKLY goals, which feed into my LONG TERM goals. I never lose site of the long term goals.

Keep in mind that even if you have all the time in the world for your creativity, you still need an amazing amount of stamina that can last a long time. *This business is not for those fly-by-nights. This business is for those who can withstand all the obstacles, do the grunt work, take focus, and stand the test of time.*

Build your day with a little bit of discipline, a lot of freedom, pleasure, creativity, meditation and exercise. Multi-task, or be linear focused – It doesn't matter. Whatever you do, though, enjoy the journey.

Have fun with time. It can either make you feel constricted, or give you freedom. If you can't seem to work within time, throw your watch away.

Personally, I don't believe in the word: time.
Something for you to ponder!

Exercise: Creating the List

With the big dreams on the wall, and the Goals in your Plan, it's time to create your to-do lists for the week or month.

Start by creating four (4) columns on a piece of paper, landscape style (long ways). Put the headings below in each column:

Column 1: HOT/NOW
Column 2: WARM
Column 3: DELEGATE
Column 4: LATER/PUT OFF

HOT/NOW	WARM	DELEGATE	LATER/PUT OFF

Under each heading, start listing the tasks and action items you'd like to achieve. It's pretty self-explanatory: Hot/Now are items you need to take care of straight away; Warm are for items that are important but not a must-do today; Delegate – items you feel you could delegate to others; and Later/Put Off – items or projects you can do later, but still want to keep your eye on, on your list.

Having a running list like this each week, which can change every week based on the importance of the tasks/items, will allow you to not only keep track of what you need to do, but give importance or lack thereof so you don't end up spinning your wheels, becoming overwhelmed or disorganized.

Keep doing this weekly, refresh and evaluate as you go. Good luck!

Exercise 2: Creating a schedule

Draw up, on one big page (whether it be a small sheet or large poster) the 7 days of the week along the top. On the left column write times of the day in 2 hour blocks starting from when you wake up to when you go to sleep.

Add your priorities and projects to the schedule. Don't forget to also add any part-time or full-time jobs, plus your creative time, as well as down time and exercise. Be sure that your priorities that you listed in the previous chapter enter into your schedule, as well as short term and long term goals.

	MON	Tues	Wed	Thurs	Fri	Sat	Sun
8.30-10.30	Plan week/ goals/ Emails	Goals/ Emails	Writing/ Create	Goals/ Emails	Writing/ Create	Writing	'me' time
10.30-12.30	Biz develop,/ Followups/ New biz	Online/ Social Networks	Biz development	Online/ social Networks	Biz development	Writing	'me' time
12.30-2.30	Break/ lunch/ 'me' time	Break/ Lunch/ 'me' time	Break/ lunch/ 'me' time	Lunch/ Organize file	Lunch/.	Errands	Create
2.30-4.30	Projects	Projects	Emails/ Followups	Creative Time	Emails/ Followups	Create	Create
4.30-6.30	Exercise	Exercise	Projects	Creative Time	Exercise	Create	Create
eve	'me' time	'me' time	Projects	Rehearse band	GIG	GIG	Create

Exercise 3: My projects

Build a project list, of all the important projects you have going on. They may include something like the following:

> The European Tour
> Record music for upcoming CD
> Build the website
> Revamp all my social networking sites
> Orchestrate the ABC Movie

Then, for each project, **set the main Goals**, and then a **Timeline**. Try and work backwards from the final date with your timeline.

Then list the **Strategies** for each project – all the things (action items) you can do for each of your projects. Give a page per project and put them on your wall to follow.

Remember, these are actual projects that you are about to do. Not dreams. Each of the Projects should look something like this:

PROJECT: The European Tour

GOALS: Tour England, Ireland, Italy and Germany through ABC promotion company. / Sell CDs and build our mailing list.

TIMELINE
March 15 – Depart for London
Feb 22, 27 – final rehearsals
Jan 15 – first rehearsal with the band
Jan 2 – CDs shipped to promoter in advance.

STRATEGIES:
Find a bass player – advertise in Craigslist, Facebook, etc.
Book the rehearsal space.
Liaise with promoter for event

And so forth. Of course, your list of Strategies should be a full page long, at the minimum. I am just getting ideas rolling...

Exercise 4: Getting today's tasks together

With your priorities, goals and dreams close by, plus your schedule in front of you, set to work on your daily task (to-do) list for the next 3 days. Put the top 3 important tasks up top on each day. Put a big fat check (tick) box next to each task.

1.

2.

3.

4.

5.

6.

7.

Begin!

When you complete each task, check (tick) the box next to the task and reward yourself!

Busy
Busy

"It is not enough
to be busy....
The question is:
what are we
busy about?"
- Henry David Thoreau

There is no shortage of time. It's
how we use it that's important.
  - Gilli Moon

TIME
© Lyrics by gilli moon

1. I don't appreciate the feeling I get when I'm clinging to my rock upside down
Why is it always me rolling around, getting pushed to the ground
I'll take a minute to stand up tall
I'll take a minute to get on the rock
And not fall
'Cause, Time is in my hands
It's swimming in my pockets
Tick tock, hickory dock
Time to go and time to stop
Time to run, time to fly
Time to sleep and, time to cry
I'm running out of moments where I sit alone and contemplate
Aching in the morning don't wanna wake up to any bad days
I'll trim the edges and lose the lost
Counting on myself to break the wall
At every cost
'Cause, Time is in my hands
It's swimming in my pockets
Tick tock, hickory dock
Time to go and time to stop
Time to run, time to fly
Time to sleep and, time to cry
...Why should I wait another minute...
There's only seconds left
Tick tock tick tick tock
'Cause, Time is in my hands
It's swimming in my pockets
Tick tock, hickory dock
Time to go and time to stop ....
Time to run, time to fly
Time to sleep and, time to cry
Time is in my hands
It's swimming in my pockets
Tick tock, hickory dock
Time to go and time to
stop

Listen to this song at gillimoon.com, click on Music, as it's featured on gilli's
temperamental angel album

13. Become the creative explorer

I love being creative. I'm like a captain on a ship on a huge life adventure across the seas. I am an Artist and a motivator. I perform, I write, I speak, I motivate. I motivate myself and I motivate and inspire others. Why? Because the main focus for my life's pursuit is: creativity. And, I don't mind *how* I invigorate my creativity. That is, if I do it for me that's great, but if I do it for others, that's great too. Whether I perform on stage, or speak on panels and conduct workshops inspiring Artists to just get out there, or whether I sell my CDs or sell my books, all this energy is good for me, and the world. I love it. Besides, I'm an explorer and this is the essence of it all... to be that constant creative adventurer.

How far would you go to **change the world?**

Who do you work for? Someone else's ambition? Fame? Recognition? Material possessions? Fortune? God? If we focus on material goals only, we won't survive. Artists flock to Los Angeles seeking fame and fortune, so I've seen it all! They come, and they leave just as quickly as they arrived. But if you're aim is purely creative, then you will be in it for the long run.

Our lives are not meant to be wasted on just **maintaining** our lives. By that, I mean working hard and spinning your wheels just to maintain the status quo you have built: house (mortgage), cars, social life, 9-5 routine. There is more to our lives! Aesthetics, beauty, creativity, nature, adventure. Step out of your comfort zone of normalcy and you will find a whole world opens up to you.

Become a great explorer!

Consider that most people live in a world that doesn't include giving to others, or even themselves. They spend their lives existing on a maintenance level, getting up and going to work, paying the bills, feeding the family, buying possessions that require more hard work to pay the bills, same routines, and are often frustrated with their lives. A lot of it has to do with fear. Most of it, however, is based on an unwillingness to change habits and get out of one's comfort zone, which is also part ignorance, part fear related. But if we can **be creative**, understand and enjoy the beauty of Art, and give to our community at large by volunteering or contributing something, then we are already well on our way of being a great explorer.

Go Forward not back

The only time to look back is to evaluate the road. When you look back as a creative explorer, you're learning from your past, and seeing how far you've come, but it's not worth it to have regrets. You made a decision, and that's that. Now it's time to just leap empty handed into the void. There is no going back, just forward. The best motto in life is JUST KEEP MOVING FORWARD.

Take an interest in the world around you.

As a creative human being, it is of utmost importance to take an interest in the world around you, as it feeds your muse.

You're a creator, not a victim.

A little note about being the creator in life: the world is not done to you, it's done by you: so EXPLORE!

And remember, the world is not done to you, it's done by you. It's not coming at you, it's coming from you. When you begin to see you're the cause, not the effect, you are no longer the victim. So, be the creator, not the victim in life. In my first book, I wrote about how some Artists take on a victim mentality. They blame their Art, their circumstances, on their lack of money or opportunities. But it all comes down to attitude. If you think you are the victim, and think that you lack, you will lack. If you think you have enough, are abundant, talented and *able* then you will have it all. Be the creator, not the victim. It starts with you.

I sat drawing in the sand today and I felt excited about my projects. Aren't you?

Exploration into the unknown can be a little scary, but it's the only way anything was ever discovered. Leap empty handed into the void.

How exciting!

Exercise: The creative explorer

How can you remove the maintenance clause of your life and become a great creative explorer? One way is to answer three important questions to yourself that are about your Intention. I call this exercise the **Creative Explorer** exercise.

Ask yourself three important questions:

What have I created over the last year?

Write down all the things you did last year. For Artists, this can be easy because we can think of all the Art, music and Artistry we created. I'm a very project oriented person, so I wrote down all the projects I did, creative or not, like producing a CD, touring around the country, speaking in some interesting workshops, painting a picture, writing a new song. I then made it even more impactful and wrote down what I felt were accomplishments for myself (not based on what others thought I should do and what would deem "successful" in their eyes, but rather internal desires that I achieved). Some of these creative accomplishments included personal growth, relationships, body fitness; and others included finishing an album, getting a certain deal, etc. Spend some time writing what you created. Write whatever you feel. It's private for you to read to yourself. By writing it down you are disciplining yourself to remember certain projects, creativities and accomplishments, which sometimes we forget, or we don't give enough energy to. This is the time to give some energy to your recent past creativities. Write it down, read it, accept it.

What am I over?

The next segment is writing down what experiences, belief systems, and circumstances, modes of operandi or behaviors that no longer serve you. Put some energy into this area but don't treat it like a negative task. This is merely an exercise in writing down patterns, people, creativity, anything that you would like to remove from your life, your daily energy. I was pretty generic with my point form list. I included things like "bad relationships that are destructive and zap my energy", and "crappy gigs where the venues don't foster positive energy", and another one was "being lazy". You can write down anything that is pertinent to you. It could be something specific, like a creativity or project, or it could be broad, encompassing feelings, states of being, experiences. Write it down, read it, accept it.

What am I going to create now?

Now with long lists and writings for the first two questions, you are now ready to let them go. Yes that's right, relinquish your past, and your dislikes. Now is the time to establish a new foundation, serve a new purpose for yourself in your creative life. This is where you tap into your higher nature and ultimate destiny. Write down what you want to create this coming year, or in the near future. You don't have to be date specific. This can include creative/Artistic projects, relationships, personal goals, professional goals; anything that provides you a positive purpose in your life. Be general, and be specific. Don't hold back. Dream the big dream, and write it all down. In this final part of the *Creative Explorer* exercise, you are tapping in to your true self, and allowing your subconscious to spring forth pure intention, from vivid dreaming. If writing holds you back, start drawing too. Visualization, as I've mentioned before, is a great way to enable thoughts into actions.

Exercise 2: Changes and accomplishments

Change a habit, accomplish a goal.
Write down 5 habits you would like to change within the next 2 weeks
1.
2.
3.
4.
5.
Write down 7 goals you would like to accomplish based on the key words below. Keep your goals attainable and not in the too distant future.

Abundance
Artistry
Health
Relationships
Business Affairs
Time Management
Joy

Ask yourself these questions:

Who am I?
What Do I Want?
and then…
Why Do I Want It?

If you've figured these out,
you're half way there.

Become the creative explorer

PART 2: PLAYING THE GAME

Realities of the biz and becoming an Artist Entrepreneur

You can do all the inner work you can, but it can't be applied without

ACTION

So let's get right to it, shall we?

14. An Artist led business

The realities of the music business

What I see now is that much of our success, which includes a realization of goals and dreams through actual, tangible results, comes not only from our outer efforts, but *also from our inner work, our inner drive, our inner inspiration.*

It's one thing to have achieved goals, and then another to actually feel satisfied and happy from that. I've met a few celebrity Artists who really aren't that happy at all, yet they've achieved financial and fame recognition.

So I think to be completely prepared, we need to do a lot of inner work. I've been doing just this for at least the last eight years, and throughout that time I've been harnessing my writing, producing, performing and business skills. I hope, having read the first part of this book, that you have now done a lot of your inner work (though it's a lifetime of discovery).

NOW, is the time for you to embrace what IS available to you, and get a whole perspective on what ocean you're now dipping your toes into. This ocean has changed. It's wilder, more diverse, and rather ambiguous. The music industry has changed A LOT. It's a whole different animal. So, without further ado, **let's get started**.

The business that we know of as the music business has changed. It's in flux, but it still has conglomerates desperately trying to keep control of it, while the independent Artist entrepreneurs are rising like military tanks on a mine field.

The business that we know of as the music business has changed. It's in flux, but it still has conglomerates desperately trying to keep control of it, while the independent Artist Entrepreneurs are rising like military tanks on a mine field.

If you're interested in reading about the last thirty years of the music business, and how CDs came along to save the business, then waned, and how the

Internet came along to save the business, and now, "has killed it", read *Appetite For Self-Destruction – The Spectacular Crash of the Record Industry in the Digital Age*, by Steve Knopper. It's quite enlightening.

We are in a world which I call the "indie music world", which is so exhilarating, actually, for Artists. Although people say that it's tough to get signed, and no one is buying CDs anymore and sales are down and no one's making money, there is a whole flip side to it, and it's not a negative status for independent free thinking Artists. I enjoyed Knopper's book because it showed me that the business goes in cycles, and the medium by which we transport the music changes. So if we are ready for change, we can accept the times and find great ways to succeed through them. But you have to be on your toes...

Wikipedia defines the "music industry" as such:

The music industry is the business of music. Although it encompasses the activity of many music-related businesses and organizations, it was dominated by the "big four" record groups, also known as "the major labels"/"the majors" — Sony BMG, EMI, Universal and Warner — each of which consists of many smaller companies and labels serving different regions and markets.

Well, they're a little outdated aren't they, now that EMI and Sony are one. So basically, there are the big "3". It'll be the big 1 before you know it. But even that will become undone.

I find it fascinating that the music industry definition is still defined as run by so few entities. But back in the day... oh just a few years ago... Artists would play the game with the Majors because it was the only way to get a look in. Basically, worldwide exposure was "bought", and any Artist trying to get their music accessible to audiences had a fat chance because you'd have to sign up to the "Devil", really. The "Devil", so to speak, were these record companies, apparently, who signed their Artists to 5-7 album deals in order to get some kind of life expectancy out of them, be able to push their music through their styrofoam towers and through all that, constructed binding 60 page contracts that left little room for Artist independence, let alone the real opportunity for them to ever make their investment back or make any money.

We had this old model where major record labels would determine what's played on the radio, sold in stores, and dictated to consumers what they should buy at the store. CDs were between $10-30 and consumers would be conditioned to buy them based on being told what's good on the radio, and that was controlled by the labels. We (as public) were spoon fed music.

Quite a few years ago, I wrote an article called "Taming of the Music Mafia". You can read it here: gillimoon.com/articles. It discussed the challenges Artists were facing back in 2002 (sounds so long ago now right?), and where the music industry is heading. The term "mafia" was not a literal term I used, but more a conceptual, metaphorically speaking way to reference certain control, monopolies and bribery that existed within the music industry, whether legal or illegal, between Artists, radio, promoters and record labels. I talked about how Artists were signed to major record companies, who then spent their money negotiating airplay or retail end cap space to sell the CDs they needed to sell to keep the ball rolling. I talked about pay to play, buying radio hits, and playing the "game" of the major record company system. Ah... the music industry... such an evolving subject these days. It's like a revolving door, with nothing that sticks.

Then the Internet happened big time for music (around 98-99), and sites like Napster came about, sharing the music, which wasn't good for the songwriters and file owners as they weren't getting paid, but it opened up a can of worms. Consumers could finally find their own music online, in the comfort of their home, and not be dictated by record companies' tastes and financial agendas. Consumers no longer had to go to the record store to buy a CD that a record company told them was great. They could find it online, thereby destroying the record retail industry. (Cut to today and the only official new CD release retail store in L.A. is Amoeba, a used CD store. What a paradigm we live in, when you have to go to a second hand store to get something new, and only the "collectors" know the true value of the old fashioned CD.)

In the nineties, where record labels were still the staunch leaders, Ani DiFranco, modern folk singer/songwriter, was one of the few Artists that were paving the way as a so-called "independent" Artist, even before the Internet. She was always very outspoken about the major labels victimizing Artists, and with her own record company, Righteous Babe Records, she was able to distribute her music worldwide without "big brother" helping her.

I feel that with my own label, Warrior Girl Music, I followed in her footsteps.

But very few others were able do the same, without the financial or marketing means, let alone the gumption to give it a try.

It wasn't until the Internet came into being, in the late nineties, that things started to change. Independent Artists, those who were setting themselves apart from the machine of signing deals (or flogging themselves to the Labels to get signed), became silently, discreetly and effectively (to the major public eye) more in control of their business by managing their own affairs and using new World Wide Web opportunities to by-pass the major system. I was one of them.

"the music industry mafia is pimping girl power sniping off their sharpshooter singles from their Styrofoam towers..."

- Ani DiFranco

By 2001, Internet sites sprung up everywhere playing music, indie or major, including podcasts, webcasts, Internet radio (many run by kids out of their bedrooms). Social networks began to bring people together in online communities.

The cold hard fact was that Artists needed to become more in control of their careers and less beholden to the deep pocket, the stifling un-creative rigidity, and possibly (probably) get screwed, shelved, or bankrupt in the process. We all know, and knew then, that the "empire" was about to unravel. While independent Artists began a surge of self-empowerment and the "indie" world ignited, so did the empire begin to crumble... as expected, and much needed. We all need Rome to fall in order for something new and exciting to transpire. Since my first article, Pandora's Box has indeed opened and whilst label executives had kept their jobs for fifty years, since 2002, the majority have lost them. There is no more "status quo". This is the movie The Terminator, except instead, the Artists are the ones taking over the world.

What has happened is quite remarkable: because of the Internet and having anything so readily accessible to everyone, the consumer started making decisions about what music they wanted to listen to. Instead of Corporate Music America deciding what we were to hear on radio, see on TV or watch live, consumers searched music content of their own choosing. They didn't want to have music forced down their throat anymore, especially when so much more interesting and abundant music was and is floating on the Net.

Then the big crack down on Napster in '01 happened to stop consumers sharing music for free (they tried to win by adopting the 1984 Betamax case in their legal case – "yeah we're just sharing music with friends... only 8 million friends, but still... friends"). Well, they lost. (You can Google the case online.)

The indie Artist quickly stepped up to the plate before a Major Record Company exec could write their next marketing plan. How exciting for an indie Artist, who has always had to think outside the box and find other ways to get to the masses: the masses at their door step. And the "front door", with people banging loudly, became the Artists' own websites, and Myspace profiles and anywhere an Artist can upload, blog, ping, splash on the Internet. By 2005, the indie Artist began to take control of not only their careers and future income potential, but take control of how music is being marketed.

Meanwhile, the Major Record Companies have had to think **fast.** Their CD sales plummeted, because consumers began to buy on the Net (downloads) direct from Artists. They let off thousands of employees. Music retail chain stores began to close (Tower Records was the bedrock of CD sales history. I was sad to see it go on the Sunset Strip, Hollywood). Record companies were closing down, merging, dissipating, watching and waiting. The Majors realized they had to come up with marketing strategies and new revenue streams to survive, and compete with the indie Artist model of guerilla street and Internet marketing tactics, that were thriving. The indie Artist's model was now the model to go by. Who would have thought?

Consumers got tired of being dished music from the corporations. That's what brought on Napster. Good or bad, Napster allowed people, in their living rooms on their computers, to decide what music they wanted to hear and when they wanted to hear it. It allowed undiscovered talent to be heard, by the millions.

This has led to a giant overhaul of the music industry, so much so that now most music marketing takes place on the Internet, driving consumers to new music through banner ads, MySpace ads, iTunes, and social networking sites (Facebook, Twitter, Multiply, LinkedIn, Delicious....the list goes on) have taken over any form of advertising as the largest vehicle to spread new music and bands. Artists can upload their tunes, create free web pages and interact with thousands of people. It has led

to a reverse shift whereby instead of Artists soliciting to major record companies, hoping to get signed, now major record companies are mirroring the indie model, even pretending/faking their Artists to be "indie-like" on the Net. Some Napster-style sites are trying to survive today, like Limewire. They won't survive on the long term, because, well they are just sharing Artists' music without their permission. But that's a whole different article. The RIAA is cracking down on them all, and all the music companies are coming up with different laws and rulings on what is a download, stream or whatever. It's still in flux, but they'll sort it out. I'm still not convinced the "sorting out" is in the Artist's favor (has it ever been?) But the climate is ripe for different styles of music delivery: subscription services, radio stations online that have subscribers, selling music in bulk to services, and so forth. Major record companies are using this model by offering their entire catalogs at a bulk rate. Record companies are scrambling to find out what to do to sell their signed music. It's definitely a singles market again where you can download 1 song on iTunes (like the 60s and 80s singles markets).

Sites like iTunes breed a new kind of consumer: one who doesn't really care about the full album anymore, but can search for 1 song, and create their own compilations (playlists) of music based on a mood or style. It does leave a large creative hole though: who will care about the Art of the Artist anymore? Who will care about what we want to deliver? And who cares about the quality of the sound of music? (I personally detest the compressed sterility of an mp3.)

But let's look at the numbers: if all works out well, Artists will get paid more for their music (although there are still middle people) and consumers can buy music directly and choose for themselves what they want to listen to.

Indie Artists can potentially cut out the middle person, sell their own songs on their website (Paypal, Itunes, etc.) or use a digital aggregator (that's an online distributor but dressed in a new title), with the Artist keeping a minimum of 80% of the sale (instead of 12% of the old record company deal model). That's good news right?

So, the money making probability is in the Artist's hands, which is great. You're making more of the money. So as an Artist you may not get $2 million or $200,000, you may get $60,000. But at 80% it's pretty good money, and you end up still owning your music masters (that's longevity).

However, you may not be getting as many customers because everybody has their music up there. We are bombarded by lots of music. It's a sea of music (and a lot of terrible music also) to wade through. We are not only bombarded with music, but we are bombarded by ads and marketing ("come buy my song", "see my gig"), and even the major labels are using every inch of Internet space that for a while was owned by indies, to sell their latest reality TV star music mogul. So much is thrown in our faces, as consumers, that we have to pick and choose. We want to stay close to just a few Artists (or a few dozen). We become... FANS.... of particular Artists, and we stick to them.

An interesting statistic from September 2010 (Los Angeles Times): "While digital music sales have steadily grown, overall industry revenue continues to fall." Yes, the biz has taken a hard slap, that's for sure.

An Artist led business

BUT, we can STILL sell music. (Gilli, are you losing it?!) No, I'm not. What I'm saying is, by harnessing your local communities, and a grass roots mentality, you can absolutely create an abundant financial career.

As Artists, we learn to focus more on our *communities* to promote our music (on Facebook, MySpace, your website, e-mails to immediate fan and friend bases, etc.) and you don't need to pay for advertising costs (not really), nor have to give away a huge portion of rights to your music. You're in control of your music (who gets it and who doesn't) and the sale. You may not have the huge international success (or you still may…. it's all still possible). BUT IT'S WITHIN YOUR COMMUNITY you created.

A great time for Artists

This is truly the heart of what I'm getting at: you, as an Artist, can be in charge of your destiny. You can be in control of your business, and your Artistry, connect to your fans, AND make money. It is all possible. While everyone is complaining about the crash and burn of the music industry, let alone the economy, I encourage you to see the GOLDEN opportunity you have right now to become Artist Entrepreneurs and see the potential of this new ground.

Today, we have great opportunities for Artists to *think*

outside the box and come up with interesting ideas on how to get our music out there. In a few years, the copyright laws and the RIAA and all the bodies will all continue to try and keep their pieces of the pie, and a lot is still in flux but it will all start to level out.

And it's a great time for Artists, as they rise out of the ashes like a phoenix. When people don't know what's going on with the music biz, and the economy, the Artist *Entrepreneur* comes up with great ideas, and they are the ones that take new risks to make a change. This is what I mean by being a Warrior Artist.

So if you are willing to be that person, you have a solid chance of being successful.

And what about tokens of reward like winning awards, radio success and fame?

The Grammy nomination system is still a frustrating experience. Out of the hundreds of nominated Artists, with some worthy albums and songs, the large percentage is trash (and still bought and marketed with millions of dollars). The best music to find is outside the traditional commercial norm: online blogs, word of mouth, iTunes, podcasts. Music television like MTV and VH1 rarely play a music video, what with lifestyle shows eating up the programming. It's partly the consumers' fault. We want reality... for some odd reason we want to get into the lives of real people and watch it on a daily, hourly basis. That's why American Idol works so well. Those Artists that win each series become hugely famous in nanoseconds not just because it's rigged (um, I mean calculated programming by TV execs in cahoots with the record company ready to release an album by whoever wins). It's also successful, and the execs know it, because consumers WANT to be PART of an Artist's development now. They don't want to buy an album by someone who is unknown and just lands on our airwaves (which is the old routine, payola and all that to get it there). No, consumers want to live and breathe every moment, every tear, every laugh, every wrong note along the way to winning the contest that they have had a hand in voting for. And then, when the record company releases the single only weeks after the last program of the series (weird how the timing is so perfect, huh?!), then the consumer is ready to buy, buy, buy, because they feel like they were part of the process of making that Artist successful.

I'm not sure if I like the idea of American Idol being the barometer of talent, but it's true to say that the cream will always rise to the top, no matter how much sh-- you need to swim through.

I'm swimming as hard as I can...

With the realities of the music business as it stands, I ask this question: Why is it not possible to do it your own way, with the Artist steering the ship? I say YES, it's very possible, tangible and in fact, more financially profitable and stable, compared to the alternative.

This book is not encouraging you to just stay indie (independent), or never sign a record deal. I have never pushed for Artists to remain "independent", or "indie". It's your choice. This business is about relationships, so you will need a team, you will need to work with people, and you cannot do it alone. (See my DIT chapter later). But I do encourage all of us to be the masters of our destinies and that means being in control of your business operation, your creative choices and your career goals. This is about being awake to the realities of the business in order to succeed and survive. If you have read my first book, all these notions of a self-driven Arts business have been explained. I recommend reading it to give you a sense where I'm coming from in this new book.

This is the real world. A world of opportunity, and it's there waiting for you.

It's an exciting era for independent Artists. In the past, as well as the present, multi-national corporations controlled mass media and pop music. They have done so before and they always will. There will always be some powerhouse company, or three, in control. It goes back to feudal days of lords and peasants... the control of the food chain. There will always be the need for quick "hits" for music and "big opening weekends" for movies, as it's motivated by money, by power and by business. As I've already said, the **music business** is about business. It's not really about music at all. Don't be sad about this. It is what it is, and I guess many Artists, including me, are dependent on the "business" of music because we want to be heard and find our audiences. We want our music and songs listened to. So we play the game and make deals with the Devil on the promise that "they, them, these others" will make our music heard through the outlets "they" have set up. Some Artists waste years waiting around hoping to be discovered by a company, and spend their whole lives constantly proving themselves to some mysterious dark wall.

Most give up, tossed aside by ignorant so-called "music industry representatives" who often like to criticize an Artist simply to keep their job. They don't realize the impact negative feedback can be on a fledgling Artist who is just living on their dream of being "great" one day.

Too many Artists are dependent on someone or something else to "make it happen" for them. But the path I prefer to talk about is called the **self-empowered** path. My first book focused on the idea of Artists taking control of their own careers, getting out there on their own and making it happen for themselves. I believe in defining success on one's own terms, not by some fading notion of commercial success that is just defined by others. What we have in our hands today is the opportunity to get out on the street, ourselves, and connect with the audiences and consumers directly. New music ideas have always started on the street before reaching the board rooms. New Internet opportunities allow us to use grass roots methodologies of spreading the word through "friends", fans and link exchanges, whilst record labels are dying a slow death in their current form. They are just not getting their sales volumes and are scrambling to catch up to what many independent Artists are revolutionizing as success, in order to survive.

Artists are now the **ideas** people in business. Wait, that doesn't make sense! I thought Artists were always the ideas people. Aren't we the ones that are creatively coming up with ideas? Well you'd think so, but for so long "they" (sales men, marketing men, paper shufflers) were in control of ideas or decisions. With the age of technology and the Internet, however, the power is creeping into the Artists' hands and we have been able to navigate our own way through the quagmire of corporate control to find our own niche, and hence, our own audience... and ultimately a successful career.

An Artist led business is the way of the future. We STILL need a team, remember, and you may sign deals with companies to get your music out there, but we are no longer ignorant and no longer sheltered from the market. We have access!

It has bred a generation of business type Artists who see marketing as just as important as making music. It has also bred a lot of terrible music. But that can't be helped when the flood gates have been torn open. All we can hope is that consumers will still continue to make valued choices in the music they buy. Demand is the power force here.

The current shift

The new Artist Entrepreneur (I will define this in the next chapter) grew out of the ashes, like the phoenix, of dying Rome. It's just plain and simple. No one should be at the mercy of a large corporation when *they* don't even know the way. Many celebrity "major" Artists once signed to major labels, have left them, and became indie, starting up their own labels (Radiohead and Simply Red to name a few). This is not just because they chose to. In some situations, the majors no longer have the power to keep up the level of promotion and finance that these Artists needed in the past. While there is still a "system" in place that the majors seemingly think they are in control of, because they still have more money to play with, it's a daunting future for them, because the income streams are so fleeting and ever changing.

Where we've arrived at is a slow shift of a quagmire – that is, it is seemingly unmoving and we don't know exactly what the next phase is, but at the same time, there are shifts happening where Artists are becoming more empowered, and labels are starting to change their face in order to meet the new business models, working *with* and *by* the Artists' playing rules. It's a really exciting playing field, and not just for indie Artists: but for the **labels too**. Everyone has had to change the way they do business and now we are all on the same playing field with bat in hand.

Artists have been able to control their sales & distribution, as well as their public awareness campaigns, themselves, and easily through Internet interfaces. The record companies, in turn, are almost modeling their marketing tactics off indie Artist ideas, for example, Marie Digby. Apparently she was so successful on Youtube.com promoting herself from her living room, playing raw, passionate original songs direct to 2.3 million friends, that she became an instant star. Following that, landing songs in TV shows and filling stadiums. Indie Artist? Seemingly. But not really. There was no mention that she was signed. Just a girl with guitar. What we discovered later was this was a calculated marketing tactic by her record label, Hollywood Records, owned by Disney, to reach the new consumers who want to discover their own talent instead of being force fed. It worked. We all loved her Youtube site, and thought this 24 year old was a self-made success, and we were all discovering her. But the label was behind the ploy the whole time.

Personally, I think it's great. It's a clear example of how independent Artists are offering the way, AND it's a solid affirmation that we are now all on the same playing field: Artists and labels - we all can reach our audiences without having to "play that Devilish game".

Where does it leave the independent Artist? Well, I still think that although the "new model" is REALITY music, independent Artists are more REAL in their marketing than anyone else. We are the first to let our fans into our worlds: our websites, our blogs, our free downloads. We want to interact with our fans, and we want them to be part of our development. Some indie Artists invite fans to become investors in their CD production which is a great new way of including them in the early days, as well as helping to fund the album and its eventual marketing.

I listened to a panel of record company execs recently at the Durango Songwriters Conference that included reps from Warners, Curb and Atlantic. I felt it was a healthy discussion because I realized that the labels now know they need to work WITH the Artists and not just force feed their agendas on them, and everyone else. Reality is, digital sales have plateaued. Only 10-12% are legal downloads and companies need twenty indicators to go off at once, not just a few CD sales as ducks in a row, to see if their Artists are going to "make it". There is a trend to go for the more organic music that shows realism rather than plastic, manufactured bland pop that represented an era that is dead. Music needs to be real, alive and shows the story of the Artist that consumers so desperately want to interact with.

On another tangent, the younger generation is so distracted with all the available "toys" in their lives, that music is becoming a lesser "want". Gone are the days when a 16 year old would sift through vinyl records in their local music store for 3 hours trying to hunt down their favorite Grateful Dead album. These kids of today are plugged in intravenously to their iPods, cell phones and portable laptops, and are scouring the Internet just for a quick, short term fix of a tune they heard on reality TV; then trashed forever while they grab another quick hit song to engulf. They don't care if it's 5.1 Surround sound, 64 channel mixed. Nothing. They take it as it is, compressed, squashed and lifeless. They are also distracted by video games (hence that is now a great music marketing area to place your songs in), blogging, Instant messaging, social networking and all that is unrelated yet related to music. They love to chat, all day long, on their little digital interfaces, and if music happens to be involved, it's fast, furious and disposable. Preferably free to them.

Where to next?

So how do we hold onto our fans and create a career then, if we are so disposable? What is the future for us Artists who love to make music, real music, that sounds big and fantastic and used to come with glossy visual CD covers that told our stories?

I see it is two fold: It's about concentrating on two areas of our lives, and forgive me for asking Artists to be a little business savvy here, but it's absolutely vital to understand business and marketing. There's no way out of it anymore. If you think you're going to be in the music "business" without being business savvy, then get out now and make way for those who can do that part, because that's the only type of Artist who is going to "make it" (however you want to define that). I've spent my whole first book speaking about Artists as business people. I also addressed the concept of "success" in that book, and I believe you need to define success on your own terms, not by some commercial token of reward, because these "tokens" are changing. Once, a dream may have been to be number one on radio. Well, my friends, I figured *that* smoke and mirrors out long ago, and it had a lot to do with payola, timing, money, and what deal you had in place.

Nowadays, a token of success could be that you land the front page of MySpace. However you see it, and whatever you want, it can all be real, but don't lose sight of the bigger picture – the longer path. Tokens come and go. **Artistry is life long.**

All we need to consider as Artists is this:
1. Create great music, and
2. Market the music.

Whether you are an independent Artist, or a major label, the two principles still apply. Indie Artists may not necessarily have the same amount of money to market, promote and advertise the music, but they increasingly have a quicker and keener sense as to what are the latest marketing tools to use. Kids are growing up intravenously connected to computers and cell phones (well not quite, but you know what I mean). It's second nature for them to blog, podcast, design websites, be on social networking sites, chat on discussion groups and forums, download music and ringtones, etc. This is the music marketing of today, and it's at our fingertips. For the first time ever, the pieces are now in the hands of the Artists to do what they want with it, rather than in the power of "they/them", (you know, those people who live behind dark veils, who keep the money and keep us in the dark).

I was sad when Tower Records closed down. It's the advent of a new dawn in music delivery. Gone will be the CD and in comes a new digital way of delivering music. I do hope that we can keep the music sounding its best. I struggle with the idea that my months of labor in the studio, and the money and time spent creating 5.1 surround sound quality masters are squashed into compressed mp3s. But we all have to realize that even the making of music will change, just like it's changing for video what with YouTube and the ability to create videos on your cell phone and upload to the world.

Fortunately Artists are very creative, so this is a time for us to put our creativity to the max, and think of great ideas to create and market our music to the world.

Arriving are 100 different solutions to spread your Artistry far and wide. Even the tools and websites I've described in this chapter alone, will go. New ones will arrive. In my decade on the Net, I've seen it all. And I'm not surprised when a new "fad" website becomes hip. All I can stay is optimistic by the opportunities that are waiting for me every time I click my mouse.

I'm chomping at the bit every day when I discover a new website or promotional tool that will help get my music out there. There is so much, but it takes some sweat, some fortitude, a lot of passion and a keen desire to do this for the rest of your life, because being an Artist is life long.

The Art should always come first, so don't let your business affairs make you unhappy. Being business minded, disciplined and organized, means taking risks and focusing yourself in channeling your creativity. All this provides opportunities. Be mindful that opportunities come when you least expect them, so keep the door open and be ready in wonder.

Opportunities aren't always far afield either. They can be in your own backyard. You just have to look for them. Many people will say to you, "oh, you need big bucks to make it or you'll fail", or "you need to do this, this and this in order to be successful otherwise you won't make it". Ignore these people who say your dream is impossible to reach and if they say they know the way. The paths are opening up every day, and there are so many new ways to deliver music. Being conscientious at what you do, working toward financial independence and creative freedom ON YOUR OWN TERMS is the *only* path.

Stay positive, optimistic, keep organized and opportunities will come your way. Besides, if you are a pessimist, you will only see the failures in life. So, put a smile on your face, get your house in order and make steps to step outside the box and just get out there.

Learn my phrase: **Optimism + Organized = Opportunity**

Exercise: The biz and me

Write down 5 Artists you admire in the music business. What is it about them that you like or are inspired by? Is it their image, story or music? Or is it because their famous or something about their success in the music business?

1.

2.

3.

4.

5.

Think about your relationship to the music "business". Are you in it for fame, fortune or the glory? Do you want a Grammy Award or a number one song on the radio, because that is what you know is "success" since other successful Artists have that? Or are you in it because you are passionate about your music and you want to share your music to the world?

It's time to get real with your ambition:

What do you really want?
And why?

The music industry is like a battle field. Tackling it, and climbing to the top, is like war, and as an artist I must tap into the warrior within, carve my own road, follow the dreams, and remain true. The Internet is an amazing vehicle for indie artists to truly shine and remain in control of their art. There is no longer a barrier to deliver self-expression. Artists can manage their careers and their record sales and remain true to their art. Vive La Independence!

15. The Successful Artist Entrepreneur

So, hopefully by now you have made some steps towards WHO YOU ARE and WHAT YOU WANT as an Artist – the big picture (your big dreams) and some goals to work towards. You would have also discovered what your current priorities are in your life. And now you have a little perspective of the ocean you're jumping into.

The KEY TO SURVIVAL AND SUCCESS in the music business of TODAY is to be a **unique** Artist, in charge of your own destiny. It means **you need to be an Artist Entrepreneur.**

I'm from Australia. I grew up singing, dancing and playing the piano since I was 4 years old. But it took me a long time, though, to find out who I wanted to be, and where I wanted to go. In fact, not until I reached thirty did I even start to figure it out, and being a singer/songwriter was my passion, performing songs I write, so I headed to the Mecca of music, Los Angeles.

When I first came to L.A. I thought that the only way to be successful would be to do showcases on the Sunset Strip, and send my tape around hoping to get signed to a major label. I had all those commercial notions of success in my dreams, like a number 1 hit on radio, a Grammy, and a big fat major record deal. The thought was "sign a deal, get a huge advance, and become an overnight success".

But when I arrived here (97-98), the music industry started to change right under my feet. It was like quicksand, and the only thing that was going to survive was a self-thinking, _**proactive**_ Artist who took no bull from anyone. Consider that this was the beginning of the Internet. This was a new era, and the Wild West, and my mouth was salivating at the chance to do something without relying on anyone else, because, by golly, I had relied on too many people 'till now in my life.

After a few set backs, and years of frustration hoping others would discover my talent, In 2000 I decided to start my own record label, Warrior Girl Music. I didn't want to wait around for someone to make it happen for me, I needed to at least start it off myself. It was my life. I started to do something entrepreneurial in a time when most Artists weren't willing to risk going out on their own. So I created my own self-made success, in a way, by releasing my own music, touring across the country, and developing great music concepts. I also developed Songsalive!

worldwide which is a non-profit organization for songwriters and it has become a huge community. From all of this, I'm invited to speak about my adventures at workshops and in my books and it's all icing on the cake. I feel like I'm successful today and I'm sharing with you how I see my life and how I see success as an Artist, to hopefully inspire you.

I don't see myself as any different now as I did then. I'm still the girl with a big dream and adventurous in spirit. I live my life one day at a time, and I'm holding on to my dream like there's no tomorrow.

To this day, we still live in the Wild West of the music industry. In fact, I'd rather call it Outer Space. We're all searching for Mars and a new frontier. We're in a flux and it's a perfect opportunity for independent Artists to think outside the box and create success for themselves. Artists need to be entrepreneurs. You need to be self-motivated, and in charge of your own ship.

Yes, it's a lonely path. You will feel very "alone" in your journey, because it's unique and untainted with any path anyone has taken before.

In order to be powerful as an Artist, you have to be very business savvy. You need to be very self-driven. You don't need to know everything about the business (you can go to experts for advice) but you are in control.

If you want it to be life long, you have to be a *visionary*. You have to be able to think outside the box and "feel" it inside. A lot of inner work is required. So while you are working on your craft and techniques on the outside, you have to work on your mindset on the inside. There is a lot of inner work to be done. Everything that I am is ALL about my mindset, my attitude about myself and where I want to go. So keep that in your back pocket.

A while back, I spoke for my second time, at Berklee School of Music in Boston. It's such an honor to be able to do this and I thank the insightful and prolific Berklee author Peter Spellman for the opportunity, as Berklee is one of the most prestigious music schools in the world. Peter Spellman also gets my vision about the Artist Entrepreneur. In fact, he inspired me to use the title as I heard about it first from him. It was very timely to speak to students there, not for the sake of the writing of this book, which I always feel inspired to write a chapter or two after a public outing, but also because it reminded me of **who I was** and **what I wanted** in life. Speaking and inspiring other Artists, reminds ME of why I'm an Artist. My audience is like a mirror to my own Artistic soul, and my dreams.

I was asked to give my thoughts on the topic of *"the inner game of music entrepreneurship"* at Berklee. This statement conjured up some fascinating thought and ensuing dialogue. The most obvious cool topic is 'entrepreneurship'. To be considered an entrepreneur in this business of music by Berklee is indeed flattering, let alone the opportunity to speak about it. With everything I do as an Artist, musician, author, speaker, label owner, Artist community builder, I guess I am indeed entrepreneurial. What is more important here though is that I feel everyone needs to be entrepreneurial, in order to be truly powerful as an Artist in this new music/Arts business. It's automatic. If we want to lead our lives, Art, or business, we need to be self-driven, business minded, and a visionary. But this cannot be just shown externally. We need to feel it and "be it" internally too.

The next part about this topic that I was excited about was the idea of talking about the word "game". Dabbling in the music business can indeed be like a game, and it conjured up really cool concepts for me to speak about the game of music, the game of business and finally... the psychological game.

This final part was the clincher in totally jumping to the cause to discuss this topic: The "inner" game is what is so cool. Everything... everything that we do.... everything we want... and who we are... is based all around our inner work on ourselves, and less on the external. I have written much about this already. Thought is very powerful, and a mere idea will turn into reality. Thought breeds action. How we perceive ourselves, what we ask for, how we operate our belief systems,

everything about our inner dialogue, emotions, desires.... *everything internal: creates the external.* So by combining this whole statement together, "the inner game of music entrepreneurship" just made me bursting with excitement to philosophize over and share.

> Being an Artist Entrepreneur means you are in CHARGE of your career: making decisions for your career.

Side note, Dr. Wayne Dyer says, *"We do not attract what we want, we attract who we are. And that is a culmination of our belief systems and everything that is about us. And we can change who we are at any time."*

That means that how we work on our inner game, who we are in our minds, creates everything on the OUTER. Put that in your back pocket because that's one of the key ingredients in being an Artist Entrepreneur: endowing it (becoming it).

So, the premise of this chapter is to ask

What makes the successful Artist entrepreneur?

Much of the success of an entrepreneur comes mostly from <u>within</u>. Yes, they have the trappings of being a creator, inventor, warrior, leader... but it all starts with an idea, and an inner knowing and confidence about WHO WE ARE.

Being an Artist Entrepreneur means you are in CHARGE of your career: making decisions for your career.

It requires Artists to think outside the box (very creative), be masters of their own destiny and to be business people, in charge of your own business.

Ok, so you get the point. (Believe me, I remind myself every day and still I'm just learning it.)

The Music Business:

Is a business

— Beyond playing, you have to understand contracts, keep yourself organized, know how to market yourself, create valuable relationships. Understand it's a business.

Can be tough

- It **IS** tough. It's one of the hardest businesses to get into. You have to be ready to put in the hard work (happy hard work, but hard work). This is not for the next year. You have to be in it for **life**, for the long haul. You have to be convinced this is something you want to do.

You need money

- You can't do it with no money. But you don't have to be hugely wealthy or have huge investors. You can do so much on your own. You have to be willing to find the resources to make things happen, and also believe and **value** your Artistry and products in order for them to become financially rewarding for you. If you believe in it, others will. So put a value on your Art. And in the meantime, if your Art can't pay your bills, get a job. There's no sense in acting like a victim and not working like everybody else in this world. A job is a means by which to gain a greater goal. Save the money, and slowly wean yourself off working for others so you can work for yourself.

People can zap your energy + criticize/judge

— They will, and it happens a lot. Be prepared to be criticized, judged, critiqued, knocked back and said "no" to many times. But at some point someone will say yes, and the door will be wide open when you least expect it. Unfortunately, even our nearest and dearest can be the most critical in our lives, because they want the best for us. But their "best" isn't necessarily the right "best" for you. Also, many in our Artistic field can be judging and competitive. Actors judge other actors, musicians judge musicians. It is what it is. We all want each other's success (seemingly), so there can be a lot of jealousies and competitive attitudes around you. The important thing is to stick to what you believe in, only allow a few close to you, and seek no one else's approval but your own.

Has seemingly less opportunity

- It's all about perspective/state of mind. One can think of the music business as a place that is harder and harder to find opportunities. I just see it as a glorious way to think outside the box, come up with new ways of doing business, and reinventing myself every day.

Creates Internal doubts/torments of the mind

— Look, the business is not easy, it's hard work. You WILL have a lot of doubts and turmoil, and frustrations. So work on your Torments of the Mind exercise I gave you, regularly, to work out those demons and create affirmations to change your mindset into a positive will power that no one else can defeat.

HOW TO BE A SUCCESSFUL ARTIST ENTREPRENEUR

1. **It takes Passion.**

2. **It's all about how you *balance* your *time*:** time management.

3. **Do it because you love it.**

4. **You need to see yourself *as* a business.**
   You need to be left and right brain thinking (logical and creative). You can learn to diversify your talents, and be able to "spin your plates" all together. Be creative with a business mind. Be persistent, conscientious and persevere. It's ALL about relationships. Find out what you can do for others first.

5. **Learn my 3 Os: Optimism + Organized = Opportunity.**
   My 3 Os are essential ingredients in being Artist Entrepreneurs. Having **optimism** - being optimistic - and being **organized**, breeds **opportunity**. If you don't have optimism, it will undermine your Art and every step you have taken towards your path of self-realization. Optimism also surrounds other nice words such as enthusiasm, energized, joyful, appreciative, fueled, passionate, confidence, inspired. The list goes on but you get my meaning. It's a state of mind. If you are optimistic, people want to be around you and learn from you. It rubs off on to them also. Business becomes very exciting and fulfilling if you are optimistic. Doors open when you show a smile. On a spiritual level, life delivers everything you want when you are positive and see the world and yourself with happiness and optimism. If you show joy and love, it returns to you twice fold. This is part of the natural laws of karma. The important thing to recognize is that life is a mirror. Smile and the world smiles with you. Right? You've heard that one before. Create blocks and you get blocks in return. Fear inside brings fear to your doorstep. Be courageous.
   Having a great, positive attitude will help you get what you truly want out of life. This can be not only about how we feel about ourselves, but also about how we feel about others. If we constantly criticize others, such as successful Artists (that we

secretly aspire to, yet remain jealous of), or if we constantly complain about our circumstances, then this behavior will not bring us joy, nor what we want.

Life's rewards are not supposed to be delivered to us on a silver platter. There will always be work to be done to achieve what we want. It's in the process of doing, with a smile on our face, and knowing that we are lucky people who have a chance to go for what we want in life, will it be delivered to us... because we give it to ourselves. Consider that many people who had poor upbringings, limited resources and little education, have gone on to be truly wealthy, successful and even famous. The key is having a positive, optimistic attitude. If you think that circumstances will limit you, then they will limit you. Your thoughts, your beliefs, your attitude will play vital roles in the outcomes of your life. If you can alter your behavior to a more positive energy, using your creative gifts and imagination, then opportunity comes pouring in.

Allow opportunities to manifest in your life by learning to create JOY in your life! Here's a little poem for you that I have kept as a mantra since I was fifteen.

> *Attitude, you know is better than aptitude*
> *With the right attitude and a modicum of aptitude*
> *You can succeed in anything you choose.*
> *If you think you are beaten you are*
> *If you think you dare not you don't*
> *If you'd like to win, but think you can't*
> *It's almost a cinch that you won't*
> *If you think you'll lose you've lost*
> *For out of the world you'll find*
> *Success begins with a fellow's will*
> *It's all in the state of the mind*
> *If you think you're outclassed, you are*
> *You've got to think high, to rise*
> *You've got to be sure of yourself*
> *Before you can ever win a prize*
> *Many cowards fail*
> *Before their work is done*
> *Think big and your deeds will grow*
> *Think small and you'll fall behind*
> *Life's battles don't always go*
> *To the stronger or faster one*
> *But sooner of later the one who wins*
> *Is the fellow who thinks that he can*
> *Attitude, is better than aptitude*
> *You can succeed in anything you decide*
> *Its all in the state of the mind*
> *-anonymous*

Being organized is equally important in the definition of opportunity. You must always be ready to handle any situation on your own. This is called self-management. That doesn't mean you can't hire a manager. You can, but always on your terms, not theirs. There are some things we can't always know how to do, like accountancy or legal advice, as these are specialized skills that require just as much time to learn as you are putting into your own Art. But let it be said that making educated decisions is crucial to the success of professional Artists. Read, study, educate yourself. Go to business night school. Whatever it takes, do it. You will always have time for your Art. Why? Because you have made a conscious decision to make it important in your life and so it will be.

Artists get screwed in the entertainment business because of their ignorance. Because they are too willing to let others do the work without properly understanding what they are doing. Sting had to sue his long term accountant for embezzling his funds. Courtney Love sued her record company. She learned about her one-sided contract only years later. It happens all the time. An ignorant Artist means a failing Artist. I say this bluntly because we have to empower ourselves with the understanding that we CAN manage our own affairs (with the select chosen experts we bring in) and that we CAN find the time to know what we need to know. It's okay to sign a contract, but make sure you understand it fully before you sign on the dotted line.

If you are business savvy, people will want to do business with you. You will know what you are talking about. Don't be fooled or be ignorant. Being an Artist does not mean you have to be naïve in the ways of the world. Be organized and develop your business skills. But do it happily and with minimum stress. It's the Art that should come first, so don't let your business affairs make you unhappy.

Being business minded, disciplined and organized, means taking risks and focusing yourself in channeling your creativity.

All this provides *opportunities*. Be mindful that opportunities come when you least expect them, so keep the door open and be ready in wonder. Opportunities aren't always far afield either. They can be in your own backyard. You just have to look for them.

Many people will say to you, "oh, you need big bucks to make it or you'll fail", or "you need to do this, this and this in order to be successful otherwise you won't make it". Ignore these people who say your dream is impossible to reach. Being conscientious at what you do, working toward financial independence and creative freedom ON YOUR OWN TERMS is the ONLY way.

Stay positive, optimistic, keep organized and opportunities will come your way. Besides if you are a pessimist, you will only see the failures in life. So, put a smile on your face, get your house in order and wait for the sun to shine!

Optimism
+ Organized
= Opportunity

6. Know thyself and represent yourself appropriately.

Whether you want to be a rock star, or a consummate Artist, or both, you need to be clear and focused with what path you take and how you are going to promote yourself. But it all begins with who you are. If you can't describe *Who You Are* well, you could be sabotaging every future step. Creating your I AM Statement is a good start. Getting to know your competitive advantage and unique selling point (marketing of you) is the next step.

7. I AM versus I WANT.

My first book was called *"I AM A Professional Artist"* and I titled it for a reason: to empower Artists to make a positive, current affirmation about who they are, based on who they want to be. If you only proclaim that you "want" something, then all you will ever get is "wanting" without any actualization. I'm not the first to say this. It's written in many motivational self-help books. Use your words carefully. Introduce yourself to the world as someone who already is. That way you are empowering yourself to be the person you've always dreamed of being. Talk about your future as if it's your present, and be convinced as to who you are. Then we will be convinced of you. You have to endow success: which means to "be" successful in your mind, inside. Permeate it in every way in your beingness: the way you walk, the way you talk, and what you do. People will feel it.

8. Get started – just get out there.

Take small tangible steps. Create a plan. I never knew how to get where I wanted to go, but I always had a dream. So write your dreams down, and be as ambitious as you want. But then, create a plan. The plan starts with some goals that you want to achieve within the next couple of years, and then start writing some strategies on how you think you can achieve them. Remember, you don't have to know exactly how to get there, but just write what you know, for now. And then the road will begin to reveal itself as you start MOVING towards your goals. The key word here is MOVE. You have to just get started with some steps.

9. Age doesn't matter.

It doesn't matter how old you are in the world of Artistry. Ignore what you hear from hearsay: you can be any age you want to be as an Artist in the Arts business. It all depends on the market you are targeting. If you want to go for the Taylor Swift or Myley Cyrus market, then sure, being under 24 surely means something, and the major record companies spend most of their budget on the 8-14 year olds. If you want to compete with that, give it a shot, but know what you're up against. The whole pop radio, video and retail machine is geared towards that age bracket. But you have the opportunity to find so many other markets, age brackets and genres for your music. You can be 65 years old and find your audience.

> It doesn't matter how old you are!

In the Indie world, being an Artist Entrepreneur, know that what might take 6 weeks for a Major Record Company to launch a record, make take 1, 2, even 6 years to fully realize for you…. and that's ok. 'Cause remember, **being an Artist is a lifelong journey.** You will not run out of time.

You have all the time you need.

If you're 35, 45, 55, 65 years of age… **it doesn't matter how old you are.** I write about this often. There's no age limit to Artistry. We are Artists for LIFE.

Again, it doesn't matter how old you are. I know it's an incredible statement in this world of entertainment, but consider this: most Major Artists these days have a short career span. They may break 1 record, maybe 2, but in this new "singles" world, if the record companies can't go Gold on the first song, they really don't have the patience to develop Artists. But you have all your life.

If you really love what you do, and you have a passion for it all (both the Art AND the business/promotion), you will be an Artist for life. So why fit into a commercial success definition of having to "make it" by 30, or 25, when you can develop your Art, put it out there and create all your life'till you're 100. There is no reason why you have to succeed by a certain age, unless you have created unrealistic expectations AND you are pushing your music to a market that is not tangible for you. Madonna is no spring chicken, but she has found her audience… actually they found her. She just does her music and her fans find her. **Find your own market, your own audience, and they will stick with you for life.** Remember, take all the time you need. Don't rush, don't get frustrated, and do things on your own terms.

Remember, Artistry is for life. This is a life long journey. So take the time you need to learn, be and share.

10. Learn but also be all knowing.

Be the student of life, but know you have what you need to be who you want to be. I have also felt like I'm at the beginning of the road, always learning, always starting. Our learning is life long and beyond college we will always be learning something, on a daily basis. Everything we do will provide us insight into ourselves and we will always be "in development". But I believe that we all have the assets and the know-how to achieve whatever we want to achieve and be whoever we want to be, now. I use the term *"commence-aphobia"* with Artists at times, when they procrastinate and wait a long time to do something, like perform or record an album. It's like they are waiting for a sign, or someone to say "ok, you are ready now". But what if we are always ready? What if all we needed to do is to take one step. I see that by taking that first step, the other foot will follow, and the seemingly foggy path will clear up and illuminate the way. We don't necessarily need to wait for someone to tell us how to do it, or have our Art approved before we put it out there. We don't need to read every single book on the business or go to every class in order to start a project. What we need is confidence and a desire to do the Art, for the sake of doing. If we just initiate the step to start, it's amazing how much information, resources, advisors, support and opportunity comes our way, because we have internally opened up to the Art of doing and we are constantly aware of always learning.

11. Seek no one else's approval but your own.

I'm not suggesting that we don't seek advice, or that we have to do things alone, but at the end of the day, _you_ must make the decision as to what's best for you.

It's a hard statement to digest at first, but when you really consider it for some time, it makes total sense. Definitely have a core few around you, which you trust, to gain feedback about your work. But at the end of the day when all is said and done, you alone are the one to decide if it's right for you or not, if you are on the right path or not. This ties in greatly to the whole concept about enacting _who you want to be_ as an Artist and the things you'd like to do. We can wait for ages to have some high and mighty record executive, or media critique, to approve of our process, but really, we don't need anyone to tell us we are doing the right thing for us. Once you agree with yourself that you have everything you need to be who you are and who you want to be, then you can enact without waiting for someone else to tell you it's okay. Everyone is unique, and, so, what you bring to the world cannot really be judged by anyone.

The journey of Art is a personal journey, no matter what competitive, commercial or public purpose you may choose to endeavor in.

Work with others, just don't rely on others to make it happen for you. Definitely have a core few around you, which you trust, to gain feedback about your work.

12. Community and Relationships.

I have learned how important community is through Songsalive!, way before there was Myspace, Facebook or Twitter or any social network. Bringing people together, and networking within your community or communities you participate in, is the key to building relationships, which is a key to success. Your music industry is inside your current community, and it's in this arena that you can develop, nurture and expand. When the social networks came along, I had already known about communities and their strength in marketing: developing loyal fan bases, customers for your music, interaction and such. So now with the online communities so prominent in everyone's lives, it's a fabulous way for indie Artists to interact in, and find new fans.

Relationships are THE most important aspect of developing your business. Nurture the relationships you make because you never know where they might take you. _Remember to ask "what can I do for you" first before you expect something in return_. It needs to be a symbiotic relationship.

Another way for truly utilizing your relationships, is to learn how to capitalize on current contacts. Think about who you may know already that you could work with, or learn from. Go through your contacts, and engage with people at parties, social events, gigs, even the local grocery. Just open your eyes to the world around you. You'll be surprised who might be in your immediate proximity.

13. Enjoy it. It is a game.

How can one possibly proceed into the world of the Arts without seeing it as a bit of fun? My gosh, we are so lucky as Artists to pursue a life with paint brushes, musical instruments and anything creative. Just think that about ten percent of the world's population has the audacity to make their world revolve around creativity and imagination whereas every child on this planet lived and breathed it before they were 7. What happened to most of us as we grew into adults? The world has gotten so serious! Always business, business, business... mortgages, living on credit, an ever present need for financial security and keeping up with the Jones's.

I must admit though, being in the music business, I have had to be more business minded than I ever would have thought. I have had to wear two hats, and more business, which I didn't realize at first, was to be. But let's use our Artistic insights to survive the biz in a cool, creative way. Think of it like a 'game' and know that this game is made up of people playing the game. As my singer-songwriter friend James Hurley says, "it's a game because people are participating in it". This business is all about relationships, strategies and dreams. Play it like Monopoly or a long thought out chess game, with patience and a sense of humor. Navigate with passion, and joy, and know that at any time you want out, you can. You can always go back to a 'desk' job in the suburbs, right? You can always just play your musical instrument because you enjoy it. You don't have to get into the business side of it. You have a choice, to play the game or not. Besides, the music business in particular is all an illusion. Everything you read about fame and fortune, the celebrity lives versus ordinary happiness... is all wrapped up in an illusion dished out in glossy magazines. The real business is business, and hard work. The 'game' of the music business can be played with tenacity, joy and passion, if you put your mind to it.

14. Everyone is unique. Know your uniqueness.

We can find it all quite daunting when you consider all the things we have to do to be creative, promote our creativity and survive it all. There's a lot of competition too. Many Artists all wanting those top 10 slots on the Billboard charts right? Wrong. There is room for everyone at the 'top'. It all depends on what you want, and what you bring to the table. You may not be Sting, Bonnie Raitt or Eminem, but you probably have something very unique about you that can tap into a market all to itself. Consider that there are more than 300 million people in the U.S., heck, nearly 7 billion on the planet. You can find your niche for your Art, if you know what makes you unique. I've always called this "finding your **competitive advantage.**"

Your talent + your uniqueness = your competitive advantage.

It might be that you play barefoot, or you have an interesting hair-do. Maybe your name is different. Perhaps you cross styles with your music, or have a different stage presence or image/persona. Whatever it is, harness it, focus on it, and exploit it. This will certainly help you find your own audience. In this day and age, for the new Artist Entrepreneur, you don't have to conform to a structure as to what you should look like, sound like, be like or the way you share your music or promote. We are in a new era where not only are audiences in control (they search for their own music based on their own tastes online, etc.), but they are busting to get something NEW. Be creative and use your imagination to find new ways to present your music and yourself. This is the time to be very imaginative and to think outside the box. I'll talk more about this in the next chapter.

15. It's a choice – you "choose" to do it.

Yes, that's right. You're not a victim here. You want it? Then do it, but don't complain about it. It's one thing to be creative, but it's another to go into this profession. Remember, you're a business person, in the business of music.

16. Dare to be different.

Are you afraid to be different? So many Artists are afraid of being individually powerful, unique and different. A lot of this is natural. Artists are innately interesting, so just being yourself goes a long way.

There is no need to conform to normalcy as an Artist. Stand up to your own individualism. That means, don't wait for the approval of others to be accepted or loved. Sometimes you just have to be adventurous and daring, and be WHO YOU ARE. Go for it!

MYTHS ABOUT ARTIST ENTREPRENEURS (not true)

You need a lot of money, or have large investments.

You need to know where you are going and know exactly how to get there.

You need to know about marketing before you start.

You need to do everything yourself.

A SUCCESSFUL ARTIST ENTREPRENEUR...

Knows who they are, and what they want, even if they don't know exactly how to get there.

Understands the importance of being a business person as well as an Artist.

Defines success on their own terms. Not by fame or fortune, but solid, daily rewards that only they can define, and not by commercial standards. They seek no one else's approval but their own, but they have a team they work with.

Writes careful, meaningful, tangible, and ambitious goals.

Has a solid plan to reach their goals, which includes who they are, what they want, and a carefully laid out strategy to reach the goals.

Has a life mission statement about themselves, that is bigger than just themselves, and contributes to something greater.

Understands the Importance of mentors / education and lifelong learning.

Sees themselves as a marketing jewel, whereby to develop a unique story, image and marketing strategy.

Is not afraid to promote themselves.

Is persistent, conscientious and passionate about their Art and their business career.

Knows that Artistry is a lifelong journey, and there is no quick overnight shortcut to success.

Is confident, and will try anything, with care: leap and the answer will come.

Dares to be different.

This is your time to be, do, create, think, visualize, and build your empire. Be the entrepreneur, and be yourself.

And so, I ask you... Are you an Artist Entrepreneur?

Exercise: I am an Entrepreneur

What is an Artist Entrepreneur to you?

How do you see yourself as an Artist Entrepreneur?
(Give examples of what you do and hallmarks of your character.)

Write down 3 entrepreneurial steps you'll take this year.

16. Going to market

What is marketing and why do I need it?

This cannot come at a better time in this book, because once you've understood that being a business person is absolutely necessary in this business of music, it's absolutely necessary, then a key component is to understand about marketing. I wish that Artists could be *just* Artists and paint, sing, play, dream... but the reality is, we are faced with so much change in the music business that we need to be Artist Entrepreneurs, and understand *the business* side, and the best way to wrap your head around it all is to **understand marketing** and to develop a plan.

Dan S. Kennedy writes in his book, *The Ultimate Marketing Plan,*

"Marketing is getting the right message to the right people via the right media and methods."

Webster's dictionary writes: *"Marketing is the process of planning and executing the conception, pricing, promotion and distribution of ideas, goods, and services to create exchanges that satisfy individual and organizational objectives."*

Wikipedia writes, *"The way products (you or your music) are sold, and to whom. Includes advertising, selling and delivering products to people. Marketers try to get the attention of target audiences by using slogans, packaging design, exposure in the media world."*

"Identifying and reaching specific segments of the population that will want you or your music."

So just as I do for my Artist clients, this chapter's purpose is to help you craft the right message for your music and Artistry, chose the best media and methods to deliver it, and choose the best 'audience' to deliver it to. I use the word 'audience' here broadly. I'm not just speaking to fans, but I'm also speaking about the media (print, radio, webcasts, podcasts, etc.), the music industry (record labels, publishers, film and TV music supervisors, ad houses, etc.) and anyone that will WANT the music for a purpose (to either re-direct to a target audience, or be the end-user/listener).

Just like Dan Kennedy, I don't like to plan much. I'm pretty much a spitfire – ready, aim, fire. As soon as I think of an idea, I want to jump in quick and see where I land. That's the Aries impulsive nature in me. However, I've soon learned that without a solid plan, with an end target in mind, I just end up swimming in a mush of ideas, half-cooked projects and an overloaded to-do list that I just want to throw away and run on the beach instead. So, in order to keep my creativity in check, my ambitions on the page, and my passion into the process of it all, I have come to realize that **planning** IS the way. It can be done tastefully and moderately, so that you don't spend too much time planning, and less doing. I like to plan as I go. A little bit of fore-thought, and a lot of action. Like splashing paint on a canvas Jackson Pollock style, I like to see how the colors and swirls end up, but I now know I need to at least spend a moment to mix the colors on the palette.

A family friend of ours, Doug Weiss, works in marketing (the real business nitty gritty of marketing) whereby sometimes he has been a consultant for politicians on how they can use the new social networks, Internet or old school marketing practices to promote themselves. His world, really, is so similar to my world, it is uncanny. It doesn't matter what you are selling, the same principles apply. So over a dinner conversation we chatted about marketing, and how it's changed in the new world, shrouded by a deluge of Internet options and Wild West strategies.

Markets are conversations not monologues. It is not about broadcasting what you want to say but engaging in a more intimate dialog. If you are going to have a conversation with someone—or many someones' it helps to:

➤ **Know your market/your audience** – know as much as you can about who you are talking with.
➤ **Know what they want** – truly understand what they want so you can deliver your Art in a way they can "get" it.
➤ **Know how to reach them** – relate to them on their terms.

I interpret this for Artists as follows: We can no longer just spam or advertise our wares thoughtlessly, out into the world. EVEN with the Internet, we cannot forget that we are reaching out to real people, with real values, needs and tastes. So how we start marketing our music and Art means we have to be in touch with our audiences and customers in very tangible ways.

Even though you create your Art and Music as something inspirational from the Gods (replace God with universe, or whatever else inspires you), once you've

created it, *it's important to know who would like it.*

I happen to have taken a very long time to figure out who likes my music. I thought it was for young teenage girls, because I likened myself to Mariah Carey a bit when I was younger, so I just followed her fans as a demographic that could work for me. But then I realized that a lot of my gigs had a large male demographic, as well as a more mature crowd. So really, I discovered my music was likened by a large cross range of different types. But what I did figure out was that they liked music that was emotionally driven, and filled with stories, as I'm very much a story teller with my songs.

So too for you, it's important to figure out what type of person (whether young, old, male or female) likes your music, and WHY. Do they like to hear hard hitting music where the lyrics aren't so important, but the edginess of the guitars and drums takes them away from their mundane lives? Do they want to dance to your music? Do they want to listen to your music while dining on camembert cheese and cabernet sauvignon? These are the questions you might want to ask yourself. What kind of listener listens to my music? When? Why?

If you know your audience, and you know what they want, then the tricky part is finding how to reach them.

I want to say something really important here. Unlike some music business authors, I do not believe you should write your songs, and create your music FOR a particular market. I believe in creating your music based on your personal passion and inspirations: and just be that consummate Artist. Think that Van Gogh or Picasso didn't set out to paint for people who might like their Art. No, they just painted from within their inspirations.

I believe that when you truly capture your essence in your Art, then the audience finds you, and you can then ALSO find your audience, HENCE, your market.

I know there will be some people who disagree with me. Some people in the business believe you should listen to the music on the radio and understand the current times, and then create music like that because there is a defined market to sell it. Major labels tend to do this because it's easier to make money from a sure thing (an already proven market place to sell). But as you know, the TRAIL BLAZERS on this planet have ALWAYS been those who do something different, go completely left of field, and come up with something new.

This is your opportunity to be a trailblazer.

How to Market

Marketing your music can be broken down without all the bells and whistles and ambiguity that record labels have done in the past. I see it fall into two areas:

1. Sales & distribution, and 2. Public awareness campaign

Sales & distribution centers around all the avenues where you can make money. How you make money from music has changed, as we all know. CDs are somewhat selling (at least I sell them at my gigs). I think of myself as a door-to-door salesman ready to sell anything I have available (*"wanna buy a watch?"* she says, as she opens her invisible trench coat). I sell CDs, my book, t-shirts, caps, mugs, posters... whatever I have that is about me. Fans love to grasp onto anything that's about the Artist.

So, merchandise is important too. As we lose ourselves in the intangible world of Internet downloads (mp3s from iTunes, Rhapsody and the like), I still believe that fans still want to "touch" something – be able to save it as memorabilia at the very least. So, yes, get some t-shirts done, or caps, or mugs, or posters, stickers or *something* that the fan can take home after a show.

Other areas of revenue include the now lucrative, but now already densely populated, film and television music placement market. Did you know that this is the number one marketing plan for record companies these days? That's right. It's lucrative if you're ready to play the game hard and get on the phone. But it's there for the taking, and Artists and labels alike are equal with their foot in the door. While labels may have "ins" with the film companies (example, Sony Music and Sony Pictures), indie Artists also get a look in because their original songs are usually easier to clear, and that makes it much easier for the music supervisor who needs to get the song in the film fast (music is always the last thing placed in the film by the director which is sad because there's less of a budget, but we can capitalize on the opportunities fast).

Anything where you can think outside the box, and expand your revenue sources from all the creative aspects of yourself, will bring in opportunities and money. The focus should be about expansion and not the pennies. For once you start thinking abundantly, and expand your horizons, the money will flow in.

Capitalizing on your fan list is the most important avenue, because in business the most important thing is to take care of your current customers. So if you can work hard at building a relationship with your fan base, and tease them with new products for sale, and some giveaways, such as music downloads and ringtones, you'll find that they will keep buying from you forever. Now, this theory works well for indie Artists who are personally in touch with their fans. For the majors, they're finding in this new era, that their targeted consumer base: young, hip, distracted, Internet teenagers (I mentioned them above) will usually buy the first CD or download, but can't guarantee even 10% of sales for the next one. Poor labels: I sympathize with them as they "move through this rough period". Believe me, an A&R executive actually said this on a panel last weekend. *"We are assessing it as best as we can, as we move through this rough period."*

Rough period? What?! Are we in the Dark Ages? Hell no. *This is the age of enlightenment, of empowerment, of Artist growth and global change.* We need this diversity, and change, and new thinking. I'm so excited to witness the evolution of Artist empowerment and people empowerment before my eyes, while old mainstream corporations tumble. You just need to know your market. Market yourself to the audience that loves you for your music, not how high your skirt is at age 18.

New distribution strategies to sell your music

Getting your music to the world is now becoming seemingly different, difficult and daunting (my three Ds). It's up to the Artist Entrepreneur to grab hold of the new ways to take the music to market. What is important to know is that the consumer has changed the way they want their music. Buying a CD in a store is the least likely means for attaining new music these days (to the chagrin of retail stores who unfortunately are a dying breed). The Internet opened up the desire for consumers to want the music fast, and direct: Downloading mp3s, or full albums (as mp3s) is the most common form these days. Understanding how consumers access their music, and keeping up with the trends is THE MOST SIGNIFICANT RESEARCH you can do. Don't assume selling a CD in a store, or at a gig, is the only way to go. One day, it won't be the way at all. So cover all the options.

Selling Direct

Let's look at the most obvious route, both traditionally and new. While it lasts, creating a CD (compact disc) still works, especially for because I find I sell more CDs at my shows, direct to my fans. It's a point of sale/impulse buy. They see me perform, they want me to sign a CD so they can take what they saw home. It's a no brainer.

I also sell my CD online on my website www.gillimoon.com. My website is my homebase. It's where I want all my fans to ultimately come to, where I can control my sales (and my Art). So I have a dedicated music page on my website to buy my CDs (I have 3rd party companies who pack and ship). I also sell downloads directly from my site through Paypal. Another site I use to sell from my own website is www.musiconlinealive.com. They provide a way for consumers to buy my virtual album, not just the mp3s but the entire artwork. Createspace.com (powered by Amazon) is also another place that does that (selling virtual on-demand CDs).

Selling through 3rd Parties

CDs can still sell through unique mom and pop retail stores (and the large chains like Target, Best Buy and Walmart who are not CD stores, but sell CDs). It won't be long though that we'll all go digital. Maybe even by the time I publish this book! Ha ha!

Creating mp3s of all your songs is, of course, crucial. (The iTunes program on your computer can convert your tracks to mp3s. See the DIY Music Licensing chapter for more on how to organize your mp3s (meta-tag). There are a bunch of great 3rd party online sites you can have direct accounts with, to sell mp3s (and market your album as a digital product). Some include iTunes.com, Amazon.com (the top 2 e-tailers), as well as slew of sites that all come in a package deal when you sign up with a digital aggregator. CDbaby.com, Theorchard.com, Tunecore.com, Iodalliance.com, and Bfmdigital.com are just a few of the big guns that can sell your mp3 albums online to hundreds of online sites.

But if you also want to tailor your mp3 sales and marketing to communities and unique audiences built into certain websites, I also recommend (in conjunction to getting digital distribution through an aggregator), these sites: Soundclick.com, Thesixtyone.com, Whotune.com (Australian), and Reverbnation.com.

More resources at www.Artistalive.com.

Out of the box consignments

Find new places to sell your music. How about cool cafes (have a CD rack for your music); unique bookstores; women's spas and beauty places; athletic stores; clubs and associations, etc. Don't be afraid to investigate setting up a direct account with a retailer, just like a distributor would. Be okay with consignments in your area.

Getting on compilations

Some are dicey, a lot are great. If you can't afford to make your own CD (and that includes releasing it and promoting it), think about getting on a compilation that at least gets your name and music out there. Songsalive! (www.songsalive.org) and Warrior Girl Music (www.warriorgirlmusic.com/compilations) both create compilations that are for industry and promotional purposes. Sonicbids.com offers great solutions to get on compilations that are trustworthy and have a track record. Compilations these days have usually one of three goals: to sell at retail; to promote to media/press; and/or to promote to music supervisors who place songs in films or TV shows.

Check into them first, ask about their success rates, before you pay any money... because they usually cost, like any advertising.

CDs - is this a mute point?

I believe that for the next 5 or so years, CDs will still have a place because people like to collect them, and the Art work, even if they load the songs onto their iPod. And if the CD does go, then there will still be another tangible product that we can touch in our hands. But I regret to say that online digital formats have taken over because they are more readily available (people want things NOW), lighter and easily transferable to their computer and of course the iPod (bye bye stereo), and are cheaper. Yes, my dear friends, music is becoming cheaper and cheaper and I don't want to get into the whole discussion about respecting music monetarily right now, though I will later. Notwithstanding, let me talk about the old fashion CD for a moment:

New packaging ideas – gone are the days when we have to put up with jewel cases that break and shrink wrap that just won't come off. Why not try digipacks, in cardboard sleeves. Notice that the more creative Major Artists are going this route (if they are indeed pressing CDs) and it's all for great reasons: cool creative concepts, environmentally friendly, and easier to transport. I don't recommend pressing large quantities any more, and consider that many CDs can be used as giveaways to new fans, the press, radio or music industry representatives. We have some cool CD manufacturers listed at Artistalive.com

Another approach is to try the drop cards as a way to give or sell something in tangible form. This is the size of a business card and it basically gives the consumer an access number to download the songs online.

Why not give people a flash drive (tiny external USB drive) with your songs and artwork on it? Some CD manufacturing companies are getting in this business. Personally, I still think this is a bit pricy.

The artwork – like your website, the CD cover, or drop card cover, or even the iTunes single artwork, is the second thing that people see to know you. (Apart from seeing you at a show.) It's all about first impressions so really be creative on your Art work. We want to know who you are but also mystery works. If you're a painter, try painting a canvas, take a digital photo of it, scan it in and work it up in Photoshop. Sometimes I get a CD that is so plain and boring, with the worst photo representation of the Artist, that I don't want to even look inside. Be creative. You're an Artist! Capture your essence. Write down 20 words that describe who you are, and what you look like. Sketch images, think layouts, learn Art programs, and be the graphic designer that's hidden inside you. Go on, I dare you!

Giveaways – think about cool ways to give away your promo CDs, like wrapping the CD in a gift voucher, or a fun little bag, or a box. If you can afford it, have extra promos of dance remixes, or the single in flat cardboard sleeves. Send promos to radio stations in your area, or use them as handouts on the street. Give a few to the retail store chicks and guys and they might just put your poster up! Hey you can even just press CDs on the spindle and fly them into the audience at gigs. "Pick me, pick me!"

A word about Vinyl and the new frontier

I'm going to be very poignant for a moment: there will always be a vehicle for music. Whether it be the cassette tape, the vinyl record, the compact disc (CD), the digital download (mp3) or something we don't know about yet. Transmission of music will always exist. We may not like the new way, but there will always be a way. I personally don't fancy the mp3 being the sole vehicle of music because it doesn't showcase the music enough. I spend time, money and energy creating HD surround sound, beautiful music that should be heard in beautiful stereo speakers, and yet it gets reduced to a compressed mp3 in tiny ear phones on your cell phone.

That being said, technology is getting better and better and I want to trust that music will be honored and glorified, because our ears demand it. I'm not here to profess what will be the next vehicle for music, but I will say that old is sometimes the new. Vinyl records have become extremely popular again as an additional (not only) product for music. What I like about this phenomenon is that we are tapping into a unique audience: the collector. Those who like vinyl records, are those who collect music. These are the ones who still have vinyls from the '60s and '70s, and who are also interested in new music on vinyl.

What's even clearer about this audience, is that they will, on average, spend more on a single record than any new teenager will on a download. Consider that a download can cost .99c, and a CD can cost $8 - $15. A vinyl can average $18 all the way up to $100 if you make it a collector's item.

If you happen to think laterally about the new area of music selling, it could become something more like a piece of Art, (like Art in art galleries). Instead of buying into the notion of music not being respected and given away for free, why don't we start thinking (and educating our youth) that music is a treasure, and worth something to collect.

If you do a short run series of vinyl records (50-100) and number them in the series like Art prints (1 out of 100, etc), then the small limit already places value on the product. If you sign it with your autograph, it could become even more valuable. If you create original art on the cover, the value increases. See what I mean?

Let's think of unique ways to create **VALUE** for what we love so much, to inspire others to value and treasure it.

Micro-marketing

Think one region at a time. Don't try and blanket promote across the country when you don't have the money nor the advertising visibility. That also goes for radio promotion. Book your gigs in advance, then, contact the media, retail stores (if they're still alive in the area) and your street teams for that region. Slowly build a fan base and move on. Then return to that market. It seems obvious, but so many Artists make the mistake on paying a radio promoter to blanket promote to radio stations across the country, when they may be wasting their money if they can't physically go to that city to perform, to back it up.

Even with touring, it's always a good idea to concentrate on one region at a time, and then you can focus on getting press, radio and fans in that region to support the gigs. Remember, you are going to have to take more time as an Indie Artist on a budget, unlike a Major Artist who may have big bucks to blanket promote on a billboard, TV ad or Facebook promotion. So start small and consider your micro-marketing will slowly expand in awareness like a spiral.

Create a marketing plan

Have a dream. Dream big. Everybody should have their own plan. Don't rely on a label to provide you with the answers, because they're right there with you wondering what the answers are too. You don't need a label, and the labels know you don't need them. But because everyone knows the same thing, there is no harm now working together on new models, deals and visions where EVERYONE benefits. At the end of this chapter I will detail two types of plans: a general business plan, for your entire career; and a specific marketing plan – for your current promotion (e.g. new album or a tour, etc.). I believe that the two are uniquely different, and collectively both important. It's one thing to dream and have goals. It's another to input them into a constructive, time managed plan that that you can implement. Every business has a plan. Every new product has a plan before it is marketed. So to you need a plan, not just for your products (music, as an example) but for you as the whole Artist.

Define your competitive advantage

We all think we're talented, right?

I'm an Artist, and I'm dedicated, and my grandmother used to love my singing, so... I'm talented right? That's what makes me special! I'm talented.

Well, perhaps you are right in a certain respect, but let me be really frank with you: so are many, many other Artists. So what makes you different to the rest? You can't just rely on your self-determining talents. And then, what about your talents? Just because you are inspiring, sing soulful music, or write lots of songs doesn't mean you are any more special than any other Artist. There are thousands of Artists out there all playing and singing inspiring songs. So what sets you apart from the rest?

It's really key to figure out what sets you apart from the rest.   That is, find your **competitive advantage**, which is your talent **+**

uniqueness

What is your uniqueness? Is it your hair? Your dress sense? your music? It might be that you play barefoot, or you have an interesting hair-do. Maybe your name is different. Perhaps you cross styles with your music, or have a different stage presence or image/persona. It could be as simple as a costume, or the image used on packaging. It can be as diverse as your voice, your musical style, or even something you do that's completely different to someone else.

When I first came to the States from Australia, just being Australian was unique and my competitive advantage. Then, after a while of developing my Artistry, I began to paint on stage while performing with my band, a movement I call "SensuArt".

Just because you are soulful, or you think you have unique lyrics, or that you are "gifted" or can touch the audience's emotions... doesn't make you unique. It is a

GIVEN that Artists have unique lyrics and it's your job to touch the audience's emotions. So, you have to think better than that. WHAT MAKES YOU TRULY UNIQUE? Think about it. Perhaps it's your accent, or the way you cross boundaries with your styles? Or perhaps it's because you play a cello like a guitar (like one of my client Artists, Thia Sexton). Thia's competitive advantage, apart from being extraordinarily beautiful, and it shows in all her glossy videos and photos, is that she plays the cello LIKE a guitar. That's unique. Everyone is talking about her in L.A. as "that girl with the cello". Now they may not all remember her name, but she is branding herself in a very unique way. Everything she does, whether it be recording an album, doing a live show, or creating ad campaigns with herself and her music in it and pitches it to ad agencies (she really does think outside the box), is ALL about her and her CELLO.

I always suggest to Artists to find their competitive advantage as the integral aspect of their marketing campaign.

Find your "edge", what makes you unique. Sometimes this is a cool strength about you. Whatever it is for you, harness it, focus on it, and exploit it. This will certainly help you find your own audience.

Let me end this chapter with food for thought: you might know you who you are, what you want, have a big dream, create goals and manage your priorities; you may understand everything about marketing and know how to spread the word; you may have developed the best marketing plan out there – but if you've got no talent… it's a moot point.

The Artist proclaims, "I've done it all but I'm just treading water."

"Well, what's the opposite of drowning?" Coach asks?

"Treading water?" the Artist wonders.

"Congratulations! you are treading water!"

Exercise 1: Defining your competitive advantage

IF SOMEONE (friend, associate, fan) WERE TO DESCRIBE YOU AS AN ARTIST, WHAT DO YOU THINK THEY WOULD SAY?

WHAT ARE YOUR FAVORITE ARTISTS WHO YOU FEEL INSPIRED BY OR INFLUENCED BY? (What draws you to them physically, Artistically, and jot down some of their characteristics as well as what you like about their image and the way they promote themselves.)

WHAT WORDS WOULD YOU USE TO DESCRIBE YOURSELF?

WHAT ARE YOUR BIGGEST STRENGTHS?

WHAT ARE YOUR WEAKNESSES?

WHAT MAKES YOU UNIQUE/DIFFERENT?

SO .... WHAT'S YOUR COMPETITIVE ADVANTAGE?

Exercise 2: Creating a business plan

Let's create a general business plan, for your entire career. Start with your **I AM Statement** at the top (refer to the *Who Are You... Really* Chapter for a reminder on how to create this). Then begin to plot down what your lifetime dreams are, short term goals for the next few years, and from there we can build strategies for each goal. Doing a plan like this keeps it visionary, yet with useful ideas on how you can implement your goals.

My Business Plan

ARTIST NAME:

Who I am/I AM Statement (write below)

LIFETIME GOALS:

1. e.g., Create financial abundance from performing and touring

2.

3.

4.

5.

6.

Going to market

SHORT TERM GOALS (1-2years):

1.   E.g., Pick up a Tour with a Major Artist that pays at least $5,000 a tour

2.

3.

4.

5.

6.

7.

8.

STRATEGIES: (how I'm going to do it)

(On a new page, for every Goal (from previous page, write the Goal, plus a list of strategies (3-10) of each Goal. Let's start with your first Goal below. You can continue on separate paper for the rest of your goals. In fact, it's best to type up your entire business plan in one place.

2.   GOAL: E.g., Pick up a Tour with a Major Artist that pays at least $5,000 a tour

Sample Strategies:

1. Research Pollstar and contact some Agents that represent Major Artists
2. Perform 4 times a week in New York to be visible to Agents.
3. Join the Musicians Union
4. Go to as many Music Conferences as I can to meet music representatives
5. etc.,
6.
7.
8.
9.
10.

Exercise 3: The Artist Marketing Plan

Along with your business plan, it's important to also create a marketing plan, to implement a strategy about a specific campaign for a product you are releasing. I use marketing plans when I release a new CD or a new book. The marketing plan can be for personal use, to guide you and your business, and/or it can be shown to prospective distributors, and music industry executives as a way to pepper them/grab their attention. When they see you have a plan, they believe in you more.

My Marketing Plan

ARTIST NAME:

ALBUM NAME (OR PRODUCT):
Contacts:
Address:
Phone:
E-mail:
Website:

Hook

Insert a really cool, short statement hook line.

Bio

Insert one paragraph only bio

Image

- Insert bullet points that describe the Artist's image
- Two
- Three

Budget

In the following area, write a breakdown of your budget for the creation and marketing of the new CD or product:

- CD Recording (including paying musicians): $
- CD Mastering: $5
- CD Manufacturing/Printing: $
- Marketing/Promo Tools: $
- Photos: $
- Touring: $
- Advertising:
- Cont. list here...
  Total:

How money will be generated. (Write here any money coming in from sponsorship or outside sources/or record label etc.)

Goals

Insert from Business Plan or Goals recently devised and written down:
1.
2.
3.
Etc.

Music Releases

E.g., the stillness, by gilli moon (2010).
You can list your past releases here, as it looks good to see a history of music releases.

Distribution

(Insert all the ways the CD will be distributed.)

Marketing/Selling Tools

(List all the marketing/selling tools to be used to promote the CD. These are usually listed on your one sheet. Some ideas: One sheet created, postcards, flyers, website and internet promotion, mailing list, P.R. Explain in detail in bullet point form.)

Radio

List radio that the CD will be targeted to.

Video

List if any songs will have music videos. Describe in detail. Be sure to have this in the budget.

Club/Other/Film

Insert how the songs of the album may be used in other areas, such as TV/Film, compilations, dance remixes, etc.)

Publicity

Insert if any formal publicity will be used to promote the CD.

Advertising/Sponsorship

Insert advertising campaigns/budget, and/or sponsorship that will be used.

Merchandise

Insert any merchandise that will be created to accompany the CD promotion. (e.g. t-shirts, cups, hats, posters, etc.) Make sure it's in the budget.

Touring/Personal Appearances

Describe the projected touring objectives in promoting the CD.

<u>Schedule</u>

Insert a year's worth (or 2) of specific dates or general months of touring appearances in different regions. This can be projected, not actual.

JAN

FEB

MAR

APRIL

MAY

JUNE

JULY

AUG

Commercial break

Let's take a moment to introduce you to an intriguing lyricist, spoken word and Hip Hop Artist, **Immortal Technique.**

(I've deleted the profanity he has used for those with sensitive ears, and so I don't have to put "explicit lyrics" on the cover of my book. I've just put an * instead. But note that wherever you see an * means Immortal Technique certainly was passionate in delivering his message!)

Also, he talks to Hip Hop Artists and MCs in these lyrics, (because he is a Hip Hop Artist) but ALL Artists of all genres, are appropriate here. Whether he inspires you or annoys you, I hope he creates a reaction:

Lyrics from "THE MESSAGE AND THE MONEY" by Immortal Technique:
(REVOLUTIONARY VOLUME 2 CD)

I would like to send a message to all the underground mc's out there, working hard. The time has come to realize you networked in a market

and stop being a *** commodity. And if you didn't understand what I've just said then you already waiting to get *** For example; a lot of these promoters are doing showcases throwing events, and not even paying the workhorses. They trying get us to rock for the love of hiphop or rock for the exposure. Now look man, I don't mind doing a guest spot for my peeps

Or, or, or doing a benefit show, but don't lie to me ***

Coz I find out I'm paying your lightbill, I'm *** you up ...

Besides, you ain't doing this for the love, you ain't doing it for the exposure

you charging up to 10$ at the door, and you ain't tryin to give me s***??

So wait a minute... you want me to go shopping, cook the food, and put it in front of you, but you won't let me sit down and eat with you? The *** is that? .... need to start playing their position, man. Just coz you throw a party a hosting event or an open mic or a showcase, or a battle

that don't make you important at all. Without me and everybody like me out there you ain't nutting but a good idea, *** So stay in your place

And to all these *** who are too lazy to come up with a way to sell records... That they keep recycling marketing schemes and imagery... C'mon... There is a market for everything man
There is a market for pet psychologists... There is a market for twisted ***etish video's. For nipplerings, for riverdancing, for chocolate

cupboard roaches.. But you can't find one for cultured hardcore reality and hiphop?
People like you: the house... executives
and them rich mother*** that own you; you the mother*** machine man!
You and all these ... talking about the same ***
with the same flow over the same candy-*** beats
But I refuse the feed the machine
And I'm not giving any magazine money
So maybe my album won't get 5 mics, or double-x-I's, or 5 discs
Whatever man, *** it
But then again; you don't own me, and none of you... ever will
If I'm feeling what you fight for I'm rolling with you to the end
But if not, then *** YOU!
And the more that mc's, producers, dj's
and independent labels start to grasp the conceptuality
of what their contribution to the business of hiphop is
rather then just the music - the more the industry will be forced to change
    ^ "THE MESSAGE AND THE MONEY" by Immortal Technique
(REVOLUTIONARY VOLUME 2 CD)

    Below, Lyrics from "FREEDOM OF SPEECH" by Immortal Technique
(REVOLUTIONARY VOLUME 2 CD)
    *** a record deal, I want development land
With my benevolent clan
And that's the reason that I only trust my fam
40,000 records sold, 400 grand
*** a middle man, I won't pay anyone else
I'll bootleg it and sell it to the streets my self
I'd rather be that than signed and stuck on a shelf
And because of this executives try to diss me
Racism frozen in time like Walt Disney
And now they say they wanna get me signed to the majors
If I switch up my politics and change my behavior
Try to tell me what to rhyme about over the beat
*** ... that never spent a day in the street
But I repeat that nobody can hold my reigns
I put the truth on tracks...., simple and plain

Why is this so challenging for most of us to do? It's just a matter of confidence. Well, if self-confidence were all it took we would, in fact, own our excellence. Acknowledge your greatness. Own it!

- Will Craig

17. The Art of self-promotion

This chapter is the pivotal place of diving in as a Warrior Artist and the ultimate Artist Entrepreneur. Promotion has changed over the years because of the Internet, whether constructive or destructive on traditional music business strategies. We now live in a time where the Artist has become the self-promoter. It is a part of an Artist's life, whether you want it or not. You must embrace it as much as you have embraced your creativity. Your Art and your self-promotion must live side by side in harmony. There is no way around it. Live with it.

When you're an independent Artist the only way to compete with the majors who have money, power and connections, is to **learn the warrior way on the street**: Grass roots, street-wise, guerilla type promotional strategies are key. You have to be street savvy, creative, quick, and different in order to compete.

The Awareness Campaign

It is critical for Artists, in order to support the sales and distribution of your music, to developing your public awareness. We have all the tools at our fingertips now: the Internet is our friend, building relationships, everywhere, with everyone. Using the Internet, and social media/networking to draw attention is the masterful plan, as well as all traditional means of publicity and promotion.

Over the next few pages I will endeavor to provide you tips and tools on creating the best public awareness campaign ever. But I confess: I still have so much to learn. Coming from the dubbed "queen of Indie", where I've implemented my own marketing and promotional campaigns for my 6 albums, 4 Artist compilations, 2 books, and several websites and tours, I think I have only a tiny inkling of the full gamut of promotional success. Every time I think I've mastered a new social network or created a new way of promoting, something new comes along. So forgive me if I keep it rather broad, knowing that anything I write here may be outdated before I even publish this book! You can keep up to date with the latest promotional tips and tools at my Artist website www.Artistalive.com.

A public awareness campaign is quite a simple notion to understand: you want to create a 'campaign' (this word started in the war, but now is used in advertising), which is *"An operation or series of operations energetically pursued to accomplish a purpose"* (thefreedictionary.com).

With this campaign, the objective is to let as many people know about what you are selling: your Art, your music (whether that be a CD, online downloads, a new music video, another type of release, or just You, the Artist and all that you are.

It needs to be done strategically, with a plan of timing and goals to achieve. You don't just want to promote ad-hoc. I recommend writing up a marketing plan and keeping track of tasks and accomplishments along with way, with specific deadlines of completion and promotion.

Why guerilla?

If you can't simply rent a billboard on the Sunset Strip (like, say Jennifer Lopez, Miley Cyrus or any American Idol star can), or if you can't advertise on the front page of MySpace or Facebook, because you just don't have the cash... then the only way to do it is by taking on a guerilla approach. That means, you will find every way possible to go through the back door, side door, and maybe, just maybe, different doors all together. You need to be a lateral thinker, able to think 'outside the box'. You need to find other ways to be heard and seen, that maybe don't require fast and huge amounts of cash or connections. You need to be ready to build your own teams who love you and your music. Street teams are it! Make a strong plan of attack, and then implement, combat style, smiles a blazing.

Be out in the world. Just get out there. That's the title of this book. It says something very succinctly, for a reason. Just. Do. It. Go to music conferences, play at festivals, get on compilations, host Artist nights, network in circles that bring new relationships, information, resources and opportunities... stick to likeminded individuals. Podcast, webcast, YouTube, MySpace, Facebook. Twitter... gosh, by tomorrow there will be 50 more sites to be on. Every day it's evolving and growing.

Most importantly, nurture your current contacts and build formidable relationships. Most of my opportunities come from people I already know, and sometimes years down the track.

Promotion shouldn't be feared. It's part of the Artist's mode of operandi. There are so many resources at your fingertips these days.

Don't' be afraid to self-promote. It's a new era, and you can do it. Ok, let's get started...

gilli moon's Self-Promotion steps

DIY WAYS TO DEVELOP A LOYAL FAN BASE

I'm going to share with you some of my tips and tools on how to self-promote. They are broad strokes for the context of publishing a book that could so easily be several books (this chapter alone could expand into a book) and by which websites and companies are a flash in the pan and change over night in this new Internet age. Again, if you want up to the minute tips and resources, please go to www.Artistalive.com for a full, current listing.

1. *Identify your product. Is it you or your music.*

Decide what it is that you are promoting and make it great. Don't put out sub-par product. Strive for excellence in everything you do. You have three choices on what to promote

a) Promote a product – e.g. your upcoming CD (or digital music release), and everything that supports the selling of that release which could be music videos, websites, live performances, dance re-mixes, you name it... it all supports the release.

b) Promote You as an artist – e.g. gilli moon, the Artist is an all encompassing polymedia artist who performs, records music, writes books, runs a label, coaches artists and is a motivational speaker. A campaign can be creating public awareness about the artist, not just the products she releases.

c) Both the Artist and a product.

2. *Write*

You need to write. I'm not talking about songs. I mean, about you. The first thing you need to do is get all your promotional tools together, and that starts with writing.

Write your biography. Have it on your website, and also in a document on its own or part of an **EPK** (electronic press kit) you can e-mail to people or print. Create a long, medium and short biography for different occasions.

Write your one sheet. This is a sheet that is one page about you, about your product (album, etc), and some reviews. It's sometimes called a "sell sheet" and there are different ones for radio/press, retail stores, and what you give to music industry professionals.

Write your website. All the copy (the words) on your website must be streamlined with anything you have printed that you give to people. All the copy should match any copy you have on 3rd party social network sites. But your website should be the crème de la crème of promoting you. Your website is your home, your hub, everything about you.

3. *Make your story inviting, not boasting*

There's a fine line between self-promotion and the "me, me, me" (promoting too much of the self). It's really important to not overdose your fans or the press with your promotions. It can be taken the wrong way. Firstly, if you saturate everyone with too many promotions (newsletters, e-mails, tweets, etc), you might find you'll get an opposite reaction: unsubscribe, delete, remove. Secondly, find a way to promote yourself but also add cool opportunities or interesting stories along the way, then people can relate to it a little more. I love to read gig news e-mails if it starts with some funny anecdote about what the Artist has been up to or a story they want to tell about some worldly cause. It grabs me in. Then, in a subliminal way, I'm also fed great gig and music news.

It's hard to be your own promoter, that's for sure. But if you don't have someone to do it for you or you don't want to use a pseudonym and write in the third person, then go for intimacy. Speak from you, colloquially, and let us into your world. Fans love to know the "real" Artist!

4. Humility is the key

In your biography, any parts of your website, your press release, or any way you describe yourself in the written form - just watch any language you use that might suggests a focus too much on glamorizing yourself by veering away from fancy words like 'outstanding', 'the hottest performer ever', or 'the new Madonna of Arkansas'. Try not to compare yourself too much and be your own unique being! Being humble is important. It's nice to be glorified, but let others glorify you instead (like the media when writing reviews about your music or interviewing you).

5. Be Unique: Milk your competitive advantage

I always suggest to Artists that when they hone in on what their **competitive advantage** is, (remember, your TALENT + UNIQUENESS) – to then Milk It Baby. When I first came to the States from Australia, just being an Aussie was unique and my edge was my accent and my story. Then, after a while of developing my Artistry, I began to paint on stage while performing with my band, a movement I call "SensuArt". Find your "edge" what makes you unique. Sometimes this is a cool strength about you. Your "edge" should ooze into everything you do, whatever is written about you and every aspect of your image and PR campaign, from your website, to your CD cover, to gig flyers, to your outfit, to your press releases, one sheets, press kits,… just EVERYTHING.

6. Brand yourself

Use your name in a cool way. Create logos, banners that use your name, with unique fonts, and great pictures. Become a commodity and use mystery to your advantage. The Artist Entrepreneur knows about branding, like any business person who knows about marketing. Consider that everything you do can be around a concept. When you think of Lady Gaga, you think of "wild", "avant-garde", "pushing the envelope". When you think of Tiger Woods, you think of "Nike". (Maybe you think other things too…!)

One of my favorite artists, Kathleen Blackwell, has created a brand not just with her music, but also with fashion. She calls it *Cougar Rock*, a trashy, fashionable way to listen to music *and* wear hip clothes. She has combined the two industries together in products that show a concept, and it's working for her. When I think of Kathleen, I hear her music and visualize her high black platform boots.

Wouldn't it be great that when someone mentions your name, they visualize a theme, a concept, a *brand* around you. Become your own self-made brand.

7. Your website, your world

yourArtistname.com is the most important portal for you in this new music industry. People should be able to find you, read about you, see what you look like, hear your music and importantly, buy your music from your site first and foremost. Your website is the hub, the home for everything. No matter where you are on the Internet with your music or information, make sure that it always links back to your website, as that is the one thing you can control, and the one area where you want your fans to embrace your music and Artistry. THIS is the new place to show everything about you, taking over the old CD cover. You can bring your visual form to life with the way you design your website, and allow fans to enter into your world, and hopefully, live and breathe it on a constant basis.

Artistically, *your website is the portal to your inner creative soul.* Use it to show everything about you: from your music, to your story, to your prose, to even perhaps your artwork and any other wonderful things you'd like your fans to grasp onto. Since we don't foresee the CD and the beautiful CD covers to engage our fans any more (as they all download compressed mp3 singles now), then get CREATIVE with your website. Fans are still fans. If they love you, and your Art, they will stick with you: so bedazzle them!

Keep it simple, effective and snazzy.

* Making your online calendar work for you – use Yahoogroups.com, or Myspace.com, or Reverbnation.com or Sonicbids.com to design an online calendar that you can insert into your website and upload your gigs from wherever. WIDGETS ARE US. Widgetbox.com helps you create widgets, but golly, by the time this book is printed, there will be hundreds of ways for you to make your website interactive.

* Add Songs/snippets to listen to - I prefer just short edited snippets, so they get a teaser. Educate the public to buy full length songs (but sometimes you need to give a little away...).

* Tell your story through every page - have your biography, a photos page, video page, blog page (wordpress, blogger are great) and anything else that tells your story.

* Buy links - Don't forget the store page to buy your songs/albums.

Link exchange – look for sites that would link your website and always offer a link in return. Post your website on all your social networks, and link back from them to your website (very important).

8. The Internet is a small community

Get yourself known on the Web. Social media is the new buzz word and the new platform to self-promote. There are so many books about this one area, you don't need me to regurgitate the info. But I will offer some great books for you to read at Artistalive.com. It's all about community – whether it be your friends and fans at your social networks (Facebook, Twitter, Myspace, etc.), or you tapping into existing communities like Songsalive!, musicians on Yahoogroups, LinkedIn groups, etc. The more you engage with others, the more they will get to know you.

9. Embrace the New Media

Straight ahead radio promotion and newspaper/magazine publicity are not the only means to get out to the world. NEW MEDIA is king and guess who has tapped into it more than anyone in the biz? That's right, indie Artists. Access and engage with online blogs, online radio (like Blogtalkradio.com), podcasts, internet news and music sites, and anything that's trendy and new online. I highly recommend learning from Ariel Hyatt's *Arielpublicity.com* and getting her books. She really knows how to engage new media and social networks the best. If you decide to work with her, go through our affiliate link at Artistalive.com, songsalive.org or tell her I sent you.

The online video world is a really amazing community where it brings music and video together. I strongly recommend that you upload videos to Youtube, Vimeo and any new video site that comes along. I know it sounds strange to promote music through visual, but it's obvious. Apart from putting songs in films and videos (see next chapter on that), it's important to promote your songs and albums through online video portals. Upload music videos, making of the album in the studio videos, you playing in your living room blog videos: anything that will keep your fans engaged and wanting to buy your music. It might not translate to immediate sales but getting one million views on Youtube is actually tangible for indie Artists, and if you "annotate" your videos then you can forward your viewers to your website or iTunes where they can buy your music. Annotation is where you add words, or websites into your video from the Youtube site. You can do this while you're uploading your video or after the fact under settings. It's really easy to do and essential.

The key to these New Media tips is this: don't just try and do promotion the old traditional way. Get out there in the new media, and taste new ways to find outlets for your music to be discovered.

10. Traditional media is still a plus

While we blast ourselves on the Internet, there is something to be said about the old-school way. People still read newspapers and magazines, and still watch television and listen to the radio. Our media is changing, yes. It's evolving to be more intravenously connected to our cell phones, and laptops. But if you're like me, I still like to read the newspaper on the weekends, read juicy magazines, turn the radio on and watch television.

It can be really expensive to promote to these traditional means (with publicists sometimes costing more than $1000 a week, and radio promoters sometimes $4000 a week to solicit your material on your behalf), but there are ways to reach traditional media your way.

1. Build a database of media contacts yourself (every time I tour I'm collecting the e-mail and mailing addresses of local newspapers and music magazines wherever I go).

2.   Send press releases to your media contacts.
3.   Send packages and *personal* letters to local media where you are travelling or promoting. Radio still loves personal letters. KCRW, the number one alternative music station in Los Angeles, will accept "unsolicited" music if you send them a personal letter, circling the songs you want them to hear. It may not guarantee airplay, but give it your best shot.
4.   Build a network of media and invite them to your shows. They might review your show, or your album, or even interview you.
5.   Keep in touch from one album release to the next. Media become fans too. As you bring them into your circle, they will support you over a long period of time if they like you and what you are about.

11. Build your fans one fan at a time

Build your fan list, one fan at a time. I now have over 27,000 on my list from doing every gig in the land... it takes time, but it's so worth it. Every time I do a show I have a mailing list.

Always collect e-mail addresses at gigs ("Sign my mailing list.") as well as have a link on your website to join the list, and keep your fans up-to-date with a cool newsletter that is filled with info, news and even opportunities and stories for others. Don't over e-mail/contact your fans. I send my newsletter once a month. I brand it as the Warrior Girl Music eNews – a little big of gilli moon in your inbox. My fans expect it around the first of the month and I try not to make it overwhelming for them. I always have an unsubscribe link at the end. That's the polite and appropriate thing to do. (Get on my mailing list at www.warriorgirlmusic.com/enews.)

Oh, a great way to build fans online and maintain your e-mail lists is at www.fanbridge.com. You can also use Reverbnation.com , Hostbaby.com, or Constantcontact or or or or... there are SO many now. But if you want to build a large list with sub groups (e.g. fans in California, or different regions) then I recommend Fanbridge and they are the cheapest for this kind of thing as I've looked around. Plus their customer service is optimum. See www.Artistalive.com to get a discount to Fanbridge.

Rules of engagement

Spend AT LEAST 5 hours a week on PR
a.   Online sites – social networks.
b.   Corresponding with media.
c.   Building your mailing list and sending out regular (no more than bi-weekly, every two weeks) newsletters.
d.   Friend your new media, and post comments. Be active.

    e.   Follow up your media and press that you mail packages to.

    f.   Offer something new every time to your fanbase: keep it new and fresh!

Get to know your local media, which includes the traditional radio, TV, newspapers, magazines.

And know that Internet promotion is equally if not more beneficial: cross linking, adding comments, blogging, banner ads, discussion lists and networking.

Be PROLIFIC in your creativity, AND your marketing.

As mentioned before, make sure your music is available for sale all over the web. Use 3rd party sites – iTunes, Amazon, digital, expose yourself over the web.

Be very open to new media ideas. Try as many radio stations as you affordably can (not just in radio promoter costs, but simple shipping to radio can be expensive).

"Uniqueness and sweetness" – Be consistent with who you are, as an Artist, and how you promote yourself. Be unique, and be persistent. Don't Stop. This is all about your ATTITUDE.

Street Promotion

Just because you're intravenously glued to the computer with the age of the Internet, doesn't mean you forget about people face to face. Street teams are it – gather people in cities you will tour, who are fans of yours to help promote you before you come to town. You'll find that your fans will work twice as hard for you if you give them and their friends some free passes or maybe even CDs.

Flyer handouts – hand out gig notices and CD release flyers to people on the street, outside other performances. If you play Brazilian music, find a hot Brazilian music concert and flyer away! Flyers can be postcard size, to 11x17 posters. It doesn't matter the size but I recommend doing different types for different venues.

Posters at venues – put up posters at venues you're going to play at.

Rallying fans – entice your fans to help you spread the word and offer cool merchandise, swag and CDs in return. They like to feel special.

Promoting at Live Performances

Unique promotional flyers – try and create something a little different to what others do. Use interesting fonts, find a cool catch phrase, or design an interesting logo, cartoon or your photo altered to attract attention. Use different paper, textures, colors, sizes.

Find cool new venues and locations – find new spaces to perform, where others aren't necessarily saturating. Find the right venue for you! Maybe an old funky café, or an Art gallery, or warehouse open to the public, or an old theatre.

Stamp your fans – Give them things to remember you buy at shows like a cool stamp on their hand as their venue entry, with your Artist name and website.

Merchandise

Chatchkies and trinkets – find little toys that would be cool giveaways. When I released my CD "temperamental angel" I found little angels to give away in industry and media packets. I threw out soft squeeze balls (those balls that strengthen your hands by squeezing them) from the stage with my website URL on them. Fans loved trying to catch them! Because I sometimes paint onstage, I found paintbrush bubble gum. Go figure! I found it!

T-shirts – best promotion ever. Have your friends wear your t-shirts and make sure your website is on it so they know where to find you. Come up with cool sayings. For example Songsalive! has "I'm Alive" and "Got Songs?" t-shirts. Warrior Girl Music has "I am a Warrior Girl" and "Enjoy the Journey" t-shirts. Sell t-shirts at your gigs, on your site, and take them on tour with you. Big fact, most Major Artists generate equal to if not more revenue from selling merchandise on tour than they do CD sales or even door takings. That's why so many promoters and record companies want a piece of that pie. Hint: if you make a deal, watch the fine print on merch in the contract!

Hats, bags and other swag – make whatever you can afford to sell and also to add to the branding of your Artistry.

Stickers – car bumper stickers, window stickers, any shape, any size. Great for giveaways.

Posters and postcard factories – What does one do when they receive a postcard? It's very hard to throw it out because it's not flimsy.. it's a solid cardboard, usually glossy card. Research shows that most people have to put the postcard somewhere, usually a fridge, on a pin board or sitting up on a desk. Postcards are very effective for album launches, releases, gigs and website promotion. Flyers are great in all shapes and sizes. The glossier they are, the harder it is for people to throw them out.

Creativity is key

Don't be shy. Again, there's a fine line in talking yourself up, and being a bulldozer. Radio is easier if you know you are touring to that area. Smaller stations love to interview if you're one of the few acts playing in town that week. Send effective press releases to street press, and don't over saturate them or they won't bother printing it. Also, write press releases succinctly and simply. Not too much flour and keep it brief and to the point.

Be real – It would be nice to have a full story in Rolling Stone but remember that they are also trying to sell Ad space and subscriptions. If you are an unknown, be realistic and start with papers that are in your local area, or support indie music. Build your press kit up with favorable reviews and interviews, and then... as you become more well-known, just watch the media come find you!

If you were to think like a record company, you would know that promotion is just as important as making the music, in so far as revenue. If they don't know where to buy the CD, they won't buy it. Being creative in your promotional strategies will allow you to at least set your own playing field in this music industry. The more visibility, the more they remember and can find you. It takes time to build a name, but if you're persistent, it will work for you in the long run. Patience! It might take a while, but remember... you have all the time in the world.

Think about my little saying: The Three Os
OPTIMISM + ORGANIZED = OPPORTUNITY

A lion met a tiger
As they drank beside a pool
Said the tiger, "Tell me why
You're roaring like a fool."

"That's not foolish," said the lion
With a twinkle in his eyes
"They call me king of all the beasts
Because I advertise!"

A Rabbit heard them talking
And ran home like a streak
He thought he'd try the lion's plan
But his roar was just a squeak.

A fox came to investigate-
Had luncheon in the woods.
Moral: when you advertise, my friends,
Be sure you've got the goods!

- Anonymous

18. The Art of production

The next two chapters are for music makers, specifically. Those who want to record their music and release it.

There is no point going on tour or starting to promote unless you have a great product. This chapter is dedicated to the musicians out there who are interested in producing music in order to sell it.
It is really important to have music you LOVE, that you can stand behind, that represents you, and it ALL starts with production.

When production goes wrong

I bet you've been there too. You've written this great song, all the musical elements are swimming in your head... yeah I hear the violin here, the bass will go, thump thump like this, and then a drum loop like that song on the radio. Etc., etc. You make a little home recording and then you decide to put the money together and go to a "professional" to make this song come ALIVE. So you take time off work, get the money together, have all these pre-production meetings with the chosen producer and at the end of all the talk the producer says, "yeah I know exactly what you want, trust me".

So off you embark in what you think will be a hit song, with a hit-making producer and you think, "yeah, my money's well spent... this is success speaking", and you start the recording process. You're in there with the producer playing your song, the musicians are all giving it their session best and the producer is throwing ideas at you left, right and center. You have such little time to hit that best vocal performance of a life time (the pressure's on, time's ticking and you're running out of money), but still the performance goes well, at least you think it does - and the producer's saying, "sweet honey, sounding so sweet", so you trust him (or her) and keep holding the faith.

Somewhere along the line the style of the song is changing, but you reckon that the producer knows best and has had hits in the past so surely he won't go wrong (what do you know anyway, you're just an Artist, right?)... and the money is running overtime but you are keeping the faith.

It's playback time and the producer is gleaming (you've already paid him, of course). You're listening for the first time, even though it's now the 50th time, but the first time without being a musician with the cans (head phones) on.

All of a sudden you start hearing things you hadn't heard before. Like a string arrangement that really puts it in the Celine Dion camp when you were really going for Alanis Morisette, or a retro 80s guitar solo that just doesn't fit in the piano ballad, but you say thank you, glad the whole process and stress is over and you go home.

A week later ('cause who wants to hear it so close to the production time, right? We all need a break from music...), you put the song on your home stereo, with some friends and a bottle of red, and you sit back to relish the achievement with your Cheshire Cat smile.

Why doesn't it sound the same? Some vocal notes are pitchy, the live full band sound is a little sloppy and that guitar player... hmmm... something else to be desired. The vocals are way back in the mix (you can hardly hear yourself singing), too much grunge, and not enough oomph. Your friends go 'yippee' but that musically apt friend on the sofa says he's heard me do better, and that the production is *dated*, and that it doesn't show off my vocal range, and, aaaand...and...anddddd. Oh my.

Been there? Why do Artists have such a hard time in producing their songs? Why do some of the home 4 tracks show the passion and style of the Artist better than the thousand dollar professional production? I have met so many Artists who come out crying from an album production simply because their story, their emotion and their statement have not been met in the studio.

Producers these days, and I'm not saying all producers, but some need to understand **that there is more than just being a great engineer, a proficient musician, or a fan of the Artist.** The producer needs to KNOW the Artist, get inside the Artist, understand the Artist, BEFORE they begin to produce. How can a film producer produce a script unless they read it. Really read it... and visualize it happening. A director begins to LIVE the script and the characters in it. So too must a music producer.

Too many producers live on their egos and think that their skill and expertise will get them through. Well it may have worked for their last projects but that doesn't mean it will for you.

And you, the Artist, needs to **be sure of what you want**. You have to communicate to your producer what you want. And if you don't know what you want, then both of you have to take the time to find it, together.

Artists don't always magically know how they want the musical style to be. Producers can help them with that. Producers can help channel eclectic styles into a more homogenous one. Hey, its OK if the style narrows to, say 'hip hop' for this album. Artists, you know you're talented. The next song can be jazz if you want. But be flexible to narrow it down for the project. That way an audience can be defined.

The vocal producer

Sometimes producers may be *hot* music producers, able to create a string arrangement better than David Foster... but they may not be so apt to VOCALLY produce. How many times have you sung that riff, with only a "great..., great" from the control room, and later you hear you were flat! Vocal producers are able to not only be flexible with you and allow you to experiment yourself (yes, you CAN do backing vocals in your own way if you want to), but they can provide ideas and encouragement and bring you out of yourself to create a dynamically better vocal performance. A swim coach makes a swimmer stronger, better, faster, and competitively ready for the Olympics...to win. A vocal producer can make a great vocalist greater and the message of the song brought forward and accessible to the listener.

Finding a producer that is strong in music and vocals is rare but possible. You must ask yourself what is the most important thing when choosing a producer.

Communication

We as Artists all have sad stories of our past. Some albums or songs we put on the shelf because we are unhappy with the production, even though at the time we had run off 2000 copies of the CD with our own sweat and money. We may say "yeah, big mistake"... or, "that was part of my learning curve". Yes it is all learning but we can avoid production sadness by speaking out early in the production process. Don't just sit quietly and agree with the producer just because you think they know best. You're the Artist. It's your song and your voice and their job is to bring the best out of you.

Communication is the most important aspect of production.

I have now become a producer, for two reasons. One, I enjoy bringing out the best in others, and their songs; and two, it teaches me how to be a better and more communicative Artist. Being behind the wheel for another Artist reminds me of seeing me in that booth, and as producer I ask the questions that I would liked asked of me when I'm the Artist. I've also learned to appreciate my own talent. Yes, there are better producers than me, but I have learned that some of those little ideas I scratched into my home 4 track demos are VALID and REAL for a full professional production. When I produce my own songs, I feel fulfilled that those little ideas can become reality. Nevertheless, I also appreciate working with other producers because, as an Artist, I act subjectively and most times I need objective opinions and support by someone who is not as attached to the song as me.

I applaud a good producer. It's a hard job. But anyone can call themselves a 'producer' and not really know how to produce. Choose who you work with carefully. Those songs of yours are meant to be on the radio forever and so they need to last.

Production stages

Ensure you produce an album that speaks to what you want to say, and produce it well. Take your time to create the best album it can be, and don't skimp on quality or cut corners. Be sure that YOU like it first and foremost. It's impossible to truly get behind marketing your own album if you are not behind it. Many Artists rush to complete an album because of a certain expectation of timing (needs to be out by Easter, or must be done by end of Summer). Really think about what that timing is based on. Is it due by a certain deadline because of some opportunity? Or are you just pressuring yourself for no due cause?

The album needs to be ready when it's ready, and I suggest not starting any marketing on it until you are at least in the mastering stage.

On that note, do not master your songs until you are completely satisfied with the mixes. Every step needs time:

a) **Producing the songs** – the evolution of recording your songs means time to record, and time to LISTEN before you start mixing. Remember that when you are listening to 'rough mixes' of the recordings, the sounds will sound out of balance, and that's ok. This listening stage is to ensure you didn't miss anything you need recorded, or to listen if each instrument and vocal is technically and creatively satisfactory to you, and the decision makers around you (label, manager, etc.)... though remember my saying, "seek no one else's approval but your own", meaning, you make the final creative decision.

b) **Mixing the songs** – Recommended to be done by a professional mixing engineer and not the engineer who recorded the songs (to get a different 'ear'), mixing is done when all the recording is completely done and technically and creatively approved by you. A mix of one song can take from 2 hours to a full 8-10 hour day, so generally it is best to do one song a day. This allows you to be able to hear the mix overnight, and then send comments in for any changes by the following morning. You should listen to the song in all fashions, not just in the studio: home stereo, in your car, on your computer, on small and large speakers and so forth. Also, recalling mixes all depends on the computer program your engineer is using. If he/she is completely automating the mix (every change to the mix is tracked through the program, such as in Protools), then you can bring up a mix 2 days or 2 years later. However, if your engineer is also using the mixing desk and outboard gear (part analog) then it may be difficult to recall a mix (unless he has taken great, detailed photos of his board). Be sure you know the parameters you have to recall in a mix before he starts, and therefore, you may need to know if you have only 1 night, 1 day, or 1 week to provide your mix comments post song mix.

c) **Mastering the songs** – The next phase is mastering. This only happens when you are truly happy with the mixes of the songs. Note that mastering is different than mixing (a lot of Artists get this confused). Mastering does not change levels of tracks (e.g. vocal higher than guitar, snare drum louder, etc.). That's done in mixing. The mastering sets the overall EQ of the songs, and of the album entirely, so that the songs are the same overall levels (some songs were recorded softer than others especially if done in different studios), and prepares the album to be played on all stereo/playable formats. Mastering also delivers the Master Disc that duplication plants can duplicate from. Therefore you want to know the track order of your album as you enter the mastering process, as well as the timing in between songs. These last two points are somewhat undervalued, but I believe that track order is essential to making a good album great, as well as how many seconds one waits to hear the next song from the previous. Sit with these 2 elements for AT LEAST 1 WEEK, if not 2, between the mixing and mastering stage, so you can really take time to work out the order and timing. Once mastering is complete and you get your Master Disc, you are ready for duplication.

No matter what, produce the album well and know that you have to be truly happy at the end of each stage I indicated above, before going to the next stage. There is a humorous t-shirt I once saw someone wearing. On the front it said,

"We'll fix it in the mix"

Then at the bottom of the front it said

"We'll fix it in mastering"

And on the back of the t-shirt it said

"We'll fix it in the next song"

Exercise: Dissecting an album

What makes an album great? Grab your favorite album by an Artist (that's not you), and listen to it with a critic's mind. Write down the answers to the following questions:

1. Why do you think this album is 'great'. What are the qualities that you admire about this album that put it in the 'great' category.

2. What aspects of the music are you inspired by, for producing your own music?

3. What are some of the technical flaws or imperfections you can hear in the production or mix, that you notice, that could be better?

4. What are some of the unique assets about the production of this album? What sets it apart from the rest?

5. What is the most important element in your music production that needs to shine? Is it your vocals? Your instrument playing? (And what instrument?) Your lyrics? The groove? Narrow down exactly what parts are to shine in your music production. Be sure to tell your next producer these answers.

19. Timeline for an album release

Creating goals as an Artist, that encompass your life visions and creativity, is very important. I've always said "dream big", and have worked with many Artists in putting their vision into practice through a business plan and a marketing plan. So let's bring it right down to a project that most **music** Artists do, which is effective in releasing music.

Now, I use the term "Releasing a CD" loosely, because in a wink of an eye there will be no such thing as a CD. But you'll understand what I mean when I use it. As most know, a CD is a disc of music, soon to become obsolete, that you can play in your car stereo, home CD player and computer. It's still the method of choice at radio stations to receive your music on for potential air play, and it's still the choice by music supervisors when they want to archive your songs on the shelf for potential placement and licensing in TV shows and films (though the iPod/iTunes is often their preferred listening/choosing method). But ultimately, Artists should procure MASTERS that are high resolution WAV or AIFF files that are not compressed into tiny mp3s when licensing tracks or making CDs for home listening. Then from these MASTERS you can make squashed mp3s for your iPod. But that's another story.

For now, let's discuss simple ways to effectively get your music out there through an official "release" of your music. I don't care if CDs go away (there will be something to replace them), and I don't care if you do 1 album or 40 in a year (the Internet allows releases to happen so quickly these days). What I do care about is the *care* you give to your music, and that means putting energy behind the release of your latest music with vigor, careful planning and a clear and concise strategy. Just putting out your music willy nilly gets you nowhere. A focused effort, using marketing strategies and plans, is vital for a successful music launch.

Because I am not reinventing the wheel here when giving advice about releasing an album I want to humbly acknowledge a few writers and resources who write about this subject in detail. Peter Spellman and Dave Cool wrote a book called *Your Successful CD Release* which I strongly recommend you get if this subject is of particular priority to your journey. Dean Henderson and John Vestman wrote a cool article called *"Marketing Your Music – 10 Helpful Tips"*. Another article is Adrian Hamblin's *"7 Tips to a Successful Independent CD Release"*. There are many music biz representatives I know that have written on this subject. Artistalive.com has some lists of cool books and articles.

Here are some integral stages to your album release timeline:

1. Who are you?

The first steps in releasing a CD starts with who you are and what you want. I always go back to this, because without a true sense of who you are, or an overview of what you want, it's impossible to realize your dreams. In this respect, the answer to *who you are* is focused on you as a recording Artist and your album. For example, *I Am an Australian recording Artist and songwriter who has recorded a CD called yaddayadda which are 10 songs about living in Los Angeles, relationships and stories, through a pop alternative production.* (Of course, all this part will be elaborated as we delve into bio writing and album concept writing, but for now, this helps you, and you alone in your quest to get out there.)

2. Create a great album

As previously mentioned in the Art of Production chapter, ensure you produce an album that speaks to what you want to say, and produce it well. Take your time to create the best album it can be, and don't skimp on quality or cut corners. Be sure that YOU like it first and foremost. It's impossible to truly get behind marketing your own album if you are not behind it.

3. What is the goal?

What do you want? Well, in this specific scenario, you want to release a CD, and possibly get some media exposure, make some money (lots of it I hope) and tour to spread your music and message. It could be that you want to release a CD to make money for a charity or spread a message about a cause. Really, it's up to you what you want. I'm just throwing in ideas.

4. Tailor promotion around the album

Next, you need to make sure that your biography, and image gets a little attention. Peter Spellman and Dave Cool emphasize the importance of four types of biographies. The long one. The medium one. The short one; and the elevator pitch (the one you verbalize in an elevator or somewhere face to face, quickly and efficiently). Write them down so they are handy to pull out when needed.

Write a description of the album: talk about why you wrote and recorded the album, and what its intention is. Having a mission behind an album, or a concept, will attract more interest, instead of it just being a collection of songs (like thousands of other Artists). If your album has a theme, e.g. songs about the Goddess, or Nature, or children on the streets, describe it. If it's about love or relationships, give us more than "these are great love songs". Talk about the dynamics of the relationship, the good, the bad, and the emotions that are felt when listening to the songs. Describe the musicians, the producer, the studio, perhaps even the recording location if it's interesting. Add *anything* that is interesting, but make it brief. Wrap it up all into one nice paragraph.

Create a one sheet that includes your short bio, description of the album, pricing, distribution, marketing and promotion strategy, song titles, album cover pic and Artist cover pic (if the Artist is not on the album cover). Also include the barcode, UPC code numbers, Contacts (label, address, phone, web, e-mail).

5. Plan the Release

Now comes the time to do an "Album Release Goals and Timeline Exercise", which I created. Check it out in the pages over. Basically, you come up with 7-10 goals on the left hand side of a page for releasing your CD. I've given you some examples. Then on the right hand side you build strategies for each goal.

The important aspect of planning is, like I've always been saying, you want a game plan and timeline to actually build it and realize it. Stick to your goals, and implement tangible strategies and actions in order to complete and realize your goals.

Brainstorm at first in pencil, because you'll come up with way more ideas than I gave here, pertaining to your own music and abilities to put the ball in motion. Once you've fleshed out the goals and strategies, on a second page draw up a grid that you can insert the Goals as headings, and Strategies as info under the headings, next to a Timeline of dates (Months). That way you can see where along the timeline of a year you will roll out your strategies for your goals. As you go along, you can modify it, inserting new goals and strategies that come to you just because you're getting out there (it's surprising how much more comes to us when we just make the first move).

Let's look at some easy steps to release our CD. Note that some of these steps may end up being in a different order for you based on your third party resources, availabilities on touring and many other factors that life likes to throw at you when you're not looking.

STEP 1: Plan an album release party, whether it's your home town, local bar, or a big stage in New York City. Allow at least 2 months to plan it, because you'll need the CDs in your hands from the manufacturer, your online distribution in place, and you'll need to get the word out to the media, radio online and your fan base.

STEP 2: While planning your album release party, which is 2 months away, **organize your online distribution** for your music such as online retailers (CDBaby.com is cool), Amazon.com, iTunes and a plethora of others that you can usually get as a bundle going through an online distributor (usually an exclusive agreement). Include other distribution ideas like ringtones, drop cards (cards with a code to go online and download mp3s makes it feasible to sell or give away to people who don't want to pay for a full album). Try traditional distributors too. There are some still around and still active, such as Independent Distribution Collective (www.independentdistro.com). They are my distributor and fantastic. They're very picky with who they sign (like any distribution company) but if you do contact them, let them know how you heard about them ☺.

STEP 3: Build your PR. Using some of the self-promotion tools in the last chapter, start with drafting up your first press release. In your press release you want to specify what you are promoting (the album), your release date, and talk about the venue, what the night will be about, about you (that's crucial) and have easy contacts at the end to find more information in as they want to do a huge interview with you and put you on the cover of *Rolling Stone*. (Wouldn't that be nice?) Send out your press release to the Media list you have collected in a specific mailing list; to online media sites; and to the music industry (also have a list you've collected).

STEP 4: While you're planning on the release party, and waiting for your online distribution to kick in, why don't you **write up descriptions of your songs**. Peter Spellman and Dave Cool say that song descriptions give *"people a sense of what kind of experience they'll have from listening to your album as a whole"*.

STEP 5: Put on a **big celebration**: have a fantastic launch celebration that can be in a traditional venue (with your band) or a cool listening place (play the CD) at your home, in a hall, down by the creek... whatever. It should be fun, and on the day of your actual CD release through online stores and traditional stores.

STEP 6: Get into high gear **promoting your album** through Media, Tours & Public Appearances, your own Social Networking and Newsletters, and being OUT THERE. Some more ideas are in my Album Release Timeline exercise over.

Exercise: Album Release Goals & Timeline

This exercise assists anyone wanting to schedule all the tasks and priorities to schedule an album release. Below is merely a sample of all the things you may need to do to prepare for an album release. They are examples, and not definitive.

Goals	Strategies
1. Distribution	- *Submit CD to CDBaby* - *Submit CD to Amazon* - *online distributor "ABC Distribution"*
2. CD Release Party	- *book venue at Such and Such* - *Date will be.....* - *Guest artists will be....* - *Invite the media (such and such newspaper)*
3. Promotional Items – flyers, posters,	- *Design promotion* - *Make postcards and posters at XYZ.com printers*
4. Other Promo/New Merchandise	- *Design promotion similar to the flyers/posters etc.* - *t-shirts, caps, stickers* - *Make promo at XYZ.com printers*
5. Media/PR	- *Create press release about CD launch* - *Send to my Media Excel list via e-mail* - *Send to my personal e-mail list* - *Call local newspapers (including, AZ newspaper..)*
6. Internet Promotion	- *Blast on Myspace, Facebook, etc.* - *Banner swaps on friends' webpages* - *Upload mp3 singles to sites using different online resources*
7. Radio and New Media promotion	- *Call radio stations* - *Hire a radio promoter/Get Joe Blo Radio Promotions involved* - *Hire a radio service or online new media service (like Arial Publicity or Music Submit)* - *Start with my home state first*

Timeline for an album release

8. Touring	- Make a schedule for the next 2 years - Use the Indie Venue Bible, Sonicbids, Songsalive! and Musicians Atlas and other resources to book gigs - Contact such and such booking agency - Regional touring, start in my home state
9. Film and TV Music Licensing	- Contact music supervisor list about album - Create at least 5 key contacts - Aim to place 2 songs from album in first 6 months

Next comes putting all these Goals and Strategies into a timeline:

Month	Distribution	CD Party	Promo Items	New Merch	Media/ PR	Internet and Radio Promo	Touring
Jan	- Submit CD to CDBaby, Amazon, Distributor	Book venue	Design promo	Design merch			
Feb			Print promo	Print merch			
Mar	Check CD is on iTunes	Prep release party	Hand out flyers, postcard		Send release 30 days before	Contact radio	
Apr		Release party 8th		Merch on the night	Send reminder release with online sales available	Facebook Prepare SW regional radio promo	
May			Handouts on tour (below)	Sell merch on tour (below)	Announce tour schedule	Prepare South regional radio promo	
Jun	Check sales on iTunes				Announce any music licensing	Prepare SE regional radio promo	Tour South
Jul					Keep sending to regional media for tours	Prepare EC regional radio promo	Tour SE
Aug						Prepare MWest regional radio promo	Tour EC
Sept						Prepare NW radio promo	Tour MWest

Timeline for an album release

Now, it's your turn to right your Goals and Strategy below

Goals	Strategies

Timeline for an album release

Next comes putting all these Goals and Strategies into a timeline:

Month	Distribution	CD Party	Promo Items	New Merch	Media/ PR	Internet and Radio Promo	Touring
Jan							
Feb							
Mar							
Apr							
May							
Jun							
Jul							
Aug							
Sept							
Oct							
Nov							
Dec							

The voyage of discovery is not seeking new landscapes, but having new eyes

Marcel Proust

20. The Art of communication

So, we've talked about the fact that what we communicate adds to how people perceive us. That is why we worked on our "I AM Statement" to be positive and reinforce your dreams and mission. But what about communication you send out as correspondence?

In this past week I received 3 types of communications from three different Artists, which in turn I tossed each three in the recycle bin. Why?

Artist 1 – I received a padded envelope addressed to my record company in the mail. There was no name, nor return address listed on it. Inside was a seemingly well packaged music CD, but no cover note. Just a CD. Oh, and it came all the way from Australia to my Los Angeles address. So they spent time and money shipping it, but no letter to accompany, nor a way to contact them back. *Toss.*

Artist 2 – I received an unsolicited e-mail with 4 attachments (a cover letter, 2 mp3s and a lyric sheet). The e-mail itself was blank in the body and there was no subject.

The attached cover letter was typed on letterhead as follows:

Dear Recipient,
To whom it may concern:
Hello! My name is Jane Doe (I've replaced the real name for privacy sakes). This is my demo package. It contains my photo and four professional and expensive! recordings, SO PLEASE LISTEN CAREFULLY, & let me know what you think.
I am 26 years old. I was born and raised in Flint, Michigan, but now live in Falkner, MS, about 45 minutes from Memphis. I love gospel music and would love to sing and record professionally. I don't see this as a "dream" but my destiny. It's only a matter of time. Throughout my life I have been told not just what a beautiful voice I have, but, more importantly, what an anointing there is on my voice and life. There has been nothing else I have wanted to do since I can remember, but devote my life to worship. Nothing is more satisfying than complete dedication to my purpose. I am looking for a record deal and/or management to push my demo with that goal. If you are interested, my contact information follows. God Bless!

Ok, so what is wrong with this unsolicited piece of e-mail?

Firstly, it was unsolicited. I didn't ask for this Artist to send me her music and the whole shebang. It would have been polite to ask me first.

Secondly, this person had poor etiquette with sending attachments without permission. It could contain viruses and the like. Best to write everything within an e-mail, and again, not to send mp3s without asking first.

Then, there was no subject, and no body to the e-mail. I would have normally immediately deleted the e-mail because it seemed potentially harmful. Asking me to open an attachment (and only that) from a stranger is rude, and could contain viruses.

Also, the letter itself doesn't address me personally. By writing "Dear Recipient" and "To Whom It May Concern" shows she has not researched who she is writing to AND I'm probably just one of many in a long list of recipients. I guess she thinks one of the e-mails will stick like spaghetti on a wall? Hmm.

To capitalize "SO PLEASE LISTEN CAREFULLY" is just plain rude. When using CAPS (Capital letters) in e-mail correspondence, it shows that you are shouting. That's just plain e-mail etiquette. And also, why should she demand something from me. She doesn't even know me. Plain arrogant.

"I don't see this as a 'dream', but my destiny." Umm, girlfriend, join the queue. Does she think this makes her any special that I should take time out to listen or sign her?

"Throughout my life I have been told not just what a beautiful voice I have, but"… err, perhaps we'll be the judge of that. To tell others that you yourself have a beautiful voice does not show humility. Besides, beauty is subjective. Best to use someone else's real quotes, than to say you are beautiful or fantastic.

What's working for her:

She has a mission. Her worship duties are beyond just her talent. I like this. She has a purpose. She is open to getting a deal or finding a manager, and that takes courage. She's young. She'll get over anyone who will judge her approach, like me.

Third letter:
Sent to about 100 recipients, with all their e-mail addresses clearly seen.

Subject: Hi There
A&R Department!
I'm wondering if you would be interested in signing me to your label, with the new commer to the scene, there is not much time at all to have a shot at breaking into my niche market! In all honesty there is huge potential for this to work! I have booked shows, but i don't have something good enough and i know it, see i hired a producer A&R guy here in brisbane, but what he produced is not up too scratch and my vocals are way more diverse then he had me sing, so i'm stuck and really need a break for someone to see the potentioal in me and my current situation! Can you guys help?? thnx

What's wrong with this letter? Again, unsolicited, but then, we all send e-mails out hoping for some form of connection. Bad spelling. It's so easy to use spell check! How on earth do you expect a record label to sign you as an Artist if you don't put the time in to write a proper letter, with back up, details, your bio or EPK or SOMETHING! Do you expect a record label to sign you because you have a dream?

NO! That is not why record labels sign you. They sign you because they see, by how you prove it to them, that you can make MONEY for the label; that you are a wanted commodity (lots of fans already love you); and that you will last the distance.

Why is it that an Artist, who may want to run away from a bad situation, or doesn't have all the resources, think that a record company is going to be the answer?

Think about it. Who's in control of your career right now?

YOU ARE.

When giving CDs/Music

When I use the word "I" or "me" or "us", that could mean anyone in the biz or media you give your CDs to.

Always ask "may I give the CD to you" first, rather than just assuming I will accept it. It bugs me when people just come up and force a CD in my hands and I'm too polite to say no for various reasons as I will explain.

When people are travelling, sometimes they can't accept CDs as their luggage is already crammed with stuff. So, ask first and perhaps a better way would be to ask "may I send this in the mail to you, I know you are travelling".

If you give me a CD, let me know "why" you are giving it, and what you need. If I can't help you, I can at least avoid you wasting a precious copy and you can give to someone who can do something with it.

Once it's clear there is a mutual opportunity for you to give me your CD, give it to me without the cellophane/shrink wrap. By the time I've figured out how to tear the wrapper, I'm ready to toss it in the bin out of frustration. Set aside promotional CDs without the wrapper to avoid your industry or media listeners going through this cumbersome task. The sooner they can hear track 1 the better.

Put your best song first. Don't give them 4 songs to wade through to get to your best, catchiest hit song. There's no secret formula you need to try. Just bring it on straight away.

ALWAYS have your e-mail address on the outer artwork (back traycard the best), nice and big and clear. Don't make us try and find it in the liner notes in an ambiguous place. Or, put your business card inside. But we tend to lose those so just put it on the art work. Don't make us have to go to your website and fill out an ambiguous feedback form to find you. A waste of time and by this stage, your CD is tossed in the bin.

Finally, consider what you can do first for others before you think what they can do for you. So, join Songsalive! (www.songsalive.org), get to know my businesses www.warriorgirlmusic.com www.artistdevelopmentcoach.com, www.gillimoon.com www.artisalive.com - and see how we can mutually benefit from each other. That goes with any industry exec or media rep you meet. It's a co-creation, this music business, and I love meeting new artists, if they truly "get" who I am too!

Be of the world

I am perplexed as to why artists complain about not getting heard, when they don't take the time and put in the energy to be heard. Some artists don't even want to engage on social networks. *"Oh, Twitter is silly, I don't understand it."*

My answer to that is: get to understand it, and all social media and ways to connect and communicate. If you don't, you'll be left behind.

I stress that it is IMPORTANT to have your own mailing list as the main focus, and then also build your fans on the social network sites, such as Myspace.com, Facebook.com, plus followers on Twitter.com.. blah blah…. So many sites, so little time… JUST CONTINUE TO KEEP IN TOUCH THROUGH ALL OF THEM.

Know that you are building your fan base one fan at a time. It doesn't matter how many people are in the room listening to you. If it's 2 people, then get them to sign the list. They'll tell their friends who will tell their friends and so forth.

What not to do: Send an e-mail out without an unsubscribe link (not cool).

Show everyone's e-mail address in the e-mail (way not cool). Always blind cc your e-mail addresses. (That means, hide the e-mail addresses you are sending to. ALL e-mail programs can do that. There are no excuses except ignorance, and that's not good enough.)

Be of the world, and the world will be of you.

21. DIY Music Licensing

Songs in Film, Television, Advertising, Games and New Media

One of the most significant playing grounds for independent artists and songwriters to truly create revenue from their music, promote their music, and access directly, has become the Film and Television Music Licensing world. (And for the purpose of this chapter, that includes Advertising and Games. I will collectively call this "NEW MEDIA".) Formerly a closed and secular business, delegated to only music publishers "in the know", this arena has now become not only accessible by independent artists and songwriters, but has become the largest marketing avenue for artists (Indie AND Major). Why? Well, my theory is two-fold:

1. The **demise of the music retail business** (CD Stores) and an increase in internet marketing has caused Artists and Labels alike to look further afield to market music and build revenue streams. Placing songs in Films and TV Shows was a natural fit (as has always been needed since the silver screen began). Let's face it, they still pay. It has become harder and harder to see money from CD sales, and quite frankly, still a little early to see how Internet downloads can really create true, valuable revenue. Landing a song in a TV show, or Game, by opposite, can give you 500 times more profit in one go. 70-99c download revenue per song, and maybe a CD sale of $8 versus, $500-$50,000 for an average upfront license fee and royalties for a song in Media. Which arena would you spend your time on more?

2. As the landscape and opportunity for **independent Artists to run their own business affairs** has increased (instead of waiting around for a Label to sign them), **music supervisors for Films and TV Shows have equally become excited to use indie songs in their projects**, versus spending the big bucks on going through a Major Label or Publisher. Not only is the cost cheaper ($5,000 to sometimes $50,000 for a major label Artist's song, versus $1000 going down to $0 for an indie Artist's song), but **it's easier to clear the song from an indie artist**. Major Label Artists songs are usually tied up in red tape: Clearing a song through a Major Publisher (or several) can take months, let alone trying to clear the use of the Master by a famous Major Label artist. Whereas clearing an indie Artist's song (which they most probably own, publish, wrote, recorded and released themselves) could take 24 hours or less. These are big incentives for Film and TV to use indie songs.

Unfortunately, a music budget is sometimes the last to be allocated in Films and TV shows, and so even though the film producer or director may want a cool famous Artist/songwriters song, they may not be able to afford it by the time music is thought of. So they look for sound-alike songs and that's where the indie Artist can profit greatly.

So, as an independent Artist and songwriter, below are my tips on getting your songs into Media (Film, TV, Ads and Games). I've also included some links to online resources which detail the nitty gritty/ins and outs of it all too, wherever I can. If you want to take up a private coaching session with me to discuss further about your songs/get feedback/ask more questions, go to www.artistdevelopmentcoach.com and sign up for a session.

7 steps to getting songs placed

1. DON'T BE INTIMIDATED

They are just like you and I with the same goal > great music in media. So, who are "they"? Who is in charge of putting music in films or TV shows? "They" can refer to several people, but usually the person that will ultimately communicate and negotiate with you is the "music supervisor", or music publisher, or a library.

Mostly, these people love music just like you. That's why they chose this business. They want to hear great songs, and are "going to work" just like you are. Know what their intentions and needs are before reaching out, and remember: they are just people.

More on who you work with, further down under. "Do Your research".

2. GET YOUR DUCKS IN A ROW

a. The 5 Ps - Proper preparation prevents poor performance

Before you start knocking on doors, you need to know what you are doing, about the licensing business, and get yourself organized. My father used to say to me as a kid, "Gilli, PPPPP. Proper preparation prevents poor performance." The first thing I recommend is to ask yourself:

WHY - am I doing this? What will I get by pursuing this field. Is it for money? For glory? For exposure? What? This will help you refine your focus.

WHAT do I need to do in order start licensing? What do I need to know?

WHO do I need to contact? Who is my target? Who will want to hear my songs? People I know? People I don't know?

WHERE do I need to go to do this? Research? Network? Communicate?

HOW do I go about this? Online and e-mails? Industry networking events?

b.   *Organize your song catalog*

Get your songs in an organized format, whether it be on an Office Excel document, or even a Google Doc. Some electronic file is handy, with rows and columns for each piece of information about that song.

It's also useful to have a manila folder for hard copy information about your songs. Each song should have its own manila folder. Inside you can put lyrics, chord charts, co-writer agreements, licensing contracts, and any other pertinent information.

c.   *Meta-tag your songs*

It is extremely important to understand what Meta-tagging is. I know it seems like a techy term, but seriously, as we are now starting to pitch our songs over the Internet in mp3 or WAV/AIFF form, rather than giving out CDs, you need to be able to put reference tags on your digital file so that it shows it is yours, as well as provide useful information for the music supervisor.

Besides, the worst thing you can do is send a digital file that doesn't show who wrote it, who owns it or what it is. Just like giving a blank CD to someone with nothing written on it (my pet peeve), if I get an mp3 from someone that just says the title "Beautiful Day.mp3" as an example), I get equally annoyed. Even worse, if someone sends me "02 Beautiful Day.mp3". All I know is the title, and that it is track 3 on an album. iTunes has the unfortunate standard of putting track numbers with the song titles when it files songs on a computer, and I find it annoying. You can turn this feature off in Preferences.

What you want to do is title the actual mp3 with the name of the song AND your name (whether you are the artist or songwriter). THEN, you want to meta-tag the song.

What does that mean? It means that all the information and details, as well as search tags are already instilled into your mp3 so that the end-user can receive all the data they require. This helps you, because it makes it easier for them to find your song if they save it in a database. And it also gives them style/genre/songwriters/publishers/pictures and even lyrics.

Most music supervisors require it.

d.   *Be a member of a PRO; Ascap, BMI, Sesac etc.*

I cannot tell you how many songwriters I've met, who come to music conferences or are a member of Songsalive! (i.e. who are actively pursuing their music career as a business) who are NOT members of a PRO. It's like shooting yourself in the foot! A PRO is a "performance rights organization" and they effectively represent you and your song for all performance rights usages of your songs in the world. Without being a member of a PRO (and you can only choose one), you will not get paid for your songs on radio, on television, over the Internet, or anywhere there is performance rights usage of compositions.

There is no reason why you shouldn't join a PRO. Everywhere in the world, except the U.S.A., there is only one PRO per country, and free to join as a writer member. In the States, there are three to choose from: Ascap, BMI and Sesac. You should research their sites and ask other songwriters before choosing one. They are pretty much the same though one is non profit while the other 2 aren't. Still, they collect royalties, in your favor, so please join one.

Let's take a quick scenario as to how they help you when it comes to placing a song in a TV show or TV film.

Your song, "Beautiful Day" gets licensed to a CBS movie of the week (for those outside the U.S., CBS is a major network, with one of the highest ratings, so placing on song on a show on CBS is up there in royalty potential).

As you would be a member of a PRO, the ONLY way you could get royalties (and this is beyond the front end fees you might get ... more on the breakdown later)... is through the PRO. That is, the PRO pays the SONGWRITER the money from the TV network. The producer of the TV show MUST submit a CUE SHEET to the TV Network, which MUST in turn submit that CUE SHEET to the PRO, who in turn pays the songwriter.

So, you have to be a member of a PRO. Period.

e.   Consider having your own publishing company or find an administrative publisher

It can get a little crazy trying to keep yourself and your songs organized. Gone are the days where you have to find a publisher to do all your work. You can do it yourself (DIY), but you may want to consider setting up your **own publishing company**, or having an administrative publisher, to ensure your publishing share gets taken care of. You can contact your PRO directly to set up a publishing company. They will ask you to search available names and once set up with them, you would also want to set up a business under that name (I'd also search the Internet for websites, (as well as your local chamber of commerce/city business license office, etc.) so you know it's not taken, before you contact the PRO). Do your homework in your city as to how you go about all this. Your PRO will guide you also.

If you want an **admin publisher**, they might be useful and the short answer to having help, yet you get most of the percentage. In an ordinary publishing agreement situation, you may be giving away 50% or more of your publishing share (sometimes 100%), whereas admin publishers take anywhere from 5% to 30%. The difference is admin publishers will generally just collect royalties on your behalf, and organize your songs (so what I wrote above they help with). Rarely do they also pitch and find opportunities for you, but some do. They can organize your licensing and contractual agreements though, when the job comes in to you.

Ultimately you want to consult your PRO, a lawyer, and other songwriters on your best course of action.

3. USE SPECIFIC SELF-MARKETING PRACTICES

a. Create a website specifically tailored or an area dedicated to songwriting

Why should having a website be only for performing Artists? I think it's extremely important for songwriters and composers to also have their own website, promoting who they are, and their music. If you are a singer/songwriter, I encourage you to have a section dedicated to your songs and songwriting, a discography, and a specially tailored biography just about you as a songwriter. I also believe that social networks play an important role in your Internet promotion (Facebook, Myspace, LinkedIn etc), but always link BACK to your website: your hub/home of all things about you. Bring them back to you!

Some songwriters say to me, "why should I have a website? I'm not promoting my band or my shows". I disagree. You are promoting YOU. You as a songwriter, your songs, and your purpose. If you are pitching your songs to music supervisors, they will want to see your credits, your discography, and perhaps a little about you. Remember, this is about developing relationships, and the more human you become (accessible to others), the more opportunities you create.

b. Business cards, postcards, flyers

Just like having an online presence, it's important for songwriters and singer/songwriters to carry with them their cards and flyers to promote themselves. A business card that is professional and clear, is a first start. I would avoid "glamour" photo shots on your business card, unless it really shows something about your music. Add a catch phrase under your name, such as "the low end Doctor" (a really cool one for bassists), or "creating change, one song at a time"), or "lyricist/composer". Whatever you write, make it cool, but CLEAR. You don't want to give a business card out that just says your name, and then no one can remember what you do. Also, do not give people a business card from your 9-5 job, and expect anyone to take you seriously. Create a card just for your music. They are cheap to make. Vistaprint.com is a good start.

Flyers and postcards are equally great to have on hand. I prefer postcards because they are small enough to put in your pocket, but too big to toss. I have copious postcards from artists on my fridge or desk, because they are too pretty for me to toss. That's a good thing! Make your postcard glossy, colorful and fun. Show us what you do, and why you are doing it. Put links to where we can read more, hear more, and discover more. Don't overdo it. Keep it simple, but effective.

c.   *What to send to music supervisors*

What do they need from you? Songs for what? Music for what? Get specific. Know what they want first, if you can. Sometimes supervisors are clear in the pitch as to what they are looking for. Sometimes they are vague, e.g. "songs about love and loss". If you get a generic pitch, don't be afraid to contact them and ask them what STYLE, GENRE, TEMPO they are looking for. Also more about the story can be helpful. Is this a love song, i.e. romance? Or a family member passing away? This means two different types of songs.

Usually, if you are e-mailing someone unsolicited (not requested/out of the blue), you DON'T want to send any mp3 files or propaganda. Just a short and sweet e-mail note asking permission to send more. ASK THEM what they want. Ask them if they want mp3s or a CD in the mail. ASK THEM if they want a biography/press kit. Or, just a URL to your website.

In the mail, once you are given permission to send, songwriter packages should be uniquely simpler than Artist packages. Don't over "flower" the package. The focus should be the music you are sending. My recommendation, to keep it simple but effective, is to send

- the CD - labeled clearly (make sure you know if they want it in a sleeve or jewel case with spine clearly marking your song so they can store it on their shelf).

- a typed sheet describing the songs on the CD and any directions on how to listen to it, and what pitch you're pitching to.

- a one sheet or 1 postcard. That's it... about you.

- They may not want your big biography. but sometimes they want to read your discography (recording/placement credits). See mine at www.gillimoon.com/discography.

- You must **meta-tag** your digital files.

4.   DO YOUR RESEARCH

a.   *What are the markets?*
  i.   Films – major
 ii.   Films – indie
iii.   Trailers
 iv.   TV shows

v.   Video Games
vi.   Corporate Video
vii. Advertising (TV and Internet)

Get to know the different markets that you can pitch to. I haven't scratched the surface with the list above, but this is a good start.

b.   Get connected with who is looking

i.   Your markets are music supervisors, publishers, music libraries, producers, editors, directors and some labels/Artists.

Music Supervisors - A music supervisor's role is to place music in Films, Television shows, Ads, Video games and projects needing music. They are usually well versed in styles of music, and know where to find them, whether through major label/publisher routes, or indie networks. Songsalive!, as a non-profit songwriters organization, is often approached by music supervisors looking for songs. If you are Songsalive! Elite Member, you can access our program, <u>Songshop</u>, where song leads are posted.

A music supervisor may work directly or indirectly with the Film/TV show director, producer, music editor, or another go-between, such as a publisher. Their job is to deliver music within the budget allocated for music in the project.

A music supervisor is like you and me. They are people, who like music. You like music. They like music. This is your first common denominator, and a great way to start a conversation.

Music supervisors will often take 25-50% of your publishing share of your songs, and sometimes the complete 100%.

Music Libraries - represent songwriters and pitch for you. They tend to sell packages to their clients (media world), so your songs might be lumped into one package as a group and you get smaller percentages, but still... you get paid. They usually take ALL upfront licensing fees, and you just get your songwriting royalties through your PRO. They often take all the publishing too. While Libraries may not be as lucrative, you may get more songs licensed in quantity.

They love instrumentals, so be sure to mix instrumentals of all your songs, before you leave the studio. Music Libraries will often take 50% of your publishing share of your songs, and mostly the complete 100%.

Music Publishers - Publishers technically represent songwriters and were the only representation songwriters had in what I call the "Dark Ages" of the music business. They also print sheet music and draw up contracts for all types of placement scenarios for songs. As I mentioned above in "Get Your Ducks In A Row", you can sign with a publisher, or an admin publisher, or become your own publisher (a relatively new phenomenon for songwriters to take charge of their own business affairs). Publishers will often take 25-50% of your publishing share of your songs, and sometimes the complete 100%.

It is important to see a Publisher as different to a Music Supervisor or Library. A Publisher takes care of the "whole you" as a songwriter. Not only representing your song catalog, they are invested into your future and goals as a writer (career growth) and you would want them to be introducing you to people in the business, other writers, artists, and placement opportunities on a 365 days of the year basis. Also you are fixed into an exclusive contract with Publishers, unlike Supervisors or Libraries who take you on a per song basis.

Get to know film makers, producers, directors, editors, and even actors. I've placed songs of mine in films, especially independent films, because I networked (and hung out as friends) with script writers, budding directors, and even music editors working on films. Dipping your toes into the Film and Media business (rather than just hiding behind the music business networking) will be advantageous.

ii.   Songsalive! Songshop - a special placement program

Get song leads where music business professionals (record labels, publishers, film producers and music supervisors) hunt songs from the Songsalive! song pool. Access an international database of songwriters where your songs can be accessed by other members and music industry professionals looking for that hit song. When the hunt is on, Songsalive! is a one-stop song shop. Songshop is one of our many programs, part of our non-profit organization supporting and promoting songwriters worldwide. LEADS POSTED EVERY MONTH with direct contacts to those who are looking! Read about Songsalive! Songshop at www.songsalive.org/songshop

iii.   Songsalive! Music Licensing Partners
Songsalive! has teamed up with a selection of Music Licensing Partners that offer tip sheets, resources and contacts for our members to find more opportunities to pitch and place songs. Check out the full list of Songsalive! Licensing Partners at www.songsalive.org/sponsors

iv.   Other resources

Find out who is offering resources and access to people looking for songs. There are a ton of music supervisor lists and websites now, where you can join and pitch your songs (some include musicsupervisor.com, taxi.com, pumpaudio.com, and songsalive.org has a list of more). They change a lot so get to know what's out there. There is controversy as to whether it's best to go through a third party site, or if you should pitch directly to music supervisors and publishers. My motto is, if you feel it's a good opportunity, go for it, and always use discretion in making your decision. Read up about the company and see what their success/track record is like. I think trying to connect with film makers is even better. Grab the latest Hollywood Reporter/Billboard/Variety (and look for who's making movies). The old fashioned way of networking in the film scene can help you create lifelong business connections with producers, editors, directors, film network gatherings, and college film schools. Network network network.

5. EASY CLEARING GETS THE JOB

As I mentioned in my opening paragraph, it has become lucrative and accessible for independent songwriters to find success in the Licensing world because, chances are, you own your master, and your song, and you can clear it really quickly. This is heaven to any music supervisor. Some tips:

a. Own the masters / songwriting agreements / own the publishing. Clear it in 24 hours.

Keep track of your ownerships in your Song File so you can contact your co-writers or master owners quickly and get clearance ASAP. Preferably, you become the administrator of that song from the moment it's written and recorded (through signed co-writing agreements, and master usage agreements > see end for samples), the minute you leave the studio. Also, make sure you get all your musicians to sign off on a Musicians clearance (that they got paid and won't need royalties).

b. Ok to represent yourself, but be professional and act as your own publisher if you don't have a publisher

Remember, your market is people just like you. Do the work, be business-like, and there is no reason why you can't represent yourself.

c. If you have a publisher, work with them to clear easy and quickly

Have a strong relationship with someone in your publishing company you can call upon at a moment's notice to help you clear your songs. Harry Fox (USA) and Amcos (Australia) are useful for **COVER song clearances**. There's a new one called Limelight

d. Aim high but be open to different ways to earn your revenue.

Ever consider creating music content for web-isodes, webcasts, online games, and college films?

6.   KNOW THE MONEY LANGUAGE

a.   *Upfront Fee for Sync and Master*

In any composition, there are two rights, the publishing and the performance rights. The sync license covers the SONG, which is the songwriter and publisher of that song. This license allows the use of the underlying lyrics and music of that song in the project. The master use license covers the performance side of the music, i.e. the recording: the "master". In many occasions, who owns the sync/publishing side (song/composition) is different to who owns the master/recording side (the recording). You may be the songwriter, but perhaps the Artist, or the record label owns the recording of the song. There could be many recordings of the song. But only the same songwriters of the composition.

I covered a version of INXS' song "Need You Tonight". The song was written by two of the band's members, Andrew Farris and Michael Hutchence. But I recorded the song, so I own the recording of it. In licensing to film or TV, I would receive the master revenue, and the publishing company, Warner Chappell Music, would receive the sync revenue, and they would pay the songwriters. (Of course, the film or TV show would have to get everyone's permission to use the song, that's me for the recording, and Warner Chappell and the songwriters for the composition).

So if a TV company wanted to use a cover version of "Yellow Submarine" by the Beatles, they'd need a sync license, if they wanted to use the original by the Beatles they'd need a sync and master usage license.

But let's take an example of a song I wrote, and produced/recorded, "Be" from my new album "the stillness". If I place this song in a TV show, I will get the songwriting/sync share 100%, as well as the master usage share 100%, because I own both shares. So I'm getting 200% of the 200% (nowadays they refer it to 50/50 which is 100%, technically more clearer).

Let's say the sync share was $1000, and the master share was $1000. That's $2000 I would get upfront for placing my song in the show.

Now, the sync/songwriting share is ALSO split between the SONGWRITER and the PUBLISHER equally 50/50. Right now, I am my own publisher with Warrior Girl Music (ASCAP). So that publishing share would come to me, if I place it myself in the show. But, if I had a Publisher representing me, or a Music Supervisor representing the specific placement (through their publisher), the sync/songwriting share might be divided again because they usually like to get a percentage, if not most or all, of the publishing share.

Let me point out that publishers/supervisors/third parties are NOT ALLOWED to take any percentage of the SONGWRITER royalty, of the sync/songwriter share. That MUST be paid BY the PRO (Ascap/BMI/Socan/Apra) DIRECTLY to the songwriter. No middle people allowed.

The publisher royalty of the sync/songwriting share CAN go through a publisher, and this is the only negotiable money. So, in the case of my song in a TV show, I may be giving up 20-100% of that share. Let's say it was 100% (and I'd only do that if the publisher REALLY did a great job in pushing my songs, but I deeply discourage ANYONE giving the full 100% publishing share away if you can help it).

So that leaves me with $500 of the sync/songwriting share, while $500 went to the publisher. And I have the full $1000 of the master share.

See how it's done?

Side note: In Australia, through APRApra/AMCOS, songwriters don't need a publisher to collect their "publishing share", as they pay fully to the songwriter if no publisher is represented.... but most everywhere else, you need a publisher to collect the publishing share. It is quite shocking to see how much money sits "uncollected" at ASCAP/BMI simply because a songwriter doesn't have a publisher to collect that share on their behalf.

b.   Back end royalties

When the TV show starts playing with your song inserted, there are no more Master Usage share monies to see. Only sync/publishing. So, you get a certain royalty rate, depending on the TV Station and its license policies with the producers of the show, as well as the actual standard rates they pay out. Getting a song on the Disney channel might not get as much as say, CBS or Fox. Network pays more. And as the show gets syndicated (repeats and licensed to other nations), your royalty gets less and less.

Networks pay the PROs, period. But they CANNOT pay unless they receive a CUE SHEET from the TV Show itself. Therefore it is ALWAYS a good idea that you get a copy of the cue sheet ALSO when placing your song, so you can follow up with the PRO on your end. (Don't wait for the TV show to submit their Cue Sheet. If they don't know what a cue sheet is, especially with indie productions, train them!)

The PROs pay the SONGWRITER and the PUBLISHER (see the 2 split sync shares above). You as the songwriter get the songwriter share directly, while your publisher pays you your percentage after they receive the publishing share.

c. What is a Cue Sheet?

The creation of cue sheets often stems from the composer or music editor's spotting notes or edit decision list (EDL). If a music supervisor is on the project, they can sometimes be responsible for collecting information on the music used as well. They MUST be submitted to the PRO so the songwriting gets paid.

d. To re-title or not?

There is a lot of controversy about whether one should re-title their songs for specific placements or not. The good side of it is that if you do, you can use the same song in many situations, through different publishers who may want 100% of their publishing share. So, I place my song "Be" in a TV show through XYZ Publishers, and they want 100% of the publishing, even though it's a non-exclusive placement, if I don't re-title the song it's hard for LMN Publishers to place the same song in a different show and also get the same publishing share. If each publishing company collected on different TITLES of the song, then everyone gets their own piece of the pie, and I can keep the original title "Be", as my own, collecting 100% of the publishing to my own publishing company.

You see, the PRO doesn't pay on the sound of the song, just the title (that's why you need to register your song titles at the PRO so they know what to collect on). I could have "Be" registered at ASCAP, but "Be With You" as a re-title of the same song, whereby XYZ Publishers claim their publishing share from the one TV show they worked on, and "Be Into You" as another re-title of the same song, whereby LMN Publishers claim their publishing share from the other TV show they worked on.

The downside is it can be confusing branding-wise if the TV show ONLY wants your song on their show and nowhere else. But then, that means giving them an exclusive right, and you would hope you're getting a lot of money for this. It also can be demeaning the original work you created, or demeaning the original publisher's efforts (what if the second publisher only heard the song after hearing the first publisher's placement?)

Several top Hollywood music supervisors are now refusing to accept re-titled material after being pitched *the same song* from different sources under different titles (and at different rates!). The potential for confusion has led at least one major studio to issue an edict stating that they will only work with writers/publishes that represent their content exclusively. *(Source: Production Music Association)*

Re-titling, though, allows the composer to place their music with many companies thus widening the opportunities for getting their music heard and thus sold. I lean more on the ability to re-title. Some publishers will ONLY re-title if they work non-exclusively for you. Very few will refuse to re-title, and those ones usually want exclusivity on your song catalog. Is it unethical? Is it illegal? What do you think?

7. DO THE FOLLOW UP AND KEEP RECORDS

a. Go back to your Song File Excel or use a management system to keep record of who you pitch to and where you place. Continue to stay organized with your song title registrations, pitches and placements.

b.   Polite follow ups are essential. Once you've pitched, follow up after a certain amount of time. Don't bombard people with e-mails, and don't add them to your fan mailing list. Be professional, courteous, but assertive.

Good luck in creating financial and artistic abundance in your world! I can't wait to hear about your success stories.

E-mail me your stories and any questions warriorgirlmusic.com/contact

Success is yours today!

You can sit in the wings, waiting to get the courage up to get out in front of the world, but like getting adjusted to a chilly pool, the best thing to do is to just dive right in. What have you got to lose?

- Jeff Carlisle & Dan Lipson
JAM! Amp Your Team, Rock Your Business

22. Finding truth through stage personas

Some of the best bands on record (meaning album) are not great live. Some bands get signed because of a great demo, but haven't had enough experience nor begun to explore the dynamics between the musicians. Developing an "act" is more than just creating good music. It's about the way the musicians play (live), the clothes they wear on stage, the way they relate to the audience, how they stand on stage, the patter in between songs... the whole "live stage persona".

For most of my performing life I have felt that if you **speak your truth**, and learn to **let go** on stage, then you can grab your audience's complete attention. But I also learned to **be the entertainer**. I learned that early, playing in smoky pubs in Australia with people who really didn't care at all about the performer. They just wanted to drink

Being an entertainer is important – it's not just about making good music.

beer and if there was a song they liked, they sung along. But to get any attention, you had to be an over the top entertainer. **The stage persona – being the entertainer - became *the* most important thing for me, because I learned the ART of LETTING go, and finding my truth as an Artist.**

It took me a long time to not take myself so seriously as an Artist. I remember the early days in Sydney when I would go into a deep sweat preparing for a show. I had to get the right clothes, have the right makeup, and have the right hair do or color. I have had every hair color imaginable: Brown, blonde, red, white, mahogany, purple, even blue, and so many styles, from short and punky to long and frizzy. In the early nineties I thought I needed to be a little Bohemian, a little hippy, a little punk and a lot of attitude. I always wanted to show off my midriff, wear big loop earrings and fancy shoes. Black was in.

I was still learning the Art of performance though. When I first started out performing my original songs live, I was very shy. It's funny because I was also, at the same time, performing in cover bands and I was very dynamic, on the contrary. In cover bands I could play a part, and imagine what the original Artist, like Donna Summer, did on stage. I could imitate the original Artist.

But with my original material I was shy and very uncomfortable playing the piano and singing at the same time. I found it a really difficult thing, to think about my lyrics, play the chords, sing in tune, and remember there was an audience in front of me that needed attention. I closed my eyes a lot.

When I got to the States, I learned to **let go**. For starters, I was able to be whoever I wanted to be, from scratch; reinvent myself, so to speak. So I decided to be brave, and be a little "out there". It worked. I wore Spandex dresses, four inch wedge heels, silver and glitter somewhere on my body (and especially glitter cream on my cheeks and shoulders), and even wore wings throughout the *temperamental angel* album tour. Being "in persona", I was able to take flight as an Artist. Always a diamond in the rough, my music, songwriting and voice got stronger, but at least I got attention.

When I was signed to Tribe Records I even dressed up as a man for a year on stage. That was fun. We had developed a band called Jessica Christ, which pushed the envelope with gender issues: actually we wanted the audience to remove the gender association with songs, and promote the lyrics, the words, to be the most important elements, so I changed my stage gender for kicks, a direct idea from the Label in order for us to get some media attention (which came). I'd start off in plaid trousers and a jacket buttoned up, short cropped blue hair and a Salvador Dali curly mustache on my face, singing sweet love songs, and full on rock and roll too. Half way through the second song I'd literally strip and reveal a short body hugging dress, always keeping my black high boots on.

Jessica Christ was a real breakthrough for my stage persona, and for releasing my inhibitions. There is something to be said about going "over the top" on stage. You really confront all your fears and learn to let go. As soon as you let go of any fears or nerves, which can be disguised behind costumes as we become a different persona, the more your inner natural self can exude. I remember doing a gig at The Gig (venue) on Melrose Avenue in West Hollywood and it was packed: girls and guys up front, with lighters lit with flames swaying in the air. Girls looked on with awe and felt the power of a woman doing what I was doing on stage. It gave them strength. Guys were curious about my sexuality, but they felt the sensuousness. They were all in love, and it didn't matter. The crowd started hooting and hollering when I'd change attire, never missing a beat on the song. It was an electrifying feeling. I really let loose and didn't care what people thought. My sexuality is tied into my expressing myself through music. When I perform, sexuality naturally exudes. For me, it was all about entertainment, and through my image development over the years, my musicianship and vocals got tighter.

Blog entry: June 2000

"We've (the Jessica Christ band) been playing the traps around L.A. to great crowds and not so great crowds (you have to take the good with the bad), sometimes rude club managers and sometimes great promoters. Playing live in L.A. is somewhat challenging because you never really know who's going to come and see you on any given night. We had all of 15 people at The Mint on Pico, but a couple of weeks earlier the club was packed with 150 at The Gig. I've been battling with the ideas flowing in my head about my music. I have had so many deep and emotional events that have taken place over the past year... the new songs are all very autobiographical... like you will hear the beginning, middle and end of the

*relationship in one sitting. The edge is interesting. No more Miss nice girl. I'm
coming alive!"*
    gillimoon.com (blog)

Following the Jessica Christ era was my "temperamental" phase, promoting my
first U.S. release on my own label Warrior Girl Music. The album *temperamental
angel* conjured up a lot of imagery and ideas as to how to present myself on stage.
For me it was about being a rebel and an angel, in the way I sung, performed and
how I sounded. I wanted to bring out different personalities, as we all are complex
individuals with many personalities and masks. I had a song called "Naked" which
was very sensuous, and the title track really spoke about my multi-personalities,
being the Angel and the Devil (or at least dealing with those different parts of us).

Blog entry: March 2001

*"I spent last Sunday trotting down old train tracks downtown L.A. in a
sticky black plastic dress with dark sunglasses, my 'don't mess with me'
boots, and white wings, while a train came by. We were filming the rest of
the footage of the "Temperamental Angel" music video. They then had me
wrapped in saran wrap, naked, in the living room. I love getting naked! Just
got home from The Gig, Hollywood where Jeff, Gordie, Ric and I played at
Mike Galaxy's Industry Showcase. I felt it went really well and we sold quite
a few CDs plus accumulated new fans. Both Jeff and I wore our wings and
Ric adorned my pink feather bower by the 6th song. I love "doing
Hollywood" because you can wear whatever you want on stage and in fact
so do the people in the audience. Tonight for me it was simply freaky colored
hair and my angel wings. The blue warriors, the honest, hunky and adorable
band who funk and groove with or without gilli moon, are knocking the socks
off everyone and that makes gilli a proud mother goose. The Whisky a Go
Go never saw anything like it last Thursday even though they've had, well,
just about everybody there. But we have paint flying - and Gordie our
guitarist enjoyed that on is body, dress swaying (that's mine), heads nodding,
boots kicking, a voice warbling, and music well, will take you away to the
MOON. It's quite funny that where once gilli moon was so sweet and a
"piano ballad" gal, she has turned almost heavy metal in her black boots but
still so calm and sultry when "Naked" comes on. The Press seem to enjoy the
controversy."*
    gillimoon.com (blog)

When I came out with the *Woman* album, I was all about the "warrior girl" -
wearing combat attire (before it was popular), with green army camouflage pants,
boots, and a cool, spunky tank top. It gave me room to run around on stage. I also
was painting a lot on stage, what I call "SensuArt". I'd erect a large clear piece of
Perspex (plastic) on stage and get my brushes and paint out. I'd stand behind the

clear canvas painting lots of female nudes and faces, while the band would solo and jam. I have painted my band members many times too. It was a lot of fun.

I've run the gamut of stage personas. It helps develop the Artist's story and removes the fear. Every gig should be special.

They have all been for me.

My "live image" changed when I started touring. I began seriously touring across the United States in '02, promoting the *temperamental angel* album. To keep it affordable, I went solo, without the band. This meant that that I was responsible for everything: getting to the venue, organizing my music, playing the keyboards (my fingers certainly got a lot stronger), entertaining a strange crowd, selling CDs (although have always had help on this from fans and friends), and packing up. At a certain point it got too tiring to "put on the big show" with the costumes and any theatrics. I started out on my first tour with a small color wheel light that revolved and changed lights as I performed. But I sold it for $50 in Phoenix Arizona into the second week.

I ended up just taking my shoes off, and just singing my songs on the keyboard. **This was the beginning of finding my true self on stage.**

I no longer wore the outfits, frizzed my hair up, or even put on any over the top makeup. I took off all the trappings (makeup, costumes, boots, the lot). Over a few years of being on the road consistently, traveling every state in the country, I **became less and less concerned about my costuming or stage persona.** I didn't have time and I was too tired. I became more concerned about my songs, my vocal and music performance, *and being authentic.*

The moral to these stories?

Because, **authenticity is the ultimate goal as a live performer.** If the audience doesn't feel your truth, then they can't relate to you. Being on the road was a huge awakening. I don't have a problem with any band going for the "glam rock" or over the top image. I feel every band has to go through that process, and it has many positives, especially when developing and you want to learn to "let go" on stage. If you are all about "image" and that's what people relate to, then that should be a focus. But I have grown accustomed with the notion that it doesn't matter how you look: *it's how you act. It's who you are inside.*

I've seen the worst bands all dressed up, with the full stage presence - lights, costumes, props... the works, and then be left unimpressed with their talent and their songs. Then I've seen the most humble of Artists get up in jeans and a t-shirt, no makeup or frills, and truly grab my attention with a powerful stage presence, talent and story.

> **Authenticity is the ultimate goal as a live performer. If the audience doesn't feel your truth, then they can't relate to you.**

The more grass roots I've become, more laid back and real, the more positive feedback I've received on my show and my music. Of course, this is a ten year overnight success story here. I'm no spring chicken. I've learned a lot. One has to get their chops up on stage for a long time to make it look natural!

Since a few years ago, when I released my fourth album, *extraOrdinary life*, I had really tuned in to my songs and writing, and I remember the story around them whenever I sing them. I go back in time, every time and live that emotion, and the audience feels that. Being able to touch souls is so magnificent, and it doesn't matter what you wear. But it does matter how you exude your passion. It <u>does</u> matter how you deliver. **Eye contact *is* important**. Contact in general, with your audience, is important. Humility is important. **Not taking yourself so seriously is VERY IMPORTANT.**

I remember seeing Celine Dion in concert in Sydney. Whether you like her music or not, I encourage anyone to see her perform live or check out her live videos. She is amazing as a stage entertainer. There must have been 20,000 people at this concert, and she had every one of us eating out of the palm of her hand. We were silent and riveted. She spoke to me like I was the only person in the room, and sung my life stories in her songs. She has a fabulous sense of humor (she knows what to say between songs), and never ends a song until she's ready. If you notice, she'll finish the song on a note, maybe an arm outstretched, maybe her eyes closed; and the band will stop, so will she - and everything is silent. We hang in the suspense. When she finally drops her arm (it could be even 5 or 10 seconds after that final note), we then applaud, as if we've been given the silent nod. She decides when the song is over. Until then, we are her audience slaves. It's superb.

I have loved my stage persona journey. I'm sure there is more to come with how I will express myself live. I have always admired Madonna's finesse in reinventing her image every album she makes. I like that idea because I love making concept albums. Each album tells a story. It has a theme, a plot, a journey to take the audience on. So too should the live performance, matching the essence of the album. Madonna is great at that, and never afraid to push the envelope.

Stage costumes can be a great ice breaker, to bring across your Artist story and concept. Developing an image is crucial, of course. But with or without costumes, if you can touch people's hearts, then you're on the right path. There is much controversy about developing an Artist's image in the music business. The media love to grab on to a story of some kind, and the business doesn't like to have to guess who you are. They like to see it in your music and how you look. They want to be able to market something. It's the same for independent Artists too. Image around your album concept, your website, your live performance persona, even your character in the general public, all tie in to who you are as an Artist. I believe that your persona as an Artist is crucial to telling your story and creating a buzz.

But in all of that... always remain authentic to your true self. Keep changing, evolving, and tap in to your passionate self. TRUTH and PASSION is everything. This, my friends, will make the difference between you being a quick, fly-by-night fashion trend, versus being an eternal, lifelong, rock star.

23. Delivering a rock star performance

"Rockin' the house" from start to finish

This chapter is for those who perform or would like to perform.

Ever feel like you want to brush up on how you deliver your show on stage, without fumbling in front of an audience? From owning the stage, to reaching your audience through your movements, voice, eyes and actions, to building your entire show on stage, **here are my tips on where to start.**

PROFESSIONALISM IS KEY

When you first arrive at the venue, be polite to the manager/owner/promoter, whoever is your point of call. Introduce yourself to the sound engineer (remember his/her name) and be the only point of call for your band (rather than all your musicians bombarding him/her with questions). Don't go on the stage to set up until you are invited by the sound engineer. (If you are performing in a theater, it will be the stage manager). When you've finished your show, once again acknowledge everyone that helped put the show on, such as the promoter, stage manager, sound engineer, even the door person or the waitresses. You can do that on stage, or go up to them personally, depending on the situation. Leave with a smile ☺

KNOW YOUR VENUE FACTS

As much as we all feel our talent deserves the shiniest of stages, just know that not everything will be perfect at a venue. But don't judge a book by its cover. I've played the sleaziest dive bars and ended up with the most amazing fans and applauses. On the other hand, I've booked beautiful theaters and had the worst experiences. So just know it won't be what you expect, but hopefully it will be better and different. The most important thing to remember is to be open to something new, AND to cover your bases with as much information as possible before you do the gig. That means that you should know as much as you can about the venue in advance, such as: the audience capacity, the type of clientele, if it's a sit down/stand up/dinner reservation/bar type club; if there is parking, load in access, a change room/green room. More importantly, well in advance of the gig, find out what money you're making (whether it's a set fee, a door deal (% of the door), a bar deal (% of the bar), meals and drinks for the band, or all of the above. Even better, have a contract with the venue/promoter that secures all this information in writing and a deposit in case the gig gets canceled.

OWN THE STAGE

As soon as you start setting up on stage, this is the time for you to "own" it. That means, get to know your stage. This will be your space to entertain, share your songs and touch your audience. Take a walk around the empty stage before you set up. Feel it. Love it. Own it. See how far you can walk to the front, sides and back. Set up your gear and get your microphone(s) to be exactly how you want them. Do you like to walk around with the microphone? Loosen the cables now, before the show. Make sure you have enough cable that is free and clear of other instruments, and your own legs. Work with your musicians to give YOU enough space to do what you want to do. Play a keyboard? Consider the options: sideways, lengthways? Which way is more comfortable for you? Be sure to bring it down stage (right to the edge) so you can be close to your audience. Oh and lastly, get those cables and microphone stands out of the way. I can't stand watching an Artist get all tangled up in their mic or guitar cables; or even worse, taking the mic off the mic stand, but then leave the stand in front of them, so it's like a block between you and the audience. Get the cables out from under your feet, put them and the mic stand in a place that leaves space for you to move and free yourself up! TAKE THE TIME to do all this BEFORE you start.

TAKE THE TIME TO GET THE SOUND RIGHT

A **sound check** is when you have time to go through part or a full song, or even a couple of songs, without the audience being in front of you. A **line check** is when you only get the opportunity to get the sound levels for the instruments just before you start singing (and the audience is in front of you). Even if you only get a line check, get your sound right. Maybe start singing a song at the beginning that's a sound check song that lasts 30 seconds. My band and I start singing *"this is a sound check, la la la, is everything sounding alright? La la la"*. Don't give away your songs, especially if the audience is sitting there. I find it odd that an Artist will sometimes sing an almost complete song, then stop, and say, *"does that sound good?"*. Then start the song again for the show. Don't give away your songs during a sound check if people are in the audience. It's very confusing for us sitting there waiting for you to start, because we may not know if you've actually started or not. So, make up a song for your sound check to help with levels.

Be brave enough to ask your sound engineer for exactly what you want. If you need your vocals up, down, or instruments up or down, let the sound person know. You can do this after your little sound check song, or you can use hand signals (point to the microphone, then thumbs up or down, as an example). Also, after your first official song of the set, definitely take another 10-30 seconds getting the sound right. Too many Artists put up with bad sound afraid to speak out. So maybe don't do your best, big song first. Do a song that helps the sound engineer get your levels but is not demanding perfect sound.

Also remember that your monitor sound (what you are hearing on stage) is different to what the audience is hearing. So your sound man will adjust the sound for you on stage. I think it's good to also have a friend in the audience who can be on your *side* indicating to you, or the sound man if levels are right as an audience member. Plus, if it's a fan, it makes them feel "part" of the show!

TELL YOUR STORY AS IF IT'S THE FIRST TIME

I know it can feel trite to have to sing your songs over and over again, but your audience deserves to hear them as if it's the first time you've played them. They want to feel the newness of it, and certainly don't want to hear that you're jaded, or that you are tired or that you care about other songs better. Each song is like a little baby, with a whole back story. We often play songs we wrote 5 years ago or more, because our fans love them or because we're still promoting an album that has those songs on it. Even though you may have moved on emotionally to new songs, it's important to give every song the same importance and weight. So how do you capture that innocence every time? Firstly, visualize the time you wrote it. Think what it was about and why you wrote it. Try and "be" back in that moment of pouring your heart out on our sleeve. And like any good entertainer, *entertain*, which means, share with us your emotion about the writing of the song and its meaning. If you broke up with your boyfriend, or you changed to a new city, or whatever, we want to know and *feel* it with you.

Empathize with your audience. Imagine how they would feel listening to your song for the first time. Would they want you to exude emotion or sing it stale? Understand that your connection with your audience is so important, and that your *truth* is what they want to feel, hear and see.

There is no need to be fake. This is not acting. This is *you* being you, in the moment of writing that song.

Try rehearsing in front of a mirror and look into the mirror to your own eyes. What do you see, feel, hear?

USE YOUR EYES AND BODY TO CONVEY EMOTION

The eyes say it all. As said countless times, they are the windows to the soul. I know for a fact that if you can work your eyes during the delivery of the song, you can convey your message and emotion a thousand times stronger. It is important to have complete control over what you do with your eyes. Next time you are at a concert, watch how the Artist uses their eyes. Are they focused, and intently opening, closing, moving, directing their eyes? Or do they look scattered, with no intention on where they are looking? *Work your eyes from the moment you start singing your song.* If it's a ballad, maybe think about starting with your eyes closed, and then opening at the pre-chorus –

when you're ready to reveal yourself to us more. Build your eye contact along with the build of the song. If you look at someone in the audience, give them the whole sentence. Don't sweep your eyes. When you look at me, I want to be part of your story, song and soul,'till the end of that statement. On the other hand, if you feel someone is uncomfortable with your stare, don't linger too long. Sense how they feel. Most people are shy. If you're song is a big number/rock/power – then show the intensity in your eyes. There's so much to describe on how eyes can be effective. I could write a whole book about it.

Not sure where to look? Having trouble identifying eye contact with people? You don't need to be looking at audience members all the time, in fact it's best not to. Find your *fourth wall*. This is an acting term whereby you find an invisible wall in front of you and claim a spot on it that you can focus on, whenever you don't know where to look. Consider that the walls to your left, right and behind you on stage are your first, second and third wall. So the fourth wall is the back of the venue, which doesn't need to be your focus point as it's usually too far away. Perhaps you see a pole closer to you, or a window, or a spot on a chair. Or nothing at all. Whatever you find, work it out in advance, before you show, so you can go to it (or several) whenever you need to, during your show.

When I was doing musical theater in my teens at school, my music teacher, Mrs. Williams (who taught me SO much and I am so thankful to her), told us to imagine your audience as being "cauliflowers" or "cabbages" or even "chocolate". Look over them towards the back and think about the end of the show, when you can gobble them all up. Ha ha, that was so funny at the time. I guess it sounds weird now, but you get my drift.

Along with the eyes, your body plays a big part in conveying your message. So many new Artists are stiff on stage, afraid to move. I strongly recommend, before starting a show, to get to know your stage, and walk around. That way, when you are performing, you are less afraid of the space you have around you. Even a tilt of the head can be powerful, or a look up to the sky. Maybe a hand wave, or a leg stomp. Whatever the emotion you want to deliver, using the body along with your voice is powerful.

I'm a piano player, and sitting behind a piano can feel limiting to move. But don't let it stop you. How you use your feet, your shoes tapping, or your legs moving, even subtle, can create a difference to your performance. You can bend down, sideways, left and right. Check out Tori Amos' performances. She pushes the limit of the use of a piano stool, for sure.

Don't be afraid to play with your voice a little. Go from sweet whispers, to giant screams. Growls, purrs, spoken-word, vocal ad lib/scatting... all can play a part in your performance and makes for a delicious change for anyone.

WHAT TO SAY IN BETWEEN SONGS, STAGE PATTER AND MEANINGFUL STORY TELLING.

> The more you speak your truth and you open up to the audience, the more the audience will relate to you and your story

The most important thing to keep in mind is that the audience wants to HEAR your STORY. That means not just in how you sing it, but also what you say, or not say about the song in introducing it. Don't be afraid to talk about why you wrote the song, so we get the story. The more you speak your truth and you open up to the audience, the more the audience will relate to you and your story. I find it important to rehearse your patter as well as your songs before your shows.

Rehearse in advance what you are going to say. One of my Artist clients had a great song about love. We all do right? But I didn't realize the uniqueness of this song until she explained it to me in a session. So we worked on her introduction for it. It ends up, this song is about how her parents met. They were complete opposites and no one thought they were a match at all. But they were destined to be together and they are still together after all these years. So when listening to the song, we had a deeper connection to her story, and it really worked.

Avoid speaking just because you feel the need. This can really kill a performance quickly, if you just ramble on with no reason, just because you feel the need to. Artists often ask me if it's good to introduce every song they are about to sing, or not. I say it depends on the whole show, how many songs, and what the song is about. Sometimes it can be more effective just to kick it off into a song without an introduction, if you feel the song will tell the story, *as they should*. If your song is on the radio, it has to tell its own story. You won't be there to introduce it. So hopefully your lyrics say it all. But if you feel the need to introduce the song, why it was written, or who it was written with, go ahead, as long as there's meaning to it. Frivolous small talk will hamper your show. Meaningful, even slightly spirited and funny, can intensely improve your show.

The funnier I get the more people love my songs. I like to tell a few quirky stories and bring a sense of humor to my show. I've only learned this over time, but the less I take myself seriously and the more I relax and be myself on stage, I find the audience connecting with me more. It's supposed to be fun! So have fun with it.

Don't forget to insert somewhere towards the end of your set your website and **how people can find /purchase your music**. So many Artists forget this. Also, and this is a really big thing: **repeat your name throughout your set**. Some people come in half way to a show, or they just didn't catch your name in the first place. Don't be afraid to mention it (and the spelling of it) several times. By the way, my name is gilli moon, that's g (as in George). i.l.l.i.m.o.o.n dot com ☺

DIFFICULT VENUES AND DIFFICULT ARTISTS

Not all venues will be perfect. Most are far from perfect. The morale to this story: **focus on your performance and the connection with your fans**. It doesn't matter where you are. You could perform in a barn, under a tree, or on a beach. The goal is connecting and expressing your Art. The key to a successful stage performer, is the ability to adapt to any environment. I always expect less than 100% when I go into a venue. I've learned that most venues are built with the music stage as the last thought in mind. The stage is usually in some corner, with never enough space, and never the adequate sound equipment. So when I see a great space and hear great sound, I am excited, because I don't expect it.

No matter whether you are in a tiny club doing an open mic to 5 people or a huge stadium with thousands in the audience: ALWAYS DO YOUR BEST. Every single person counts. No half baked songs or lethargic performances. Give your all, for every person, in every situation. If it's a tiny venue, you never know who out of those five people may tell someone, who will tell someone, who will tell someone. Every fan counts. I write more about Venues in the next chapter.

There are a lot of Artists who take on a **prima donna attitude** in venues. They want certain sound, certain stage requirements, and pre-show these types of Artists are usually very difficult to deal with. Trust me, having put on a music festival and many rock shows and touring events, I have come across the gamut of prima donna Artists in this world. When I co-produced the women's festival in Los Angeles in '07, we had a particular Artist who was, quite frankly, a pain in the neck. Not only was she difficult, but so was her manager. They complained about everything possible, even before they arrived: from the stage requirements to food/drink rider, to the contract, to the promotion. Everything. And when they arrived, the Artist had little humility, to the point that this Artist decided to run over their time slot (that they agreed to in writing) "just because", and didn't care that other Artists who had traveled a along way to perform, would not be able to because this Artist took their time. While this Artist was talented, I can't say that they should have been treated any more special than the others.

Let me say that it's usually the least experienced, least talented Artists that have given me the most trouble, while the more talented and seasoned Artists are a pleasure to work with, and are very humble. Lesson? Stay humble, no expectations, and be nice to everyone, no matter the situation. Remember the first time you ever performed? Was it in your living room, on the back porch or a hokey open mic? Remember that feeling of excitement, and don't let the venue or the situations dampen your spirit to perform. If the sound doesn't work, unplug, take your shoes off and let everyone come up close. No tantrums with the sound engineer required. This is supposed to be fun!

LET GO, LET GO

The most important aspect of a live performance is the Art of letting go. I would imagine that the premise of my entire book is in the essence of letting go.

You have the opportunity to express your inner you. If you are a stage performer, this secret makes the difference between connection and non-connection.

Don't be afraid to reveal who you really are. We, the audience, want to know you so much. If you feel that pretence and façade is a stronger performance strategy, well, you're wrong. There's only so much of that bravado, and falsity that we can take. At a certain point, we want truth. We want to look into your eyes and yours back at ours, and reveal the deepest of the human spirit: all our emotions, weaknesses, vulnerabilities and dreams.

I hope you can step up to the challenge.

Exercise: Rockstar Performance 101

Set yourself up in front of the mirror with instrument and even better, a mic and mic stand. Consider the following when performing your song and answer these questions along the way.

Stage costume – to dress up or dress down. Which way will you go? Put on an attire that suits your mood, your music and your persona. It can be either glamorous and over the top, or you can go the jeans and bare feet. I've done both in my life. It's important to get into your "costume" for this activity, though, as it puts you into "stage mode".

Stage position – consider where you are standing, sitting, or how you are holding or sitting at your instrument. Where is your mic stand? Do you have room to move?

Eye contact – try being really focused on how you use your eyes. Do you start with your eyes closed, then open at the 2nd verse? Where do you look? Find your fourth wall, and don't move your eyes too much in one sentence. Watch where your eyes move to and catch yourself each time. If you find yourself not focusing on this area, start the song again, and again 'till you get it right.

Body and voice – try new things with your body – bending down, sideways, head tilts. Learn to smile, and move your hands or stomp your feet (on particular lyrics even better). Change your voice to whispers in the quiet parts, and strengthen in the crescendos. Try and implement dynamics into your song with your voice, as well as the way you play your instrument.

Set list: Work on a list of songs (for this exercise, choose up to 6), and put them in an order that tells a story, and creates a theme for your entire show. Think about what each song means. Consider up tempo songs versus ballads and create a dynamic rhythmically for your set.

What to say: write some ideas in advance on what you could say to introduce each song (or not). Think about the story behind why you wrote the song. Keep it brief and simple, but effective.

Rehearse your show solo (or with an instrumentalist if you don't play an instrument), so you know you can pull it off with the minimal requirements. If you have control of you, it's easier then to fit in musicians when and if they are necessary.

Most of all, enjoy it. Let go of your inhibitions, have fun, and speak your truth.

24. A venue breathes a thousand words

Out of the box gigs

I did a show in L.A. once where I performed with a nineteen piece big band. The band, put together and conducted by Tim Davies (who also plays drums in my band from time to time), comprises of a 12 piece horn section, bass, drums (Tim), percussion, keyboards and guitar. I sang three of my original songs with the band ("Tiny Diamonds" from the *"Woman"* CD, "Naked" and "Temperamental Angel" from the *"temperamental angel"* CD) plus a Peggy Lee cover, "Don't Smoke in Bed". I performed with Tim's band a few years ago for the first time, and going back for the second time tonight, was equally satisfying. Tim orchestrates my rock songs to fit the full big band, and charts all the instruments. It's so impressive. Gordie Germaine, guitarist, joined me also, and he got a kick out of it too. I mean, there I am singing "treat me like an angel, a temperamental angel..." and all of a sudden six horns go off to my left with a snappy jazz routine that blows my mind.

It was an utterly amazing experience and one that is so unique, describing it here in writing just doesn't do it justice.

As an entertainer, I have traveled the World performing for close to twenty years, but there are only a few performances that I can say are memorable, unique and inspiring. This is one of them. Memorable gigs keep us Artists alive. It's important to treasure the gems because on average the venues we are subjected to have the heart cut right out of it before we enter the door. We fantasize that being a "rock star" means living the life of luxury when it comes to performing, but most of the time you are dealing with bitter club owners, jaded musicians, no money (or little), smoky smelly bars, limited time to perform, late night slots, no parking, and skeptical audiences. Performing Los Angeles for ten years, you can certainly say you've "paid your dues." So when those magical gem nights come along, cling on to them and fill yourself up with passion again, reminding yourself why you are an Artist in the first place.

I remember opening for Simple Minds at the Celebrity Theater in Phoenix a few years ago. I got the call the day before to go. They needed a solo act that would open for them for $100. I said ok. For me, I saw the bigger picture: a huge band, a huge stage, a huge theater. I performed to 2000 people, on a revolving stage, with phenomenal acoustics. I could hear a pin drop. By the end of my set I had people wrapped around the building waiting for me to sign CDs that they already had bought. They were just waiting for me and they had never met me before. My performance sold them. I was stoked.

A few years ago I performed at Australia House in London to 100 of the top Australian media and businesses. The room had a 20 feet high ceiling with Baroque style architecture and a cathedral feeling. I played a Steinway grand piano, and was handed flowers and wine when I finished by the Consul General. This gig went into my top 10 gigs of all time. Another one was this year playing in Morro Bay, on a boat that circled around the Morro Bay rock to 60 eager locals. I played a mixture of jazz and originals. On the walk way before entering the boat was scribbled in black pen "gilli moon from L.A. – sold out". It was such a memorable night.

I have played to 6,000 people with Eric Idle (from Monty Python) around theaters across the United States and Canada. I've played festivals to 50,000. The Morro Bay gig to 60 people was just as cool, to me.

My music business successes are based on my personal memories of what made me feel fantastic.

I found an old diary entry about the L.A. club scene. This will be entertaining:
Past Blog entry: July 2001
Ok. Just so you don't think, by reading all this diary stuff, that gilli moon's world is all bubblegum and balloons, let me air a little of my frustrations about living and working in Los Angeles as an Artist. Last night was a typical example of the Hollywood bull---t I deal with on a regular basis... well everyone deals with. It just makes me want to GET OUT OF THIS TOWN! So, we arrive at the club for a promised 7pm load in, for a 7.30pm sound check, only to be waiting in the wings 'till quarter to 8 before we even get a glimpse of the stage because the other band who's after us feels the need to rehearse every line of their set! We finally get on stage and we are sound checking and I ask politely to the girl behind the bar, who seems as cold as a fridge, if we could "please have our drink tickets" to which she replies with a tongue like ice, "you have to get them from the manager in the back room."

She's oblivious to the fact I'm sound checking nor gives me any nice sentiment what so ever. I realize, on another note, that my name is not on the bill outside even though I booked the club months and months in advance to be featured (I've played this club many times before). Uggh! Then I'm called into the ticket booth to be once again harassed by the guy at the door who looks at my 20 industry door list and says, "you can only have 10 free entry." I sigh in exasperation... I mean, we're playing for free, we give it up for free, we work our butts off, and this is the kind of treatment we get in return? So I go back stage where the bouncer at the back door is a bull dog and he literally picks up my roadie by the shirt and throws him back inside not letting him exit via the back door. Nice neighborhood! He yells at me for not indicating who's in my band - like he NEEDS his power trip today. I then try and find some quiet minutes on my own backstage but need to pass the front to go to the bathroom, trying to avoid the audience (it gives me the jitters if I see anyone before a show) and the Blondie at the bar yells at me to come over. She NEEDS to talk to me she says. I ask if it can wait 'till after. I don't want to be seen. "No", she yells, so everyone hears her, "I NEED TO TALK TO YOU!" I reluctantly show my face and she then says, "so, who's in your band to get free drinks or is it anyone who says 'Gilli' that gets free drinks." I say, "no just the band thanks." (I wasn't going to give up my credit card for everyone who knows my name). She says, "well how will I know who's in the band?" I'm thinking, surely they have a system to work this out by now. How many bands do they have every night? But I reply, "anyone with blue paint on their cheeks." (My band wears blue paint). She just didn't get it. So I'm trying to deal with her, shouting over the crowd who are agitated waiting for the show to start. I'm trying to avoid the people and have some kind of mystery by being invisible before I go on... and all I want to do is GET BACKSTAGE. Oh no, the door guy wants another word with me, so once again across the room I go... Ouch, I just want to go home! ANYWAY... the band and I did a huge, great show. We had props, I painted 2 canvases, danced, jumped, felt high as a kite, it was SO much fun. Maybe I need tension before a gig. After I get off stage of course the bouncer immediately pushes us out the door so the boys' gear is literally sitting on the sidewalk. Not even a minute to repose. These clubs do it every time. NO RESPECT! Can't they think of two simple things?

One, supply backline. Wouldn't it be so much easier if all 4 or 5 bands who play on the night can use same drum kit and amps? It would save time and space.

Two, offer a secondary room goddammit! I mean, I played the Whisky a couple of weeks ago and it's brutal. Last song and you are sitting on your amp on the street on Sunset Blvd wondering "how the heck do I get my car here to load the gear, before someone steals it, and then be able to park the car again (parking is the pits) so I can schmooze a little which is why I do this goddammit Sunset Strip gig in the first place. Sh-- I'll just go home!" I had a crazy come up to me and try and squeeze the life out of me in a bear hug that was close to needing a restraining order. Weird people in Hollywood. Then I'm dealing with some 20 year old industry person (no, that's not 20 years of industry experience, this was a 20 year old shmuck) who thinks he's the answer to everything and gives me his feedback of the show. I'm all keen asking him how he liked my set. I felt I did a great set - lots of power and energy, dancing, painting, vocals tight, band tight. I was ready for the feedback. Twenty years old and this A&R rep from Capitol thinks he knows every answer as to why I won't get signed or how I will. "Hey babe, nice set. Pretty outfit. It's all about the hit song though babe.. Deliver us the hit song and we can talk."

I walk away in complete shock. Why do they hire such kids!! I go home and all I think about on my windy Canyon drive back over Beverly Glen is... I gotta get out of this town. I can't tell you how much energy I delivered, how much the band gave it up.I mean we did a great, great show... AND FOR WHAT????? We sold 2 Cds. 2 is better than none I guess. But in the long run, what's it all for? Hollywood children who run the business and have no idea about Art? They say, "give us hit songs, that's what we really need." Well that saying is old. We gave 10 hit songs, a magic show with dance, action, energy, visual Art and color, an awesome rock band. Those who don't see it are naive. Record Companies out there - you are

hiring the wrong people to scout talent. I'm so tired of the music industry bull---.
But I love my Artistry. I'm passionate, strongly passionate about that. Goodnight."

A venue breathes a thousand words. Performing in the big cities where it's like fighting tooth and nail, can suck the life out of you. Small towns, for that matter, can do the same. You can be performing in the same little bar with the locals for years, and feel like you're never getting ahead. It's all relative.

For me, it's about finding those gems of performances that are unique, memorable and feed me first and foremost. It can't be always about the business, otherwise we'd die.

If I can feel passion for it, others will feel the passion seeing me.

Tour blog, March 2003 – New Orleans
I performed at an Original Music Series at O'Flaherty's Irish Pub on Toulouse, central French Quarter. Wonderful pub with 3 rooms for stages, we performed upstairs to a select songwriter crowd. I experimented some more with my loop station which is really giving me the opportunity to improvise there and then on stage. I'm loving it. The show was a lot of fun and I downed a cheesy nachos and 2 red wines - later, Port O'Call for a burger (I had a yummy baked potato and mushrooms.) By the way, it is quite well known that people eat A LOT here. You don't see the tummy tucked sizes of Hollywood in these parts. Food... and Spirits... are a central force of life.

Back to the little pad above the noisy club... Toni and I settled in the living room to sleep and dream of pirates and ghosts. Wednesday was going to be our tourist day. Up again to slimy (mmm yum more) coffee, and we hit the streets to see what the French Quarter was all about. We had more cafe au lait and beignets and then it was mask and harlequinn buying. We wandered down Bourbon street by day as they were cleaning up to go to sleep, and we sat by the Mississippi watching the paddle boat. Cajun shrimp for lunch, more walking down Royal Street (the upmarket Art district), consignment of cds at the hip and cool Tower Records on Decatur and then back to O'Flaherty's for my One Woman Show. I performed 3 hours at the pub in the ballad room, with great sound, and a cool vibe. I was SO excited to have my own show right here in the heart of New Orleans, surrounded by clubs that hosts the finest music there is. Here I was, gilli moon, amongst the greatest jazz and blues. I was thrilled. I will remember this forever. I improvised a lot with my new toy, and played my piano with the soul that was around me. I was in my element. I brought 3 people to tears and Sandy, the Manhattan girl at heart, was already insisting that David Letterman was my next port of call and that she was going to make the call the next day. Ha Ha. I just wanted to see an alligator.

After what I thought was an awesome show Toni and I headed off for a night of partying on Bourbon Street. "When in Rome do as the romans do...." The street, at midnight, was Packed with college kids, as well as retired tourists in their 60s and the locals who dressed in beads and crazy headware. The clubs and pubs, next door to each other on either side of the street, were pumping with music, from

R&B, to Jazz, Dixieland, alternative rock and dance. It was all happening. Crowds were leaning against the railings of club balconies with girls taking their tops off while the cat calls issued below. It was like New Year's Eve and this is every night of the week. Girly bars, 'one drink per set' minimum bars, daiquiri stands, and hot dog stands line the streets. I knew this was going to last all night, but I had seen enough after 2 hours and so we scooted down the quiet Royal street admiring the beautiful terrace houses along the way. We passed many interestingly dark and bohemian bars that lent themselves to a total Twin Peaks, macabre atmosphere. Let's just say, this is a really dark town ,and secrets behind the doors one could only imagine. There is a lot of history here, a lot of superstition, legends and myths and contemporary characters that make you wonder if we are living in a dream.

Blog entry: Houston TX, March 2003

So I loaded in my gear, grabbed a drink, and chatted with the locals. The Rhythm Room is a great room to perform in, in Houston, and the sound is impeccable. The lighting was terrific too. This time, I decided to record my set on my DAT player. I hadn't done this yet. I had by now 2 weeks to master this phrase recorder/loop station so i was ready to hit the peddle to the metal. I once again experimented with some vocal harmonies and percussion with my toy.. I'm really enjoying the spontaneity and improvisation I'm doing lately, thanks to my toy. Plus, the jazz improvs of New Orleans has really started my juices flowing. I played a 45 min set and was very much at peace performing, enjoying the tape rolling and the cool vibe. My lighting was fantastic, with every lull and thunder on the keys illuminated by the change of lights by the engineer, Jerry. John the manager of the club/ cum bar tender, supplied some nice red wine as I sat signing CDs and chatting with new fans.

Taos, New Mexico, March 2003

At 6pm we found Cafe Tazza, my gig for the evening. They had a piano which was cool, so I left the keyboard in the car. But it was snowing tonight and that means, ... not many people. I came back from the car with some of my cables and was followed in by a local Indian guy who was asking everyone off the street for money. I sat down to drink my tea and watched him sit next to a woman from the Oklahoma/Texan border with a huge turban around her head. He asked her for 45c so he could buy a cup of coffee, to which she replied "I only have tea bags." He took it, smelled it and asked if he could take it home to his family. They subsequently picked up a conversation, quite in depth and I thought "wow, a match made in heaven." I began my set to about 5 people in this adobe style coffee house wondering if I was going to make it through the 2 hours. But I did, and some people came and went and overall it was fun: I sold a few cds, a book and got some tips and .. a tea bag.

Blog entry: Manhattan, August 2003

First night was right in the heart of Greenwich Village, on 4th Street, near Blue Note, and all the cool venues. I was in heaven. I used their keyboard which was hilarious because the middle A note was really, really, loud compared to every other note so every time i played it DONGGGGGGGGGGGGGGGGG. I cracked up during a sensitive moment, vocally, then hitting the DONGGGGG again. Who cares. It's Art.

Everyday becomes one subway blur of holding on tight to the subway poles, sub-terrain heatwaves (it's like Singapore down below) and staring at the subway map long enough to know that you really are in Manhattan! Blue, red, yellow lines on the map going this way and that. No wonder I'm getting dizzy! We hit university town, around Hudson and Christopher (christofaw!) that night for a songwriters night at Caffe Sha Sha. A she she kind of caffe with a double ffs to make you know it's she she. I found it comforting and cool except that the as much as everyone was quite talented (they really were) I just realized how different us L.A. folk perform to the New Yorkers. I guess 9/11 hit their hearts pretty bad because nearly every song was sad and dark and slow and weepy. But it was fun nevertheless.

The next day I headed on down to the Bitter End on Bleecker street for a last minute awesome show. They have this honky tonk piano that you can tell has been played on by the best of them and a lot of them over many years as it was almost crunchy to play. I had to stand most of the time to bare my weight down on it to make any cool sound, otherwise it just didn't move, and it was slightly off pitch which most old famous pianos are. But the room was, well, awesome. Playing the Bitter End is like playing the Whisky or the Troubadour in L.A. It's a famous haunt and a "must".

I had an AWESOME gig for Sony /Columbia Records and Mary Guibert for the Jeff Buckley Cd and DVD launch. If you're not familiar with Jeff Buckley, please read about this talented soul who left this world too early, at www.jeffbuckley.com. Mary, his mother and taking care of his Estate, put on a most amazing event at Sin-e, a venue that Jeff used to perform at regularly. Now on Attorney Street in the East Village, Sin-e was always supportive of Jeff and other singer-songwriters. Tonight was a celebration of a DVD interview and new CD of recordings Jeff did at Sin-e when he was alive. With a bunch of Sony dudes sitting on seats in the corner, and the rest of the 300 crowd standing afixed to the stage, Mary hosted several Artists who were inspired by Jeff Buckley (personally "grace" is on my stereo every morning almost!). I was the first Artist and I had 300 eyes watching and standing and applauding. very honored to have been chosen to perform as an Artist inspired by Jeff, in front of all his diehard fans. People traveled all over the world to get to this concert ;) what a blast!!!!

Blog Entry: Atlanta GA Sept 9, 2003
Eddie's Attic is the hot spot of Atlanta to perform in.. and it's the Monday night Open Mic that is the tester for all new Artists coming in to
town. People come from all over the world to sing on a Monday night, and tonight gilli moon was steppin' up to the plate.
Having disembarked my little PSR282 Yamaha again and spent the 15 minutes building the keyboard stand (ya need these screws and screwdriver to get it set up but travelling disassembled it almost fits in your purse) I got my traditional before-gig merlot with Toni, and waited for my time on. We also spent time with Joanne's friends Lisa and Alyse.No.5 and I was up for two songs. Got them hooting and hollering with some clap along songs - Temperamental Angel

and Tiny Diamonds.. and then back to my merlot to try and appreciate the rest of the Artists.... I discovered that this was a professional open mic competition where there would be 3 chosen out of 20 to play again, and the winner gets .. a big fat wad of cash.. all of $60. Well we'd been on the road so what the heck, we needed the money, even just to pay for the food and drinks for the night! So I sweated and poured my soul and heart out. And besides, we all waited 'till midnight to see who won. What a long long day... again.

Well long story short, I didn't get chosen (was it that jinx on me as I never win a competition and is that why I hate them so much?) - but Kim Shar-Meredith was chosen and won so at least someone I knew got the gold. Besides, she came in from Hawaii, sung like Melissa Etheridge, stomped her foot and winked at you a thousand times so I think the winking and stomping certainly deserves $60 don't you?

Blog Entry: London Canada, Sept 20, 2003

I've just realized we are doing a zig zag tour. I thought I was the only Artist who designs silly tour directions. Not that Eric (Idle) had a choice to go in a straight line.. sometimes you have to be at the beck and call of promoters and of course, venues, and their availability. But this Canadian leg is quite absurd... Check this out. We started, going north from the State of New York, by going to Toronto. We then went about an hour to Belleville, then staying in Toronto we went the other way to Kitchener. Back to Toronto, and then we went north 5 hours or so to Ottawa, ... then 6 hours south past Toronto to London where we are now. Then we have to go all the way past Toronto, past Ottawa to Montreal in Quebec. What a riot! Anyway, we can pretty much sleep on the bus most of the nights we drive. See what we are doing now is no longer staying in hotels for a bit. We drive overnight to a venue, pull up while we are sleeping, and when we arise we saunter in to the venue, shower and start loading in (me, I'm on deck around noonish for the crew.) We work all afternoon setting up, then we eat dinner, and... yabbadabbadoo, it's show time around 7.30/8pm. We do the show, standing ovations, and then we load out. Back on the bus and English and Mike, our bus drivers, drive us to our next destination while we sleep rocking gently like on a motor boat. I'm loving it. Others... well they miss the 5 star hotel!

Travel stats of my tour with Eric Idol: 15,705 miles in 3 months, across the United States and Canada, to 49 venues in 90 days

Morale to the entwining story of my touring?

Enjoy the journey.

Tips on touring for performers

1. TOUR – get out in the world. Get out of your living room, be brave and share your Art with the world.

2. There is no point in touring if you don't have anything to promote.

3. Be your own booking agent. Don't be afraid to pick up the phone. Use online and book resources like Musicians Atlas, Sonicbids, Indie Venue Bible. Songsalive! touring map of the world, and so many more. There are more resources at artistalive.com.

4. Think outside the box – different performances – try different gigs like house concerts in your home (there is a website of the same name), art galleries, cafes, book stores, cruise boats, parks, street performances at malls and markets, and online virtual performances (ustream.com is fun for this).

5. Consider only doing effective performances that are promoting a particular thing, like your new CD, or a new band line up.

6. Try changing your performance so it's a little different. Consider different musicians (harp, electric violin, street rapper) to add flavor to your shows. Wear interesting costumes, masks, or a signature hat. Don't be afraid to go beyond your comfort zone and risk! That's what Art is all about!

7. Make relationships with the venue bookers. They are part of your network. Build your best venues that you can keep going back to.

8. Work with others, but just don't rely on others to make it happen for you. Try picking up the phone and booking yourself. It's not hard. It just takes time.

9. Substantial yet effective performances. (don't get over saturated) – I don't believe in lots of gigs. I believe in selective brilliant gigs that showcase you well and also don't fill up your fans' e-mail inboxes. Be out in the world, directly to your fans. It's not just a digital world. At least not yet. Space out your shows or find new regions. If you bombard your neighborhood, you might run out of people wanting to see you!

10. Back up your tours with effective public awareness campaign (see my *Art of Self-Promotion* chapter).

11. Always have a product to sell (good, great music/merchandise, plus some giveaways).

12. ALWAYS have an e-mail list and send out effective newsletters and update your online blog, inviting your fans to stay with you on the journey.

13. Micro-marketing/regional touring – start in one place and then slowly expand the region (say, state by state). Do the North West, then the Mid West, then East Coast. Or if in Europe, perform the U.K., then make your way to France, Italy, Germany etc. The idea is to create a groundswell in one area, go on to the next, but then keep going back to where you started. This is a spiral effect.

14. Touring is important. It doesn't have to be worldwide. It doesn't have to be in the back of a combi van, with 5 smelly musicians sweating and starving. But it's important to be out in the world.

*There should be albums like "The Wall"...
that starts in a place and takes you on a ride
through highs and lows and brings you out at
the end. I can't just go into the studio and
record a couple of songs.
- gilli moon*

PART 3: THE MASTER

Taking it all in, and living your Art and your dream

Relinquishing control
is the ultimate challenge
of the spiritual warrior
The Runes

25. Freedom warrior

Life on the road as a touring Artist has its stories, and also its lessons. Four hours sleep doing the red eye from L.A., via Atlanta, I arrived in Knoxville, Tennessee. I had no idea where that was on the map except that it is a three hour drive from Nashville and is also in Tennessee. But that's where the commonality ends. Instead of music being its heart, the Smoky Mountains is its claim to fame, amongst also having a reputable university, and once a World Fair.

The first thing I noticed about the Knoxville airport is sandstone walls. The gates and whole airport is built with a very nice indoor facade of sandstone. Then, as you walk down the corridor to baggage claim, there's a gorgeous water fountain, with dozens of live plants. It's, well, pretty. I never would have thought I'd use that word about an airport. It is a welcome relief to the dank grayness of LAX.

I'm performing and speaking at this year's Indiegrrl Women in the Arts Festival/Conference at Knoxville this weekend, and just checked in to the Holiday Inn World's Fair Park. In 1982, this is where the World Fair was and the famous Rubick's cube was revealed here. In fact, in the lobby is the huge Rubick's Cube statue (it's basically a giant Rubick's cube) that was displayed back then. I feel like I'm living part of history. I'm staying on the very exclusive 11th floor (you need a key to access this floor in the elevator). It's a touch of class, amongst a hotel that I don't believe has been renovated since '82, except for my room, which is pretty swanky I have to say.

Cut to 3 days later... I have spent this time performing at showcases, and speaking on panels. I also conducted my "Successful Artist Entrepreneur" workshop. I spoke to a hundred women and men about the essentials of being the "Warrior Artist" and the "business minded Artist". I also conducted several one-on-one mentoring sessions.

Basically, many performing Artists converge together for this power packed weekend to perform, learn, network and build long lasting music friendships. Most are indie Artists, all doing their best to make a career of their music, and become successful. Not all were looking for a record deal. In fact many loved the notion of staying independent and learning the ropes to record their own music, release it, promote it, and hopefully make a living from it. Others were seasoned pros, wanting to be amongst like minded Artists for a weekend. It truly is powerful and unique, to be amongst like-minded talented Artists.

In my teachings this weekend, I discovered there was a common thread amongst the Artists and what they were searching for: **FREEDOM**.

Freedom to tour and perform whenever they wanted; freedom to pursue their Artistic dream, without being inhibited by a day job, lack of money or lack of resources; freedom to write songs; freedom to be who they want to be in their lives, and not trapped by past thoughts, fears, people's perceptions, responsibilities; freedom to create and pursue this naturally challenging career with the time it takes to invest in it; and so forth.

This desire for freedom, although not necessarily mentioned directly, was definitely the underlying current in the questions I received, and the conversations and discussions that took place.

As an Artist, I am constantly exploring freedom in my creativity. I have spent quite a few years studying the path of the spiritual warrior and the essence of being that is the pursuit of freedom. You'll see by my company name, Warrior Girl Music, and my nick name "warrior girl" that I carry this mantra close to me.

> *"I realize that I am always free to let go*
> *and observe my life"*
> *- Wayne Dyer*

Freedom in the music business means the *ability to be in control of your own career* and at the same time not be in control

of anything, and let the winds of Heaven guide us in our destiny. Let's take a look at the first part of that phrase: being in control.... It's an amazing opportunity to have a sense of freedom with our Artistry, without having to be dictated by companies that are guided by budgets, competition and the commercial machine. Independence from that means you can drive your own career, and be free to create whatever you want - from writing your songs, to producing unique music albums - different, alternative, out of the box - to performing with uniqueness and diversity.

Who says we need to be like the formula on radio? Embrace the fact that you can be different from all that. There are enough people in this country who will love your music without you having to be number 1 on radio which is part manipulated anyway. Many bands fall under the radar of so-called "commercial success" (radio play, MTV video rotation, street press, Grammy awards, etc.) yet can have a lifelong, financially abundant career with a huge fan base. This can be done through being totally unique, different and out of the mainstream, by touring extensively, and knowing how to brand themselves on an independent level.

Being an independent Artist means you can create what you want, and then allow the right people who love what you do, come to you, rather than create packaged songs to an already saturated market which is commonly referred to as the "lowest common denominator". You have the opportunity to be different... to not just spew out the same ol' music that most of us are tired of hearing. We want something fresh, new, unique. The once loved mp3.com, Napster.com and now XM Satellite radio and iTunes are true representations that people are ready to hear something new, even if that means going on **that arduous** search through the Internet waves to find a little piece of unique **"gold"**

So who has the gold? You do. Artists have **that** divine gift called "imagination" that allows us to be totally different with what we create. So *be different.* There's an amazing sense of freedom in that. Freedom to discover new sounds, new packaging, new marketing ideas. From the beginning to the end, you have that freedom to do what you want, how you want, no strings attached.

Freedom is also about coming from a certain place of non-attachment with our Art. Having "no" control in the process can also be a very liberating thing, and avoids any deflated expectations. Sometimes we have to just "let go" and allow the process of our creations, and our destiny/careers/dreams, to unfold on its own accord.

Let's take a look at the writing process for a moment. Writing songs, or creating anything, even a painting, is like tapping into a creative source that speaks to us. We can't force it, or we get blocked. We just have to be open to it. Once open, we can be very prolific. I'm always surprised that my best writing is when I just brainstorm and let the words flow. Sometimes I even "let go" of trying so hard (maybe even turn the TV on or something to take my mind off the pressure), and all of a sudden the song comes to life. How many songs have you written in the car, or doing something completely different? The words can't stop coming at you can they?

In the studio, the Art of production is about the freedom of allowing the song to tell us what it needs. We can't force it. We become the observer... allowing the pieces to come to life, as we merely conduct.

Being the observer doesn't mean we no longer care about the process. No, what it means is that we don't let our mind, our thoughts, our emotions or our worries get in the way.

> "If a warrior is to succeed at anything,
> the success must come gently,
> with a great deal of effort but with
> no stress or obsession."
> ~Carlos Castaneda

Being open to a different path

Let's take a look at career projections. I always talk about defining success on one's own terms, rather than the commercial model. I also remind myself and others that even though we can have all these big dreams, and create plans.... it will never turn out the way we planned... and that's a great thing. We may project a certain future for ourselves, but ultimately, the universe, destiny, fate, whatever you want to call it, has other plans. These plans are part of the divine mystery of "why we are here" and as Artists we can respect that because it's all about creativity in the end, and all about freedom. By not being so **attached** to certain outcomes, we will never be let down. Instead, we will be offered wonderful gifts, which is part of the magic and mystery of it all.

I had an "aah haa" moment with an Artist at this Indiegrrl Conference this weekend. She had a one-on-one session with me and we were talking about how she wanted to leave her day job, as a social worker, and go into full time music as a touring and performing Artist. But she didn't know how to transition from earning a strong salary as a social worker, into the music world where she was currently making no money doing coffee houses and the like. She also wondered if she was talented enough to compete in the music business and couldn't really figure our her competitive advantage (her talent + uniqueness). Still, her passion is music and she really wanted to transition over. I asked her, "what do you sing about?". She responded, "about relationships, my truth, and sometimes the stories of the kids I counsel through my day job."

I offered a suggestion to perhaps explore some of the venues and outlets through her work, where she could perhaps perform to the kids, or the parents or other social workers, and thereby taking a different path (rather than the traditional music venues) to sing at. This was an ahh haa moment. Her eyes lit up and she started to smile. For the next half hour we brainstormed all of these ideas about how she could build some shows in her arena, where she could sing positive songs that would help in healing and be therapeutic. She saw visions of herself singing at schools, and even to general adults about abuse prevention, and various strong topics that she wrote about. She no longer felt blocked in not knowing how to access traditional venues, and realized she knew way more opportunities in her work field, than she realized previously, as to get her music out here.

In 30 minutes, this Artist became free. She freed herself from the bondage of her expectations of *having* to pursue her music career like everyone else, but instead find her *own* path, a different path, and quite possibly a more abundant and higher purpose path.

With discipline comes freedom

The book, "The Way of the Warrior" talks about the warrior who sets aside all distractions such as self pride or the desire to waste time or energy on the mundane. *"Eliminate the unnecessary", with a Zen perfection of "free-mindedness".* With freedom from distraction, the warrior becomes "emancipated to pursue perfection in all things". For us, the Warrior Artist, that means to cut away, like a sword, all that doesn't serve us, in order to pursue excellence as an Artist, and have the freedom to do what we want. This takes an incredible amount of discipline.

How can we find freedom to create, pursue our career, and manage all the business side of music along with being the Artist? How can we find the time to be free, unconfined by the walls of a day job, financial burdens, so many hours in the day, the multitude of tasks we need to get done as a creator, and a business person?

It means that we need to adopt discipline in our day to day lives, in order to accomplish it all. In my view, that means practicing, on a daily basis, some very important and effective warrior THINGS. Here are mine:

- **Clear the clutter**, and the superfluous from your life- all that is unnecessary. That may mean as simple as getting your desk in order, to something complex and life changing as a job you don't like doing, or projects that are wasting your time. Focus, instead, on what DOES serve you, that is part of your broader dreams and goals in life: and focus/zone in on them.

- **Remove the obstacles**, both external and internal. Perhaps you live too far away from the hub of the city you want to perform in. Work towards moving. Need some money? Get a job. In a sour relationship? End it.

- **Find clarity.** Get really clear with who you are and what you want. This can take years. By doing the exercises in the first half of this book, I hope you get clear a lot quicker. Finding clarity also means getting specific. If you want to increase your financial yearly wealth (so you can do the things you want to do), get specific on how much that is. $50K? $100K? $1mil? How much do you want? Write it down.

- **Feel inspired.** Finding the inspiration in your day to day process is so important. Lose the stuff that doesn't inspire you, and move towards things that do.

- **Use discipline** as a tool for personal freedom: use my time management exercises, build your priorities, understand what it means to be organized.

○ **Keep it simple**. Too many things, desires, wants, tasks, projects, avenues, ideas, create too many distractions, lost opportunities, missing arrows: don't let your head get too fuzzy. Just keep it simple. *You can do it all – but you can't do it all at the same time!*

○ **Being one** with the universe and its timing might sound esoteric and airy-fairy, but if you believe in a higher power, or a universal law, then you'll understand that you don't have to FORCE your success to come to fruition…. Most of the time, you just have to get out of your own way and let it happen, its own way, when the timing is right.

○ **Trust that all will be taken care of** speaks similarly to the above point, with the added notion that you need to trust in your path, your instincts, your gut, and that everything happens for a reason and it will ALL BE OK.

○ **Seeking no one else's approval but your own** – I repeat this notion throughout this book because it's important. Listen to others, learn from others, take feedback and advice. But at the end of the day, you are the ONLY one to approve of what you want to do and the choices you make. This is YOUR life and it will be different to anyone else's path (you are unique).

○ **Do whatever it takes to make it happen**: this is very much about pursuing excellence on a daily basis. You want to not only do your best, but you want to do what it takes (within your reality and with proper reason without hurting anyone else to make it happen). You have to be willing to defend your vision and dreams to the world, and stand by it with conviction. Nothing else matters.

○ **Have personal freedom as the goal**: it's a lifelong journey, but freedom is truly an amazing place to arrive to, either far away in the future, or little glimpses of it on a daily basis.

○ **Create change**, within and without: your mission, if you choose to accept it, is to create change in YOUR life (grow as a human being and transcend to a higher awareness of yourself) as well as CREATE CHANGE in others. This is where having a life mission comes into play. Through your Artistry, you have the responsibility to create a SHIFT around you (consciousness, thoughts, etc.). Think about what you write about, sing about or create about. What is it that you WANT TO SAY? What is your STORY? What do you want to change or affect in this world? Mine is a commitment to inspire passion, creativity, freedom and love in each and every one of us through my songs that I write and perform, as well as the stories and teachings I offer.

○ **Take the path least traveled** - no struggle - with the least resistance: We are here for a good time, not a hard time. I like finding the path of least resistance (that doesn't hurt me or others, or make me feel like I'm on a rollercoaster ride), yet at the same time be a DIFFERENT ROAD. I don't want to live someone else's life. I want to live MY life, and it's a unique life. How I emulate that as an Artist will actually make me UNIQUE and therefore a marketable Artist, with music that people will want and shows they will want to watch. BE DIFFERENT, and try new ways to navigate this amazing journey that is your life.

All of these sound easy in writing. The reality is, it's a life long journey of practicing Warriorship. I'm still a baby at it, and that's ok: I'm a lifelong Artist so I have all my life to pursue my Warriorship, my excellence, and my Artistic passions: that's why I say I'm "LIVING MY DREAM" because my dream is in the process of doing and learning it all.

Blog feedback:
"This really came at a good time for me, with an album recently completed and a bunch of fear rising in the face of my ambitions for the next steps. It's good to be reminded that it is a journey. I'm reminded of a Joseph Campbell quote,

"Sometimes we have to give up the life we've planned in order to have the one that awaits us".

So, thanks,"
- Brett Robin Wood, Artist

gilli moon's *silent warrior:*

The silent warrior is in all of us. It's not about war, nor fighting and definitely not about struggle. It's about an inner peace and a whole lot of courage to face all fears in un-chartered waters, finding the path least travelled and at the same time, finding the path of least resistance. I take responsibility for myself. I follow a preserved set of personal freedoms. I am not without flaw, and in tolerating that I see and use my strengths. The warrior, the Artist, the professional, can only be effective when free to make decisions on their own. The biggest secret is to do what you love most. Take on the Zen spirit! I am a warrior girl and I encourage everyone to tap into their warrior within.

26. "DIT": do it together

I seem to be asked to speak on quite a few music industry panels, at music conferences, about DIY (Doing It Yourself). It's the big catch phrase of the decade. "Yeah, I'm a DIY Artist", "I'm Indie all the way, man!" ["Indie" meaning "Independent".]

Having been one of the first DIY Artists since the Internet came out, I realize that DIY is now changing as a definition for indie Artists. I think most Artists grow up into being DIY as a norm these days (more so than starting out wanting to be a signed Artist to a major label). The current shift in the music business has molded Artists to automatically market themselves as "Indie" and "DIY". With the Internet and social network era that we live in, it's so easy to put your music up on the web, and communicate with your fans directly. Social networking online has taken over from face-to-face meetings and gatherings. It's so accessible to us, now, to reach people right across the world. So we don't wait so much for a big company to "come sign us". Instead, we're out there, wearing our DIY sign on our forehead as a matter of normalcy.

But what we are facing now, in this new music revolution, is a new wild west, where no one really knows what is truly going to be the next dawn. So we are all navigating our way through it all, trying to create revenue streams in this ever decreasing revenue market for songwriters and Artists who, ultimately, "make" the music business exist. Yet DIY Artists are struggling because everyone is doing SO much, touring A LOT, constantly WORKING it and never CEASING with all the doingness.

Is it time that Artists make smarter decisions and choices so that they can build revenue? Does one just continue to go, go, go, as an answer to finding success? Does one continually plow forth alone, doing everything? **I think not.**

I think it's time to change the phrase DIY - do it yourself,

DIT - Do It *Together.*

"DIT": do it together

I don't think becoming a successful Artist is about doing things yourself. I think it's about **building community**, of like minded people, to create shared revenue, visibility and success.

OK so here's the crux of it. Listen good: **there is no "us" and "them" anymore.** "They", "them", "others" that are the BIG industry moguls, against the tiny Artists. This notion has died.

There is no fight, and there are no sides to take... anymore. You can be Indie, and you can be signed. You can be self-released, and you can be commercially distributed. There is a "we" that we need to recognize now, in order for the music industry to survive, and for the music that we make to be respected and protected.

"DIY" – Do it yourself, is an overly used term. It's almost painful for me to hear it over and over again, as if it's an Albatross hanging from your neck. Sure, go ahead... be DIY. But here's my new theory: **DIT: Do It Together.**

I am quite invigorated with the state of the music industry because Artists and labels now have an opportunity to work together on a new future. Labels are making new deals where Artists are more in control. Joint ventures are cropping up, and 360 deals are a buzz word (basically labels are taking a share of all revenue Artists' make, not just CD/music sales.) It might sound a little fishy, but in reality, it is asking for Labels to work harder now on the other areas of an Artist's life, not just on recording their album. Labels can help with their web presence, their merchandise, their touring, and be accountable too.

DIT means that Indie Artists don't have to feel like they're doing it alone. They are independent, yes... building their business as any entrepreneur should. *But you can't do it alone.* You will need people who support you: your team. We are in this world together, for common purposes.

I'm inspired by the opportunities at hand. They are what you make of them. You can go back to your coffee and TV after you read this chapter, or you can get on the Internet, turn the music up loud and take advantage of the sea of possibilities awaiting at your fingertips.

Collaborating for a higher purpose

After spending my twenties navigating this music industry alone as an Artist and dreamer, I decided to reach out and ask for help. I didn't feel like I had the energy and stamina to face the obstacles alone. So I decided to sign a record deal that I thought would secure a place in the world for my Artistry. I also took on a manager and had a booking agent for my gigs. I spent money on classes to learn more about the biz, and I paid producers to produce my music. That record deal fell through and I ended up releasing music on my own label which kind of made me well known as a staunch independent Artist: the **warrior girl** – "she can battle any obstacle and leap tall buildings in a single bound!" Those key people have changed in my life over time. I dropped the managers and booking agents and producers, and decided I could do things better myself with my own record label. I certainly achieved a lot on my own since making that decision to run my *own* affairs, and my fans loved that. Other Artists looked up to me and wanted to become a patriotic "Indie" just like me.

My competitive edge has been that I was one of the first "truly DIY, Independent" Artists, and that I am known to be self-made and self-empowered. However...

...unbeknown to most, I really haven't done it all on my own. I've worked with a myriad of people who co-create with me, consult to me, and provide services to my company. The key to success is being able to know how to access resources, and then be able to use them to benefit yourself, and others, in a positive moving-forward way. This collaboration is called 'co-creating'.

My road travels have provided me an amazing opportunity to meet, connect and share with many Artists of all forms and genres. It's through their gift to me that I have learned about *collaboration*. This is an important word, and some Artists find it a hard word to grasp. Actually not just Artists, people. We see it misused in politics, in large institutions, in business and amongst kindred souls/Artists and the like. Heck, siblings learn about it and find it tough. The opposite of collaboration, to me, is *competition*. We live and work in a competitive world. But the new paradigm is **collaboration**: building positive relationships, fostering good-will amongst each other, nurturing others' talents and applauding them when they "do good" rather than criticize or judge.

Collaboration for Artists can provide amazing opportunities from the very seeds of creation. In the songwriting process, a song can be even better working it out with a co-writer. In promoting yourself as an Artist, team building and street teams, working with others for a common cause is the vehicle for success stories. We don't need to be doing this alone. There is strength in numbers. I find the Artist-to-Artist (p2p) networks (now called "social networks☺ have been such a positive vehicle for me and other Artists to get our music out there, sharing gig nights, swapping gigs (you play in my city and I'll book you, and I'll play in yours and you book me), cross linking on each others' websites, cross promoting with flyers. The whole phenomenon of online discussion groups, meeting rooms and blogging have built collaboration to be the answer to building fan bases. Artists become fans of other Artists, helping each other, chatting online, supporting, providing tips, opportunities, advice, road ideas, touring opportunities. It's all through collaborating.

The new music business is an **Artist driven business**, where collaboration dominates competition; where deals are written and created for both parties' interests, and where everyone can prosper. Artists have more to negotiate and barter now, having more to offer, developing themselves, seasoning themselves. These are important times. I hope Artists also understand that building relationships is not just being "noticed" and "discovered" for their talents as musicians and songwriters, but because they can *offer* something to the labels, to the retailers, to the businesses they begin to do business with.

Find out what **You have to offer others** first before you demand to know what they can do for you. Just because you're talented, doesn't mean you're worth doing business with. Collaboration means discovering what you can provide for someone else, too.

We are asked in life: Why Am I here? Why Am I doing this? I encourage you to find a larger mission in life, beyond your own internal dreams and egos and desires - a bigger picture, a larger purpose. Whether it's global harmony, or changing perspectives, or doing good for others, or bringing a higher consciousness - our music, our Artistry are powerful in creating amazing things, beyond our little goals.

Once you tap into that higher purpose you will find many, many people will gather around you to support you in who you are and what you do.

Enjoy this journey...
...it's life long, you know... and you don't need to be on it alone.
gilli moon

27. Defining success on your own terms

"The one thing that can be more disappointing than failure is success itself, because success doesn't always bring us what we thought it would."
- Ernie J. Zelinski

Think successful to be successful

In my first book, I delved into the notion quite strongly that as an Artist you must define success on your own terms, and not by some other commercial standard. In this chapter, it is important that I reiterate my 1st book's sentiments here, to pack a punch, and I'll expand on a lot of new things too. I wrote, that success **does not necessarily become apparent to us**; and two, **success does not always mean money**. If you think that making a lot of money will make you a success, then ask yourself, "Why do I want that money?"

Is it so that it will give you the resources to continue creating? Is it so that others see you as successful and therefore make you feel better? Or is it something else?

Your reasons are important because if you don't get that award, or the bundle of cash, or reach for that goal, you will have to ask yourself, "What if I never succeed?"

As Ernie Zelinksi says, "Ultimately, you will make yourself successful or unsuccessful just by the way you define success."

If you want to be successful you have to think successful.

Have your own definition of success

In the Arts industry, in the entertainment industry, in the writing industry...well, in any industry really, achievement has always been equated with a level of success. But what is success? Is it measured by what others think of us? Do we have to reach a certain echelon set by our peers, before society, before we become successful? Is winning a Grammy Award, an Oscar, or a literary book prize the proof of success?

> "We don't always know what makes us happy. We know, instead, what we think SHOULD. We are baffled and confused when our attempts at happiness fail...We are mute when it comes to naming accurately our own preferences, delights, gifts, talents. The voice of our original self is often muffled, overwhelmed, even strangled, by the voices of other people's expectations. The tongue of the original self is the language of the heart."
>
> -- Julie Cameron

It has to come from within... your measurement of success. Perhaps, if we see that our goals have been realized, we can then say, "Yes, I have succeeded!"

Sometimes by giving yourself small achievable goals along the way we can then see the achievement. If we long for that burning, pie in the sky goal, we may never attain that or perhaps it's a long way down the road. Does that mean we haven't been successful until that moment of achievement? What happens in the meantime?

It's how you see your Art and how you truly measure your achievements that will answer these questions for you. Only you can answer them. Don't wait for others to answer them for you. As mentioned earlier, **seek no one else's approval but your own.**

To succeed, spend more time investing into your own growth and progress, rather than winning the approval of others. *That* is such a waste of invaluable time.

You could spend your entire life wasting time trying to impress others. That's wasted energy. You have to do your Art for *you*. No one else. If success comes in ways you or anybody else hadn't thought it would (which is usually the case, for our outcomes are rarely how we plan,) then that is what is right for *you*. Just because you see the Celine Dions and Britney Spears's of the world selling records, getting airplay and so forth, it doesn't mean that they are any more successful as professional Artists than you.

What is success to you? It's not all about fame and fortune, nor other's definitions. Perhaps it's simply about happiness and joy, personal fulfillment, progress (it's not about the end result) and personal excellence. Seek no one else's approval but your own. Don't fear anything. Be persistent. Have drive, commitment, focus, energy and.... **PASSION.**

A great way of defining your success patterns is to write down your achievements. Go back within just this last year and write down all the accomplishments you have achieved. Then go back the last five years, then ten, then back to your childhood.

Then, draw a straight line forward and plot down the stepping stones you'd like to target along your way to the future. Consider these bus stops. This will help you define your true goals, both personal and professional.

Note that your direct line really takes on a zig zag course. Nothing will be straight ahead. Expect deviation to your course and be encouraged that this journey is what life is all about!

	LIVE ON THE BEACH AND RECEIVE ABUNDANT $
GRAMMY AWARD	
	FAMILY PLANNING
HONE MY GUITAR CHOPS	
	TOUR THE U.S.
RELEASE MY CD	

Success is the journey

While you may put a goal in place and even a direction, don't get dismayed when you find yourself running down a different track. Life is like that. Many people are afraid **to change for fear that they will be seen as copping out.** Many people have way too high expectations which just leads to discontent. Move with the times, follow your instinct. We are not destined to run a straight course, for then we will never experience what we need to experience. Edward de Bono wrote in his book, *I Am Right, You Are Wrong,* that we follow a "zig zag" course, that we hop from left to right, still going forth. Remember though, that if an avenue is not working for you, don't beat a dead horse. Press on. Learn to nurture all your gifts for **success may come to you in many disguises.**

We may not know our direction all the time, but if we listen to our thoughts and heed them, we can only move forward. If we think high, there is no doubt of success, whatever that may be defined for you.

If you accept absolute responsibility for your life and your success, you will become the person you truly want to become.

It's not luck, nor in the stars, nor happening by circumstance, this life of yours. You can't blame the economy, the weather or a dead end job. It's all you. You are responsible for who you are. It's funny too that only the self-proclaimed successful people will be the ones that take responsibility. They know it is self made.

Success is a journey, not a destination
- H. Tom Collard

My husband Jeff and I, were on a Fijian Island. It wasn't a glamorous beach resort. It was right in the middle of the island, nowhere near the ocean. It was hot. About 110 degrees Fahrenheit (40 degrees Celsius). There were mosquitoes, flies and the air was still. We decided to try and hike to the sea, to see if things would be different there. So off we trekked. I kept on asking, "How far do you think the sea is?"

"Not sure. I can't see the water from here. Must be miles away!" Jeff responded.

So we started walking down the hill. The ground was rough, and dirt. There were shanties along the road with Indian Fijian's living in them, washing their clothes in the river, and some bathing from bore wells on their property. They lived in poverty, by Western standards, and yet they waved and smiled at us and seemed so happy. They had a cow or a goat, and maybe a dog. The vegetation along the trail was exotic, luscious green and filled with plantations of corn and some bananas. It was jungle like. We walked for about an hour, and as we traveled we asked the locals where the water was. They pointed "that direction." We still couldn't see the water, but it was fascinating to talk to the locals and witness the inland countryside of this island.

Finally, we came across some mangroves. There was some sand and an old broken down boat on the sand. We had arrived. But where was the water? In amongst the mangroves we could now see the water: a muddy pool of shallow water embraced by the mangrove trees. It was basically marsh land for about 100 yards before any actual ocean. We would never get to the ocean itself, and we wouldn't get to swim.

But I learned something poignant from this experience. I learned that although we had succeeded in reaching the water, the end result wasn't necessarily the highlight: it was the journey that was our success. We loved the walk there, and also the walk back. Doing the walk was EVERYTHING, and way bigger and cooler than where we were aiming.

Enjoy the journey!

Cool definitions of success

Every day, in the U.S newspaper, **"Investor's Business Daily"**, they print, on the Leaders & Success page the **"IBD'S 10 SECRETS TO SUCCESS"**. I'd love to share them with you.

"Investor's Business Daily has spent years analyzing leaders and successful people in all walks of life. Most have 10 traits that, when combined, can turn dreams into reality.

- o   HOW YOU THINK IS EVERYTHING: Always be positive. Think success, not failure. Beware of a negative environment.
- o   DECIDE UPON YOUR TRUE DREAMS AND GOALS: Write down your specific goals and develop a plan to reach them.
- o   TAKE ACTION: Goals are nothing without action. Don't be afraid to get started. Just do it.
- o   NEVER STOP LEARNING: Go back to school or read books. Get training and acquire skills.
- o   BE PERSISTENT AND WORK HARD: Success is a marathon, not a sprint. Never give up.
- o   LEARN TO ANALYSE DETAILS: Get all the facts, all the input. Learn from your mistakes.
- o   FOCUS YOUR TIME AND MONEY: Don't let other people or things distract you.
- o   DON'T BE AFRAID TO INNOVATE; BE DIFFERENT: Following the herd is a sure way to mediocrity.
- o   DEAL AND COMMUNICATE WITH PEOPLE EFFECTIVELY: No person is an island. Learn to understand and motivate others.
- o   BE HONEST AND DEPENDABLE; TAKE RESPONSIBILITY: Otherwise, Numbers 1-9 won't matter."

Some great stuff there, yeah?! Let me say that I stumbled across this towards the end of writing this book, and I felt pretty cool in feeling like I had summarized these points similarly within both my first book and this book. It's a nice reminder.

I hope it inspires you today.

Don't focus on working hard, work hard on your focus

— J.Walker

My secrets to success

Revisiting from my 1st book:
> **Define success as a personal outcome**, not measured by what others think.

Watch and be surrounded by successful people - those you deem in your eyes, for all the good and righteous reasons to be successful. By observing them you are closer to understanding and touching success yourself.

Enjoy the process - If you're hooked only on the goal, the end result, you are going to be miserable. If you enjoy the process, and love what you are doing, that is success in itself. Life (and Art) is a journey. If you don't "make it" by a certain date, don't be disheartened. We are all works in progress. Life is a step by step process. Enjoy the process for it is in the steps that you will ultimately find true happiness in what you are doing. Besides, we are here today, not for some unknown time tomorrow. You never know where you'll be! It's not going to happen in one day. Enjoy the ride.

Focus on your strengths - Do what you do best and don't get distracted. Narrow down your scope to really harness your talents. Luciano Pavarotti's dad to little Luce would say, "Deve scheliere. (You must choose). Choose one chair, for if you try and sit on two, you will only fall between the cracks." Stop doing everything you're mediocre at or that you don't enjoy with a passion. If you are feeling burned out by an activity you do, it's probably not your strength.

Persevere and be conscientious at what you do - Know your mission, and work towards your goals. Take one step at a time and be diligent about it. Use all that you've learned about being a good business person whilst striving for personal, Artistic excellence. Go for it, no matter what. Pursue it to excess. Then you will excel. Think about it, write about it, do it, talk about it, live it, be it. Success is a steady, conscientious effort towards progress. Be responsible and endow your perseverance and efforts. When you are in control, you will find it much harder to give up.

Endow it - To be successful you must position yourself as already successful. Become who you want to be by living your life the way you see it in the future. Be confident, be optimistic, be organized and await the opportunities.

Relinquish - Sometimes by giving up to the will of Heaven, relinquishing strategy and relying on synchronicity (read Julia Cameron's *"The Artist Way"*!), all will be delivered to you. Sometimes the less effort creates more achievement. Listen to your intuition and your heart. They will guide you. *"Ask and you shall receive."* Whether you are religious or not, these words of Jesus Christ ring true.

Exercise: What are your definitions of Success?

Write down what success is to you. Make a great statement or paragraph here:

Write down 5 definitions of success in your life, that relate to your dreams and goals

1.

2.

3.

4.

5.

Fame can be as fleeting as a 4 minute pop song

gilli moon

28. It ALL is all of me

Something about L.A..... this city tricks us into thinking we have "got it going on" but then we could really be spinning wheels.

This city makes it really difficult to concentrate on just one thing. You end up spinning plates, which is not a bad thing. I've always talked about 'diversifying talents' in order to gain opportunities in this business. Spinning those plates means several fingers in several pies. It all tastes good... just... maybe I should go on a diet.

There are so many distractions; so many projects; so many people. So much to do, so little time. Ha ha!

I sit here, in my quiet paradise in this city of angels, with my lava lamp on, paintings around the room, cool groovy music playing, and a huge pile of unfinished business in my computer inbox, plus a stack of papers and projects cluttering my desk and floor, staring at me saying *"start me gilli, fire me up; work on me gilli, I'm going to make you millions; write me gilli, I'm your next important creative project..."*.

These projects plague me so much I feel guilty, as if I haven't handed in an important assignment or essay to my teacher. But the only teacher here is me. I'm placing pressure on myself and I feel bad that I can't get to everything.

I'm happy though. I feel like my piles of to-dos are company for my restless mind, ready, willing and able to just fly into any territory and conquer. I am a servant to my creativity. I have no problem with creative flow. I know so many people have read Julia Cameron's *"The Artist Way"* to help them unblock their creativity so they can be prolific in their Art, or writing. As for me, I have it going on too much. I am a "yes" girl, and love to want to start new projects all the time. But then I have a laundry list of them to complete.

It's funny how we think we know who we are, that we have it all worked out in our minds, and we know what we want. Dreaming big, visualizing and then planning it can be daunting to most, but not to me. I'm a huge dreamer, and a great planner. I love to plan. I love getting the calendar out and plotting out my course of action. This month I'll prepare, record, write. Next month I'm off to Ireland to mentor budding songwriters at a songwriters' retreat. Plus, I have promotions to do for the new album. Following month, a big CD launch in Hollywood, then off to Texas to speak at a music conference and perform. By June I will have released the new Females On Fire compilation of thirty female Artists, started writing my musical film script and recorded a whole album for my new Warrior Girl Music Artist, Holly Light. Then more dreaming, visualizing, plotting and planning. This is all true. This is my life for the next three months. I have a full-on creative schedule called "my life".

I dream of lying on the beach with a margarita in my hand, contemplating how many sand particles are in between my fingers as I dip my toes in the warm ocean.

It ALL is all of me

Life happens when you're not looking.
That's what my friend and music Artist, Max
Sharam, said to me once. It's funny how weeks go
by, even months, and sometimes you can't even
remember what you did. In this city, it can be
because there is SO much to do, and we do SO
much, that it's hard to remember what we did
yesterday unless we write about it.

So write about it. Write about what's
going on with your creativity. Purge it out. Write that to-do list, like a big fat note on
your bathroom wall. Then start crossing off the superfluous stuff: the tasks that you
don't need to do. Eliminate the extraneous and get down to the nitty gritty: the truly
important stuff.

When we begin to see differently, we think differently and we do differently.
Just because everyone else out there is spinning their wheels and pushing along 'till
they burn out, doesn't mean you have to. One amazing project might be better than
a thousand little ones that don't get your full attention.

My whole philosophy of surrendering to the universe is really working.
Lately, I've been listening to what I want to do "in the moment", rather than let my
scattered mind control me and leave me restless. When I truly listen to my inner
self, I start to see the divine plan.

It's stranger still when I realize that the most amazing accomplishments
are ones that didn't get on my to-do list. They are the little things that sneak in
when I'm not looking, and end up being champions. I signed up as the director of a
summer music camp for kids. I thought it would be a quick summer project later in
the year. Little did I realize that this project is becoming a lifelong dream fulfilled, to
share and nurture children in the most beloved area I know: music. I am so excited
that it has consumed my attention for three nonstop weeks as I've been hiring my
teaching staff and promoting the camp for student enrollments. I literally dropped
everything off my list to concentrate on this.

It was a natural choice. Unbeknown to me, when it comes to kids, I melt.
I've spent my whole life dedicated to education and I didn't even realize it. I even
have a Bachelor of Education and thought I'd never use my degree. I've spent the
better part of the last ten years, while pursuing my own music career, also
conducing workshops, speaking on panels and now writing my second book, all
about educating and empowering youth and young adults. I just didn't realize it was
such a strong passion inside me, until I saw these kids jamming on stage the other
day at the camp open house and I realized... gee Gilli.... this is who you are too.... a
teacher.

When I wrote my first book, I was on the speaking circuit and did media
interviews, but all through that I denied I was actually an "author". I just thought I
was a musician/Artist who happened to write. But I get so many letters from people
who've read my book, or seen me speak, or come to one of my workshops, and for
some, it has changed their lives. They feel empowered, and invigorated after

reading my writings or seeing me speak. The teacher in me is probably as strong as the Artist in me. Coming to this realization, and accepting this, is powerful for me.

Listening to our higher destiny is crucial for our happiness and ultimate success. As you know by now with what I write about, success is defined by you, on your terms. So when you begin feeling fulfilled and you know that you are on to something satisfying in every way, creatively, financially, and more, then you know it's right. That's success right there, when you've found your niche.

Pushing in several directions is ok, but when you stop pushing, and you allow it to come naturally, you'll find it all becomes a lot clearer. It's becoming clearer for me. I have nothing to prove anymore when it comes to being an Artist. My fifteen year overnight success story is simply this: I've come to understand who I am, and I'm confident in who I am. I'm talented, happy and much wiser today than yesterday. Everything I know, I'm willing to share, because there is certainly enough to go around.

You don't need any credentials to know who you are. Just faith: faith in yourself and the confidence to go out there and put it all into practice.

What would you do if this was the last year of your life? For one, you'd delete all the little stuff and get on with what matters the most. Secondly, you'd probably not be so concerned about being famous. Fame is fleeting. What's much cooler is the Art of doing.

My husband, who is a very talented Artist, and I were talking about music demos we did when we were young on cheap 4 track machines. We shared a common teenage-hood of staying up 'till the wee hours of the morning tracking seemingly amateur songs and beats, loving the process of creating. It wasn't about the big record deal or being famous; it was about getting through the night and creating an awesome song. Listening back to our demos, we both reckon some of them are better than the expensive recordings we've outputted today in our respective studios, for big albums. There was more creativity and uniqueness flowing in our demos that is inspiring us more right now than anything we've heard! I wrote more songs before I was 22 than I've done ever since. Isn't that wild? I was a creatively flowing tap, never ceasing. Same for him too.

Since those years I have always been creative, but I've also become a producer of projects, and a teacher, and an author/writer, and a business owner, and continuing as a performer. It ALL is all of me, and I'm joyous in that. I might have a lot on my plate, but it's only because I've put it there. I don't have a boss adding tasks to my inbox in a job I don't enjoy. I'm lucky. I'm my own boss. I might be a little hard on myself, and push myself a little for many reasons (to achieve personal best, financial security, project deadlines). But at least I look at a view of my backyard and can wake up when I want to.

Whether you do a lot, or you do a little, it doesn't matter. It's ALL of you. You can be a consummate Artist, prolific in your writing, or you can be choosy and selective, outputting seldomly. You can work part time, or full time for someone else, and still be a professional Artist pursuing your creativity. You can run several businesses or none at all. You can do whatever you feel is right for you. It doesn't

It ALL is all of me

matter. There is no blueprint you have to follow. You are the master of your own destiny.

So do it, do it, do it, or don't. Whatever you do or don't, enjoy the process.

29. The Art of detachment

Real stuff happens in and around our lives. But it's how we respond to it that makes the difference; whether I attach to it or detach from it.

- gilli moon

I have painted my first canvas in over a year. This is a major breakthrough. The flow has returned. Strange that I say this? No. It's actually quite a meaningful point I want to make.

I don't know about you, but I've had a remarkably busy year. Busy, busy, busy. Productive, busy, creative, busy. Get the picture? Busy.

I've conquered many mountains, and been victorious in my endeavors. It's been "business as usual" and I've written songs, performed songs, recorded songs and done many other things in between. But have I also had quiet time to just sit, reflect and ponder the universe? Not much. When I *can* do that, my favorite way is to pour a glass of merlot (I can only average one glass of wine in a blue moon), and with a white, blank canvas inviting me, imploring me... I splash a multitude of colors on it and my mind is able to drift into another world.

Letting go of the world

The world in which we live in constantly demands our attention. It's like a spoiled child insisting on having his say, and we are forced to succumb to it, through the television, the radio, traffic, people, and the Internet: **The big "I"**. We are consumed by the Internet on our computers, on our cell phones. We may as well connect an intravenous tube straight into our brain so we can download music, e-mails and every bit of spam the world wants to throw at us.

But I am as much the culprit as the world is. I hanker for attention; I hunger for a new stage to express myself. I am an Artist of course. This is part of me. The music industry and all that it entails, the good, the bad... has also been part of me. I've been living it, feeling it, dreaming it all my life. It's been my major ambition, to perform, to entertain, to star (from the smallest to the largest stages, I've wanted it all.) I don't think that's bad. It just is... innate: the desire to be heard, to communicate to the world, and to have one's music enjoyed; and out of all that, maybe create some change on this planet. Who knows?

But there is a time to turn it all off, even just for a moment. It is really important to take time out to just "be". I have a song called *"Be"* on my album, "the stillness", that goes like this:

I wanna swim in the sun
I wanna dance in the rain
I wanna feel our hearts beating the same
I wanna be with you....
I am ready this time around, to just... be....

Are you ready to just "be"? Are you able to take a moment and listen to your heart beat, or feel the breath you breathe in and out? Do you know how to stop and take a break? Go for a walk, a swim, a horse ride? Make sure that in the doingness of your lives, you can 'undo' even for a moment, but regularly, to just be... still. It's in this stillness, this emptiness that dreams percolate like a good stew or spaghetti sauce. Sometimes the ingredients aren't the ones YOU create with all your might. Often the magic happens in your life when you're not looking. So stop watching the kettle boil, and go out and play. (Heck, do it right now. Take a moment away from this book for 10 minutes and go watch the Sun, rain or whatever weather outside.)

10 minutes. Count it.

Ok, how did that feel?

Letting go of what you're supposed to feel...

Forever in my dreams, I've been restless... until today. **I am still.** Even as I carry out the motions of everyday living, being and doing, **I am still.** Meaning, I am calm and present, and happy with where I am. I can look back and say, "Hey, It's been OK. I've had a great year. I am in a good place." I couldn't say this before. I was too restless, always wanting more, always being my own self critique and saying, "Well, it was an OK year, but next year will be better, as long as I do this, this and this." Now, however, I can look back in retrospect and appreciate the journey I've traveled, and be happy with where I am at this point in time.

I can also see what lies ahead better. It was always a fog, looking ahead. Now I feel the peace, and feel the abundance. I am amazed at how calm I am able to accept my own fortitude and prosperity.

This is not something one would normally go around exploiting, one's own sense of abundance. They might think you're up yourself, without looking at the major concerns of the world. I mean, how can you feel so abundant, when there are all these major crises on the planet, perhaps even in your own neighborhood, in your own family?

Here lies the problem. Many people don't allow themselves to be thankful for a certain prosperity (not necessarily monetarily) that they have, feeling guilty because others don't have it. This is one of the problems of ambition. **Sometimes we don't realize our dreams because we don't feel we deserve it, and it's not so much because of our own capabilities, but by the pressure around us that we face.** If we see some people living on the street, or war in Iraq, or our own family may work in dead-end jobs, sometimes that influences our own potential. We get caught up in their circumstances, their perceptions and reality.

But this is your reality. YOUR STORY. We will constantly face challenges in the world, but the most important challenge is for us as human beings to become "enlightened". For, if every individual could do that, we wouldn't need Amnesty International or Greenpeace, or soldiers fighting on foreign soil. We would all be at peace with one another. In our own backyard, we would be able to achieve what we wanted, without criticism, because everyone would feel achievement for themselves.

I know, it's a big topic, and I certainly don't want to make this book about global change (though I've thought about writing a book about that). What I mean to show through this is how effective it is to truly be comfortable in your own skin, and not be so affected by dependence on the world in order to achieve personal and creative greatness.

By all means, don't ignore what's going on in the world. In fact, through your creativity, you can create change and healing. But it's important to not collapse into being a victim of your circumstances.

Being a Warrior Artist in this world today means you need more tenacity than ever before. Most of it comes from your inner ability to cut away from the throng of exterior influences, and to remain connected to your inner dreams and goals: *your inner voice.*

Letting go of expectations

Having a certain detachment to the "business/industry" side of things helps too.

Previously, every spark of joy was defined by achievements I made in the music industry. It was like a drug. I needed to have a great gig, or produce an awesome album, and then sell a certain quota, and many other things... in order to feel fulfilled. But now I have detached myself from that notion. **I am no longer beholden to my successes to make me happy.** It is part of me, but it doesn't own me.

I don't need even my Artistry to make me happy. That's a hard one to really fathom, as Artists are so connected to their Art, of course. But if something doesn't occur with your Art, are you going to be disappointed, or even depressed?

There's liberation from not being so dependent on your Art. I've had to let go of a lot of notions about my Artistry in order to feel joy. Otherwise I could be majorly depressed. I've had feelings of my Art holding me captive, and if I don't do something with it, or if it doesn't feed me, then I feel like I have failed my mission in life. This feeling is almost a co-dependent relationship, just like any love relationship that creates disharmony.

Here are some examples:

- ❖ Feeling the need to write a song every day or regularly, and if not, feeling bad about it.

- ❖ Feeling the need to practice your instrument every day, and if not, feeling like you'll lose your "touch".

- ❖ Beating ourselves up (metaphorically speaking of course) over not *doing enough* in one day, whether that's creative, like practicing, performing or writing; or business wise, like e-mailing, phone calls, or connecting with people on our huge to do list.

- ❖ Having a certain expectation that our Artistry (music, writing or otherwise) needs to make us financially self-sufficient, i.e. earning our income solely, or at least mostly, from our Artistry. I don't see a problem with making a living from our Art. It's usually the goal. But to have the expectation can cause enormous psychological pressure for us in the years (and it can take years) before we start getting that.

❖ Having an expectation that our gigs, every single one of them, should give us the ultimate high and that we should feel fulfilled by it and loved by our audience. Some gigs are just a means to an end or could be fulfilling to some but maybe not to you. They may feel disappointing based on your expectation (whether it was filling the room, or selling a certain amount of CDs or not making mistakes on your playing), but yet could have possibly been rewarding in a far different way and you just didn't realize it. Maybe one person went away from that gig and years later becomes your record company exec and remembered you back then, or maybe you changed a person's life by hearing your emotional love song. Who knows

❖ Having an expectation that we have to be just as successful as other Artists we see in those glossy magazines, or even that other indie Artist you met at the conference. You are different. You are unique. Don't even start comparing yourself. And please don't even start to think you're not as talented as someone else. Firstly, talent is individual and unique (what you offer is different to what they offer), and secondly, talent is not really what got them to a level of success that you might be envious or desiring of (there are so many factors that go into commercial success: for one, who you know. Secondly, loads of money (I'm talking hundreds and hundreds of thousands), and who you know, amongst other weird things like timing, being at the right place at the right time (whatever "right" means, 'cause it may not be "right" for you).

As far as I'm concerned, the least attachment we have to our Artistry and the music business, to success, and to OTHERS... the better. One reason is **because most of what happens around us is out of our control. So why try and control it?**

So I opt for detachment. Not in a bad, cut throat way. I am always conscious of the world around me. It actually feeds me for my writing, and I am a humanist. I am very aware of what's going on in the world, and do my bit to create the miniscule of change. But on a daily basis, I cannot be caught up in it all as it will consume me. I cannot be a victim of what people may say or not say about me. I sometimes have to turn off the news. I cannot listen anymore to my own personal demands on how I should excel, do, be, achieve, perform. What is it all for, really?

Is there a reason why I have to write a song every day, or practice my piano every day?

Really. Think about it. Is it perhaps our own personal need for perfection that insists we must be a genius at everything we do? Some singers can not play for months, not even need to warm up and then walk on stage and belt their lungs out amazingly. Others need to practice, and go to lessons, and work hard on their creativity. It doesn't matter where you fit in, in all of this. There is no judgment here.

What is called for, though, is to be able to **detach oneself from this personal expectation,** from this insatiable need to achieve, to do, to be, to perform and the dependency on the business to feed us... and to just be able to be still while the world revolves speedily around us.

My Artistry is a choice I've made for expression, but it doesn't define the complete me and I am not held hostage by it anymore. By releasing the need to be so driven, to the tokens of worldly achievement and to your own sense of excellence, you can enjoy an amazing sense of freedom.

So, today, I learn to detach and let go of all of the "stuff', all of the to-do lists, all of my personal self-demands, and I enjoy the Art of Art making, for the sake of Art alone. I return to my painting with my glass of wine. Cheers.

Blog comment
Great stuff!
It seems that an Artist has to strive to liberate oneself from other activities that day to day life impinges on us... to be free to create.
Like the imprisonment of daily/yearly chores versus finding that elusive time to be free creatively.
You never know when you may get that chance but seeking that freedom is an earnest endeavor.
It's hard to survive and find the time when your creativity doesn't pay the rent, many established Artists have found the key to making their income from their creations but that's only from initial hard work or... luck!
Finding the balance is the key.
Gilli's Dad.

30. Contributing to the world

Beyond the "me, me, me", there is something wonderfully fulfilling about making a contribution to the world.

I surround myself with like-minded people who also foster this same philosophy. I'm very blessed to have a voluntary team of over thirty songwriters and like-minded individuals who make up the Songsalive! team, running our non-profit showcases and workshops around the world. I didn't push them to volunteer. They have always contacted me over the years to be part of our altruistic endeavor. Songsalive! runs on the principle that whoever contributes to it, whether that is by the team or the members who donate as low as $40 a year, will all receive invaluable gifts in return. These gifts can only be measured by the individual. It might be something like a cool promotion, or opportunity to perform, or a new resource, workshop or article that helped their education, or a lead to pitch their song to someone looking for songs. The gifts are in abundance but it really all depends on whether the individual "sees" them, and appreciates them for what they are.

There is only one reason why we do anything in all, and that is to express, experience and become our truest selves. This self-defining process is what I call "creativity" in its purest form, and it is ongoing, every day, every moment. As we express and experience, we are contributing to others' development and in turn touching our own lives. Touching your own life is the highest of it all.

Some people contribute their energies to non-profits, voluntary organizations and groups, even bands (as musicians) and then complain about it later. They give of themselves and then swiftly retract it thinking that their energy is not appreciated or money not well spent. Or they feel hard done by because they find out the pay wasn't good, or they didn't get a certain exposure they expected. This happens a lot with Artists who perform at a show or festival for free and spend time and money to be involved, but then feel jaded after when they don't feel they got anything out of it. I've had songwriters complain that they didn't get a record deal or get signed in some way from a CD compilation we've produced with their song on it, even though what we did provide was worldwide promotion. It's like they expect us to be their saviors.

They paid some low-cost amount (that is way cheaper than if they release the song on their own CD) and did nothing else except expect the whole world to land on their feet offering them the moon. They didn't see how much effort was put into the project, how much it was promoted and distributed and the value of the exposure. Publicists and music magazines get the same criticism. Artists often think that if they pay for an ad or pay for PR services, that they expect to be signed or get a full house at their next gig.

You can't expect others to make it happen for you like this. Sure, exposure in all these forms is great. But they are merely tools to add to your existing momentum. Get exposed and promoted in every which way you can, but don't complain if those resources don't provide you with fame or fortune. You never know, maybe your song sucked! Or the image wasn't to people's taste? All these can contribute to it.

But the real reason is that everyone has their own story in life. Just because you put your stuff out there, doesn't mean everyone is going to hop to it and listen to you, call you, or come see your show, make you a star. Everyone has their own agenda and sometimes circumstances play a factor, like the weather, current economy, being unknown in a certain region, not enough of a story about you to instantly like you. It takes time to develop a buzz. If you're doing it all on a budget it can take years. That's ok. Because guess what? You are an Artist for life. You have all the time in the world. There is no end-date here. (Only in your mind.) What's important to know is you are responsible for everything that happens to you. **There is no one else to blame. Be the master of your own destiny, and take the heat, because it surely isn't right to blame others for your Lack of Whatever, because YOU made the decision to be here.** Right?

Be mindful that we get a lot out of everything we do and give in life. It's all based on perspective. Plus, it's opportunistic to be patient, for what may look like a bad decision may, in the end, be the best thing you've ever done for your career, given time.

If you have expectations undermining your initial voluntary contribution, it will totally backfire on you.

Here's an example of how expectations ruin what really is a wonderful experience and opportunity.

One weekend I asked my band mates in L.A. to drive down to San Diego to play a small acoustic show in a female gay bar. Firstly, my band mates (guys) were totally turned off to

a) perform in a gay bar (not being phobic or anything, they just like the Sunset strip rock-out atmosphere)

b) drive the long distance

c) not getting paid much

d) not being able to amp up. Playing acoustically was the last thing they wanted to do.

I urged them to do it because I felt it would be great for our exposure, a new experience in a brand new market, and we could also try some cool stage ideas. I asked my bass player to play an upright bass (those huge things that are hard to lug but sound amazing), I played keyboards and my guitarist was on acoustic guitar. We did the gig and the place was full with people who had never heard me but were becoming fans there and then. People signed the mailing list and we sold CDs. We even were treated to a meal.

The following day, both my band mates resigned from my band. I was shocked. I didn't understand. But they said that doing such a gig was the final straw of playing in places where "no one cared, the venues didn't pay and the sound was terrible." I told them that I cared, and that, yes, the people cared. They may not have been so visible about it to them. That didn't go down too well. I mean, here they were playing with me often for free, under my name (not a band name) and I guess they felt their contribution was not serving them enough. I acknowledge that it wasn't "their" band but rather the "gilli moon" experience. However, I couldn't see what they needed in return for their input. I didn't understand.

You see, I believe that if we do anything in life we do it because it's for our own self-growth and for who we are and who we want to become. I don't ask for favors from anyone. If I contribute my time for someone, I'm not sitting there waiting for a return, or expecting some result that might never happen. I do it "because". I do it as an experience I need to do, and an expression I need to make, for my life. So if I was in someone else's band I would be in it because I wanted to learn, contribute, play, share... all of these things. I wouldn't hold the band to making me famous or expecting something unforeseen. But that's just me.

I saw such immense value from doing that San Diego gig. I believe in building one fan at a time. So if only one person was in the room, who signed my mailing list, then I know they will spread the word to two others, who will spread to four, then eight and all of a sudden I've reached a group of people I'd never reach before. But in fact this gig was packed. They loved what we did. We were able to experiment with new sounds and instrumentation on stage. Even that in itself is what Artistry is all about right? Who cares about the business side and the venues; isn't writing songs and performing all about that expression first? Aren't we as musicians supposed to enjoy the creative pursuit in performance and experiment? If we don't have joy in THAT what's the use of even doing anything else?

Doing that gig has not only brought these small but immeasurable experiences to me, but on that night I met a journalist who then reviewed my album, which then spread the word up the North coast and over to Arizona, which opened up whole new playing fields to perform in. The domino effect is big.

These days I have one strict rule about playing in my band. Only one. Play with me because you love creating and performing. If a musician comes into it with a hidden agenda of some notions of fame, fortune or anything business like, then they are out. Los Angeles is a tough town and the reason why people get jaded here is because they bring their career expectations to their music playing. If a gig doesn't go right, and 'such and such' isn't in the audience to see them play, or they didn't get paid, or the PA sucked, or there were only 5 people in the room, most musicians complain and complain until eventually they lose the desire to perform at all.

But if you go into the performing circuit hanging on to your initial passion for the Art form, and don't expect ANYTHING at all, but just create your Art and your circle of influence, then not only will you ENJOY the performance, but, ironically, the opportunities will actually come flying at you... because you least expect them. This is a universal law.

Contributing to the world

Everything that goes around comes around, and what you do for another, you do for yourself. Simple as that.

Go in to it with joy, and come out with more joy.

31. Levels to nowhere

Some people around me, like managers, producers and team members, believe that they have the authority and know how to say they "want to take me to the next level" as an Artist. But I want to challenge this. Whilst it's flattering that they wish to do something of the sort, I ask them, "and what level might that be?" If I were to attach my notion of success to commercial success or any kind of token reward, then I might buy into the notion that I need to go up a level or two to reach that success.

But I'm successful already, and I encourage you to feel the same about your own life course. I define success on my own terms. I don't believe in "levels". I see our creative journey as simply that, a wonderful journey, and I don't feel like I have to climb the steps to any pearly gates in order to be a better Artist or be successful. So... in my opinion, there is no level to climb. It's all one level.

I find it bizarre that others think that their expertise and know-how is what is going to take me anywhere better than I already am. I can only say that understanding fully that I am a student of life, that I am always learning and I always am open to reaching my highest potential.

However, no person is qualified to be our personal savior in this life nor has the ability to "make us" a star or "take" us anywhere we aren't already supposed to be. This is universal law. Only you yourself can do that for you. This is your journey. Taking ownership of your success and creative freedom and being fully accountable and responsible for your own growth, is what is appropriate. Besides, anyone who is around you, whether it's your manager, producer, mentor or office assistant, have their own objectives and motives in the co-creation process with you, and so they should! You wouldn't want someone to be in your creative life just to help you. You would want them to seek their own potential in that too. This is "inter-dependence", when two or more creative beings come together to a middle ground to create something beautiful and powerful.

We are all equal in co-creation. We are all assisting and supporting each other's creative vision and to shine our best in ourselves. Instead of accepting that someone is there to "take you to the next level", why not see your relationships as a glorious opportunity for everyone, not just you, to achieve their highest potential in that co-creation.

Next time someone tries to push their ideas on you simply because they "want to take you to the next level", ask them... "and what may I do for you my dear friend?"

There are no levels. You are exactly where you need to be, right now.

Levels to nowhere

This Blog was posted on my website, which procured different comments, including this one –

Blog comment:
Right on, Sista! I'm so there with you on this. True collaboration and mutual support is beautiful and a blessing, but where would we be as co-creators and greatnesses if we didn't stop to smell the flowers and let ourselves be inspired by the moment instead of letting ourselves be "bum rushed" up the "ladder", right? If there's anything I've learned from my 3 or so decades as an Artist and entertainer is that life is happening NOW and planning ahead and being grounded about your business and partnerships is great, but totally pointless unless you're really willing and able to live a life and learn a lesson or two every moment you're breathing... Odd, isn't it, that so many people seem to be living their lives towards achieving something so vague as this notion of "success"... I mean what is that, really?? Is it living off your Art, bringing people together, making tons of money, making something beautiful... or is it jumping through enough hoops so you can't go to the Mini Mart without getting mobbed by adoring fans (?!) If you think about it, the whole "success" thing is really too vague to be anything but silly unless you think about it long enough to figure out what it means for you personally...and then think about it again when people try to help you out by helping you get to "the next level". And ask questions like: "where is that illusive "next level" anyway? Is that even somewhere I WANT to go? What, exactly, will I being doing there that's so much better (for me, right now) than what I'm doing now on my own?? And MOST importantly, have I really connected to where I'm at right now?? Because that's the human element that people will connect to, you can't paint a picture (with words or paint or music or whatever) if you can't convey what you're feeling and you can't tap in to that unless you can hang out long enough to feel something even if you're just
trying to convey that, you have to feel it or it won't work...So I guess I'm thinking: A) where is the "next step" for me, personally, and B) do I really feel compelled to go there, because if I don't I'm not bringing anything valuable to it and am in direct violation of the laws of mutual support... Wow, that was quite a ramble, any thoughts??

- Cyhndi Mora, Artist

32. Dispossessing the old, reinventing the new

I'm down-under writing this chapter. The sky is an incandescent glow of luminous grey of the clouds, mixed with the blue of today's Australian beauty of a day. The wind is up. Which is a good thing, because it would have been over 40 degrees Celsius (110 F) today. It's cooling down.

It's so green here. Bright green in fact. We've had rain. Abnormal for summer. Might even rain tonight, like a hot balmy summer's tropical rain storm. Usually, it comes quickly. We see the bolt of lightning, and then, a minute later, hear the thunder... deep and guttural. It tells us that Mother Nature is indeed in control. As it approaches, the lightening crack and thunder are closer together. Sometimes we get a flash of light in the house and a huge crack of thunder, the sky goes green, as we are in awe of the magnificence of nature. Sometimes we lose a computer or a television from a lightning strike. These are the things we put up with living in paradise... the occasional loss of a possession. It reminds us of what is truly important in life, and what isn't.

I've spent the last 3 years or so learning the Art of dispossession. It's an interesting concept... to simplify the clutter in our lives. Gaylah Balter, the author of *Clean Your Clutter, Clear Your Life* says that "Getting rid of clutter is not about letting go of things that are meaningful to you, it's about letting go of the things that no longer contribute to your life so that you have the time and the energy and the space for the things that do."

So I've spent a lot of time, in the two places I call "home" (Los Angeles and Australia), going through my stuff. From old diaries, paperwork, clothes, collectibles and, yes, even music CDs, I have put aside what I felt are no longer part of my current life. I've either sold the good stuff at yard sales, or on Amazon marketplace, or given the treasures away to people in need, thrift stores and even friends.

I have realized, through this cathartic effort, which takes time and is ongoing, that I have been a collecta-holic. I've clung on to things for that "just in case" time. Maybe one day I'll need this? Maybe it will be useful. How can I let this go when it provided so much sentimentality? Well, the truth is, so much of my possessions are a blueprint of my past, of what I *was* and not who I am now. Sometimes I feel I cannot progress, become anew, if I continue to be attached to possessions that weigh me down from the past. I am not saying I am getting rid of everything. No. But I certainly feel it is a huge weight off my shoulders and my mind if I SIMPLIFY my life, and dispossessing is by far the best first step.

Dispossessing works with any attachment we have to anything, and it's not only with objects. I started cleaning out old letters and diaries which harbored negative energy on past issues, past relationships and experiences that hurt. So then, by removing those pieces, I felt so much better. But then I also have used this methodology with people, with tasks, with food, with thoughts.

In my first book, I wrote about how people in our lives can be energy zappers, and create negative impact on our lives and our evolution. To dispossess any friend that no longer provides a positive impact or a positive return, is an amazing feeling. Why continue to allow someone to pull you down? Friends are not always lifelong. I know it's hard to believe that sometimes, but just because we label them a "friend" doesn't mean you need to take on all their stuff. If you feel that the balance of give and take is not there, or it's a strain to deal with a person, over and over again, you know it's time to dispossess. I don't mean to say you must cut off that person from your life, but certainly you can set parameters to only allow a certain relationship and certain communication in your life that empowers you, nurtures you as much as you've nurtured them.

It is sometimes hard for Artists to acknowledge this notion, as we are usually very giving, and gullible (we are the innocent creative people on this planet... wanting to give so much, and believe in others so they believe in us). We look to music executives (managers, record companies, agents) to offer us the way to fulfill our hopes and dreams; we believe in what the critics and press say; we are disappointed when an audience isn't captivated by our music performance. We can be taken for a ride, easily, because someone says they'll "make us a star". Finding that barometer in reading people will be a first step in avoiding and dispossessing energy zappers. Learning to let go of the people who can harm us, and our dream, is difficult, but necessary.

Like people, things can bog us down. I had a to-do list a mile long. I have gone from my Outlook Tasks list to huge scrapbooks of lists, to now a tiny notebook that fits in my purse. I have reduced my list. I have started to cross off what is no longer important to me. Being busy is no longer the goal. Achieving the task should be the goal. But if we have so many tasks, how on earth can we achieve them all? We are not super human. (Some of us think we can be though!) So I've started to eliminate tasks that are superfluous, that just spin the wheels and don't accomplish anything of substance. I've learned that I can't do everything in life, in this month, this week, this day. I just have to do what I can and do it in the best way. So my task list is now in a tiny notebook, and even that has become too big. I want to bring it right down. Maybe, if I can't remember what to do, I shouldn't do it. The old farmer down in the valley on his farm, with his cattle and horses, doesn't have a task list. Yet he gets what needs to be done on his farm. It's all about using his memory.

I've been taking a strong look at food. My diet is usually good, but I know I slip now and then. I believe in "everything in moderation", but I also believe our world eats way too much. We consume so much food. Our society is filled with disease, overweight problems and lethargy. I go out to an American restaurant and my plate is so full that I could eat the same dish for the whole week and be satisfied. Most people discard so much food and it all gets thrown away. Do you know we could cure the entire world's hunger problem by feeding the hungry with what we leave on our plates? It's totally messed up. The first step I took, 10 years ago, was to become a vegetarian, with an enormous respect for animals and our plant life. It's still not enough. I don't want to begin a discussion on that right now but pick up a copy of Vegan News in your local community and you'll understand it all by reading just one article.

I am also learning, within my diet, to eat only what I need. When I'm full I think to myself - don't be gluttonous just because it tastes nice. Eat for need, and yes, surely, for taste. Gosh, I love food. I love the smells and taste sensations of cooking a beautiful pasta sauce or delicious guacamole. But stop when you are full. Dispossess the mind-set of needing to eat for survival, and needing to eat because your parents told you you had to finish everything on your plate. Cook less. Prepare less. Understand ecology and the lack of resources in the world. Enjoy eating with another. That's where it's truly at: sharing a meal. A meal is all about sharing your life, in that little moment. Really appreciate that moment of eating, like it's the only meal you'll eat for the rest of your life. Don't rush it. Enjoy it. Savor it.

Moments are meant to be savored, each and every one of them. Living in the moment is the largest lesson I've learned in these recent years. I used to look so far beyond into the future I didn't even know the present existed.

What a powerful thought - enjoying the current moment. It has a lot to do with our thoughts, how we perceive things. Being a born-again moment lover, I am really inspired by the idea of living in the NOW. Another wonderful author, Eckhard Tolle, lives by this motto. He has written a book called "The Power of Now" where he expounds on a simple notion: "Much of the fear, anxiety and guilt that all humans experience can be traced to our inability to live in the present." The NOW moment is the only thing that is important. For me, time has stood still. I feel time is irrelevant in my journey. The past, present and future have become all one. I am who I am, ongoing, living my destiny, in a creative and communicative world. I work hard to keep my thoughts positive. When I have a negative thought, I meditate on it and work on - dispossessing - that thought, that reasoning, that logic, that reality. Any thoughts I think are real. Thoughts are creative, as Edward de Bono says. If you think something, it becomes reality. Therefore, any thoughts we have that are negative or take us away from who we really are, and who we want to become, we need to dispossess. Let go. Don't harbor them, or they will become us. Simplicity is the spice of life.

No bird soars too high
if he soars with
his own wings
-    William Blake

33. Be the bag

Sometimes, we want something to come to fruition so badly, we push so hard it hurts us. Sometimes, even with all the pushing, the drive and the effort, we don't even get what we set out to achieve. Why is that so?

I was brought up to think that if you work hard you can make anything happen; that if you put in the required effort, and you stay focused on your end goals, everything will happen.

When we set out to do what we want to do as Artists in the entertainment business, many Artists feel that they cannot let anything get in their way of achieving their desires, ambitiously keeping to their life purpose. Actually music business representatives (labels, managers, producers, etc.), tell them they need to be like this too. Then, they take on a pit bull like determination, with a "never give up" attitude, often sacrificing personal joy. I know that many have seen me this way in my life. I'm always seen as joyous, but certainly with a determined streak! They notice my unsurpassable resolve to stride forth, take on many challenges, and make mountains out of mole hills. I've always seen myself as highly ambitious, determined and a super achiever. I remember being told by quite a few "know-it-alls" in the business that I had to "choose" what I focused on for my career. I had to be totally dedicated and committed to being a music Artist, and not let anything get in the way, including personal life (that cut out relationships or having a family), or other career options. *"You gotta be in it to win it"*, they would say.

For the last ten years, I dedicated my life, every day, to my music career. I have been extremely committed, changing continents, moving to the heart and center of the music industry, L.A., to achieve my dreams. I have conquered so many hurdles to be here, including immigration papers, making money, getting to know the right people, everything. I won't say that I "sacrificed" alternate options of life (leading a quiet life on the beach could have been one of them), but I certainly remained focused on my mission in life. True - this is always what I've wanted to do. I was never the type to do a nine to five job or marry young. For me, performing, entertaining and making albums was everything, and I took on a ruthless, "go get 'em" mentality to achieve my dreams.

I would say that I have achieved many of my dreams and I continue to live my dreams on a daily basis. But I have expended a lot of energy in my past that quite frankly could have been better served if I had understood my intentions more, if I were clearer on my mission. I have done a lot, tried many things, and achieved much, mostly with trial by fire. But many things I did were because I didn't know what I truly wanted. I knew the overall idea, but no specifics, and I often focused on a big picture outcome (the big dream), based on some idea of commercial success that the industry has drummed into me as being the only way, rather than building blocks one step at a time on my own terms.

There are no complaints from me though. I certainly have achieved many things and continue to. But more recently I've begun to believe that it's not about the work nor the effort, and definitely not the *push*. It is more about **intent**. It is about dreaming, about thought, about visualizing and about surrendering to (and enjoying) the journey. I have learned to define success by my own terms and live more in the moment: connected to my journey as an Artist.

I remember watching the movie, *American Beauty*, starring Kevin Spacey, where the boy next door filmed his favorite home video and he showed it to his girlfriend. The video was of a plastic bag, just a bag, floating in the wind. It drifted here, then there, and up, down and over. It drifted with ease; it was light and in his mind, the most poetic and visually pleasing subject.

Be the bag.

There is much to read into this simple, small piece. In my mind, being the bag is about surrendering to the journey. Letting the wind, and the universe, provide our path, and trusting that path. It means that the outcome, the goal, is not so important. Yes, it can be a guide, and sure, stay ambitious, but if we are attached only to our end destination, and not about the journey, then we may only be disappointed. You see, life delivers us amazing things, but the most amazing are along the way, not necessarily at the end of a long hard journey, nor should we work ourselves into the ground along the way.

I notice that the more I am in touch with my inner intention, that indefinable force that attaches to my dreams and thoughts, things come to fruition more quickly and effectively. Large efforts or hard work are certainly great personal growth processes, but not necessarily goal realizing. While it's important to have a strong work ethic on the outside, it's the work I'm doing on the inside that is really allowing me to master my Art and my life, with freedom and joy. This all comes down to the powerful word of "intention".

Whatever I focus on, whatever I give attention to, whether I want it or not, I will create. This is where it gets really awesome for Artists. As we are creative more often than not, our thoughts, desires and dreams build most of what will happen Artistically and opportunistically in our lives. You get what you think. So if we focus on doing a lot of "hard work", we get a lot of "hard", a lot of "work" and a lot of "hard work" back. If we focus on a positive action or creative outcome, it will occur positively. But more accurately, if we focus on something we want... and then let go of it... and surrender to the universal forces... it will definitely occur, and with great results, because not only are you giving power to your thought, you are also allowing the universe to share the power and help realize your dreams, plus provide you more freedom to truly create what you want and who you want to be.

Remember that saying, **"if you love someone, set them free"**? Well, this is true also for your Art. If you love your Art, set it free. Don't cling onto it, push it, or force it. Surrender to the universe and let it be. It will feed you abundantly if you find the freedom. This all starts with intention.

Dr. Wayne W. Dyer, author of *"The Power of Intention"*, has dedicated a book about intention, about how to make your dreams come true, about freedom and about surrendering. His writings are one of the new approaches and philosophies that has brought me to a new attention about fulfilling lifelong dreams. Ever since I saw the movie *"American Beauty"*, and since reading many Toltec philosophy books, some by Carlos Castenada, Dyer's books and Don Miguel Ruiz books, I have come to a better understanding about the Art of "letting go" and allowing the universe to show me my true path.

Dyer, like Castenada before him, sees intent as *"not something you do but a force that exists in the universe as an invisible field of energy"*. It means, in a nutshell, that we don't have to do anything to create intention and any action and goals following that, but instead "allow" it to happen, almost as if there is an invisible force field manifesting our dreams for us. It means connecting to our natural selves and letting go of total ego identification. Dyer expresses four steps to intention:

1. Discipline - training ourselves to perform as our thoughts desire. When our bodies are healthy and connected to our mind, the whole body can take on anything.

2. Wisdom - wisdom combined with discipline fosters our ability to focus and be patient as our thoughts, intellect and feelings work with our body.

3. Love - loving what you do and doing what you love. I have always believed that you need to be passionate about your Art for it to come to fruition.

4. Surrender - my favorite part, for the exercise of this chapter: your mind and body let go of being in charge, and you move more into intent. When you surrender, you lighten up and be more in touch with your inner truth, and it will take you wherever you feel destined to go.

I am fascinated with Wayne Dyer's words and although he focuses on life development, it is equally fitting as a focus for you as an Artist. I'm sure I will touch more about intention as we move forward in this book.

What is the opposite of surrendering? Clinging on.

Attachment. If you are attached to the outcomes of something, so much so that you push for it, you will only meet with resistance.

So in summary, as we navigate through this book discussing all the cool ways to "just get out there", remember that it all starts with your intent, your intentions: what you really want. From there, everything is possible.

Be the bag

There's a great movie you might like to watch. It's called *"The Secret"*. It talks about the law of attraction. Casting out to the universe what you want, combined with the universal law of intent, attracts what you want... and so the cycle goes.

When I say "just get out there" what I really mean is "go within." Ooh, now we are really getting somewhere!

Be flexible.

Remember my saying, The Three Os?
Optimism + Organized = Opportunity.

Opportunity comes when you love what you do, and you are positive, combined with being organized and business savvy. It also comes when you are open to the possibilities that life can bring you. To get the most out of your life, keep your options open and be flexible to what might come when you least expect it. You never know when that door will open, or the phone will call. So in the meantime, be flexible to the wind, so that you are ready for whatever might happen.

Life is an adventure. It's not a rigid course, set in stone. Read different kinds of books. Watch different movies. Listen to music you might not ordinarily listen to. Go to events that you wouldn't normally attend (you never know who you might meet!) Listen to the wind, open your mind, open your heart, and be the bag.

Online blog entry: Mt. Shasta, Northern California, Aug 2003

I am seeing

I see
I see how I can dispossess the stuff
And repossess myself
Escaping hell
My own silent jail
Embrace me, light so clear and pure

Ever get the amazing sense that you must go somewhere because it's drawing
you? We were driving up the 5 north and we hit Mt. Shasta, one of the 12 sacred
sites of the earth. We spent the night sleeping in our car on the mountain.   We
really wanted to stay up near Portland because it would be a long drive up to
Seattle for the Tuesday night show. But when we saw the sign to Mt. Shasta and we
stopped for a late lunch, we ended up staying the whole night. We couldn't leave.
The one road street is filled with spiritual books, stones and paraphernalia stores,
nicely done, which drew us in the read, notice and become aware. Having found a
KOA camp ground just outside the town for $14.50 a campsite, we then drove up
the hill wanted to touch the snow-capped mountain of Mt. Shasta. We reached
6,000 feet and suddenly came across Panther Meadows, one of the 12 vortexes in
the area. It was quiet, serene and meditative.   We could see, although hot
summer, the snow capped peaks ahead. People were camping... for free. We had to
do it too. Even though we had paid for the campground down below, we decided to
stay up here, go for a beautiful walk through the springs infested meadows, and
then camp in the back of the car here like others. It was nearly a full moon, and
perfect for our souls.

6am and we packed up the car again and headed north up the 5. We
knew we were to return to Mt. Shasta again, very soon. We drove 256 miles to
Eugene Oregon and dropped off my CD to KVRM 91.9 Public Broadcast radio
station where I will be interviewed on Friday. We had breakfast, before Eugene, in
a small town called Glendale, a lumber town.

After Shasta, I knew my journey now was something bigger than just my
"next big gig".

Life is really simple,
But we insist on making it complicated.
Nothing is more simple than greatness: for to be simple is to be great.

© Max Steingart

34. Learning to relax

Fresh perspectives, fresh ideas and new starts, that's what a new year is all about. I've spent the day wondering why I am continually on the computer, busily going through my to-do lists, thinking I should try and relax. It's hard to relax in Hollywood, where I live most of the time. But I have the candle lit, the incense going, some spiritual books lying around, trying to gain a sense of calm as I slowly go through my e-mail inbox. But I can't seem to make headway with it. Every time I file an e-mail away or delete the superfluous, more come in. So I go for a walk around the block, sit on the beach and ponder. Then I get bored, go back to my desk and go through my to-do list again. But I'm not sure I actually accomplished anything. Then again, I really want to relax. How does one relax when they are only 'trying'? The only way to truly relax is to let go of the expectations on myself to achieve and complete projects. I just have to let go. It's a hard thing when one of the tasks on my to-do list is to write everyday. I am writing a book. The pressure is on.

Makes me think about life. If we push too hard, we just don't get anywhere. If you set a huge list of tasks to do, you tend to not get them done, maybe not even one of them, because it all feels too much. I think I have to simplify my objectives. The more clutter, the less I accomplish. The irony is I also am trying to relax. I want to accomplish major things in the least amount of time, and I want to relax. I want to write a whole chapter for this book, quickly, then relax. I want to plan a few shows, a tour in a certain region of the U.S. for this year, and relax. I want to organize the production of one of our new Artists' albums in the studio, and relax. I want to update my website, but relax. My current conundrum: Do I really know what I want? Through all this thinking about what I want to do, or in fact need to do, I end up not achieving much. Nor am I relaxing.

So, learning how to relax is a bit of an Art form. Even for me it's a challenge. It's difficult for many of us creative types because our minds are so active. Also, the pressure is on for Artists this day and age to be task warriors, to be in control of our business, to have a "go get 'em" mentality. We always have to be on the ball, alert, thinking outside the box, strategizing, running all the affairs of our business. But, we also have to allow time to relax. It might have to be planned. Fitting relaxation time into the schedule requires discipline. It's all about time management. There is in fact enough time for everything. I mentioned that in my last book. Time and balance: balancing tasks so that they get done in a day; factoring in down time. Most Artists complain they don't have time to create. We waste a lot of time procrastinating, or watching TV. Switch it off and get on with the task.

For me, I'm switching off to relax. I think I'll run and swim in the mornings and stay as far away from the computer as possible. Then I'll focus two or three hours on work (I'll even time myself) and then do some writing late afternoon. In theory, it sounds perfect. Let's see what happens!

...in order to become empowered warriors, we learn the Art of letting go...

Gentle warriors are joyful warriors who have no need for harshness in their lives. Gentle warriors are balanced warriors, warriors who find harmony and beauty in the contradiction of awareness. Gentle warriors are fluid warriors, warriors released to the magic of their own finesse...

("Creative Victory", by Tomas)

35. When the going gets tough

Recently, I felt unmotivated. I know... it is hard to imagine that isn't it? Most people see me as such a motivated whirlwind, but it's true. I've had a long period of this recently. I won't go into how long my moment lasted, but I can at least say that I experienced many feelings during this moment of non-motivation. This included a physical feeling of being tired, to the point that I got so run-down mentally I had two colds in two months plus other physical ailments. On a mental plane, I had no desire to complete any of my projects, or start new ones. I didn't want to sit at my desk and look at my computer, nor even my piano. I "maintained" my days with checking e-mails, replying quickly, and then not really getting my teeth into anything creative or productive. I had no incentive. What was wrong with me?

My direction as an Artist, in this big world called the music business, lost its meaning and joy... momentarily. All I could think about was all the negative stuff: how corrupt the music business is, how venues are so tough and disrespectful of Artists (not paying, or pay-to-play), how little opportunity there is to truly create a living, etc. I had doubts. Nothing went easily and money became a focal point of my day; how to make more, where to invest it, doing my taxes, running out. Everything became overwhelming with odds. Even having written a book, toured the world motivating other Artists, created six studio albums and set up my own record label plus continued to expand Songsalive! with chapters worldwide... I had lost the spirit of my own advice. How was I supposed to finish *this* book?

I started to feel my age. I started to look my age. I have always felt young and free-spirited. But I became oddly aware of my real age, my timing in life, and that time was seemingly running out.

I stocked up on more spiritual books by Neale Donald Walshe, Don Miguel Ruiz, Wayne Dyer, Carolyn Myss and Louise Hay. I stopped playing piano for fun. Only at gigs. Even then my fans noticed I looked bored. I stopped painting. I didn't write much (only when a project forced me to). I became disconnected to my purpose. I began to question "Why am I here?"

As an Artist, I have always considered myself a pretty focused and creative individual. Finding my purpose in life had never been an issue. I always knew who I was and what I wanted to do. My objective had been based on an elusive, intangible goal of stardom. Yes, I admit, even with all my writings and workshops, and how I motivate other Artists about "living the journey", I was a victim of wanting that "Holy Grail": stardom-fame-fortune. Of course I had always seen it in a realistic way, because I was so confident about my abilities, I felt it was a given: I was going to be hugely and utterly successful. Fact.

I didn't realize, until recently, that the definition of my success, including the glamour of the Hollywood music business, and yes even including the cool grass roots indie way of doing things in this music business, was really... a lie. I had lived for 20 years towards a goal that in the end is one big fat lie. There is no pot of gold at the end of this rainbow. This music business is rough, corrupt and illusive. It's all about who you know, how much money you have, and how sexy your dress style is. Whether you're a major Artist or indie, business is still business. Fact. There is little room for true talent, raw ambition and a global mission for harmony in this music business, because it really is... a fashion business. Take a look at the music videos on VH1 and MTV now. That is, if you can find any, and those you find are full of glossy "pimp daddies" rapping to their sexy mascara-laden girls with big lips, bikinis and big everything else except their waste line. Is this Art? You tell me.

I didn't sign up for this when I was eighteen. I just wanted to express myself, through my music and poetry, and let as many people in the world hear it. But I surely didn't expect to have to lie down in front of the corporate world, and 25 year old A&R "dudes" who have no idea what a good song is, to do it.

So I know damn well why I have been tired. I've been tired of the BS. I've been tired of people telling me that you have to do it a certain way to get heard. I've been tired of people telling me that there is no place for CDs anymore, after I just spent 2 years (and the rest) in the studio recording an album, with high definition sound, wonderful musicians, and heart pouring out with emotion (let alone my pockets pouring out with money to do it). To see my music, and my Art squashed into a tiny mp3 and channeled into an iPod where people don't give a damn about the sound quality, the Art work, the concept, the journey of the beginning to end of the CD... even the Artist behind it... makes me puke. It makes me very tired, and very unmotivated to do it all again.

This business is still a "hit song" game. If it doesn't hit you in the face immediately, or if it's too long, or if it doesn't have a hook in the first 20 seconds, it's done. "Done like a dinner." If you're not writing with Sting or James Blunt, or you don't sound like James Blunt or Maroon 5 or Lady Gaga or Mariah Carey (I used to love her songs, now they are just clipped, pitch corrected beats and rap that truly has lost my affection for her), then you've got no chance. If you don't look like a preppy, nerdy, or on the other end, "whore-ish" 19 year old, then you're too old. That is, if you want to play with the big fish. I spent hours researching L.A.'s KCRW's program director list for each radio segment, and sent my new CD to every one of them, with a personal note, and ideas on which songs would fit each program (as my album is as eclectic as their station). PASS. No comments, no "thank yous", just PASS. This is a radio station that used to take unsolicited, interesting music. Are they just like the rest of them now?

Yeah, there's an opportunity to play like little fish in smaller ponds, and that's what I've been doing.... I'm like a hugely known Artist in America amongst Artists and secular markets, but flying completely under the radar. Yeah, I can earn a living, and be independent, and enjoy my journey, etc. But, *is this all there is?* Does the buck stop here for me? Am I going to stay in perpetual festival and coffee house land, loved and admired by many, but me doing the same thing over and over again? When can I get some sleep? Doing it "indie" aint "easy".

I have written a book about success, defining it on one's own terms, and seeking only one's own approval. Well I did that. Here I am. I've approved my own Art. I've proven myself and paid my dues. What now? Do I spend the next 20 years slogging it hard on the road, going from one hippy festival to the next, like Ani diFranco did and still does? I was just up at Harmony Festival in Santa Rosa, Northern California. It reminded me of Woodford Festival in Australia, but way more commercialized. I liked the energy, but there was still bureaucratic red tape and mishaps just to get on the bill. Being on the road is hard work. Sure, you can sell CDs, but it's still a hard life. You either love it or you don't.

I enjoyed touring with Eric Idle (from Monty Python). We traveled the U.S. and Canada for 3 months playing to 2000+ seat theaters. I loved it. But it was still hard work. We would load in to a new theater at noon, dress the stage (I was the stage manager and a performer), sound checked and performed the show, then loaded out at midnight. We'd hop back on the bus and travel all night to the next town. Load in at noon, and so forth. Fun for me. Consider that a celebrity such as Eric, having been doing this for perhaps 40 years, still has to schlep across the country in a van too. That's the life. It's not as glamorous as you think.

How about radio? It's no use anymore trying to promote to every radio station across the country, if you can't compete with the major Artists and the record companies that still buy their way to the top 5 listening spots. It takes money and if you don't have money, there's no point in doing a national campaign. You'll just spend your money just to see a nice rotation report each week that is meaningless if you can't actually be in that small or big town to promote the airplay. Besides, there's more than radio now, what with the Internet, satellite radio, and the iPods, including podcasting. There is a lot to choose from. Sure, spend every waking hour hopping on to every band wagon to give it a shot. I dare you. I have. I don't sleep.

How about MySpace? Facebook? If you want to meet people, create your own site, blog and promote, these are great sites. I was told, in its infancy, that the more "friends" I had the better I was. Well now I don't know. A lot of these "friends" are other Artists, all wanting to be heard themselves. Not everyone likes to communicate online all the time. What happened to picking up the phone?

Gigs. Pay to play is still out there. How do we survive the market and make a dollar doing gigs? When will venue owners start paying a fee for original Artists? Why do Artists always have to be mini promoters too and constantly have to sell door tickets to get a small percentage of that? Surely their talents should be appreciated and paid for, like any other cover gig that often gets paid somewhere. And what happened to people actually going out and seeing live shows???? I don't think I can push my friends anymore to come see me live. They've supported me enough. I can't abuse that friendship all the time. So what to do? Not play anymore?? I get out of town. I tour. This is a 365 day job.

So what's the way? What is the path of least resistance with maximum success? What do we, as Artists, need to do to survive the corporate melt-downs, the grueling indie road, the business corruption, and make a living? How do we find a way to enjoy this journey? The "indie revolution" has certainly been a great leap forward for independent control over our music. The Internet has been a great champion for taking our business into our own hands. But we the Artists, having to be everything all at once, cannot possibly take it seriously, or realistically, if we can't make a living doing it and can't enjoy the process. Besides that, when will indie Artists truly get a break, like the major Artists, without having to sign with the Devil? Is it possible?

I don't know. I just don't know. What I do know is that we, as Artists, are here for a much higher purpose. Art and creativity never runs out, even though we may tire with the business end. There is always an abundance of creativity and musicality in us. I don't think I have ever heard an Artist say, *"oh, I ran out of things to write about"*, or *"all my song ideas disappeared"*, or *"I don't like my guitar anymore"*. Being Artists is innate. It is what fuels us to keep going.

So what IS the purpose of life, after all? Is it to make sure we get to stand on our soap box and collect coins for doing so? Or is it to see who collected the most awards, hit songs, deals and airplay? Is this supposed to be a competition?

Or is it something to do with our inner selves tapping into a much higher mission in life, through our creativity?

I know that there is always enough creativity to allow us to be who we want to be for the rest of our lives. We don't have to rely on the Arts business to confirm that, or acknowledge that. We can do that for ourselves.

I already feel motivated because I'm taking the time to write this to you. I have been writing my second book for 6 months now but I took a month off because I was stuck on this chapter (what you are reading). I was trying to work out how I should go about saying what I really felt, and was thinking of subliminal ways of saying it. But in reality, I had to just sit down and write what was truly on my mind. That's part of the process of writing this book.

Being truly honest: this book is called "*Just Get Out There*" and yet I am constantly "going within" with my thought processes here. Most of my readers want to know the ins and outs of getting out there with their Art and music and they look to me because, in their eyes, I have done so. Yes, I agree, to a certain point. But I will say that it truly is all about the Process. It IS about going **within** and tapping into our truer destiny... in order to actualize it in reality. Once we discover who we really are, and what we really, and truly, want, we are half way there. This takes a lot of INNER work.

The process unfolds as we create it, and the process unfolds by itself, without us even knowing it. We are merely playing a part. The cool thing about this, is that while we maintain our lives and careers, plotting and planning, being motivated or unmotivated, being creative or business like, the **process** is happening subconsciously and if you truly believe in yourself (THIS IS THE KEY), then it will ALL WORK OUT according to the higher plan... your higher mission in life.

I have quite a few Artists ask me often, whether via e-mail or in person, "how to get out there". They want to know all the steps and often show their frustrations that they don't know the steps to take. But in fact, by making any step, in any direction, will bring you closer to your higher purpose. Just making the step is important. The facts, the direction, the tips, tools and resources come to us in our traveling. We pick up a book, or we go to a website (www.songsalive.org really is filled with resources and tools), or we go to a seminar or class, and we learn something new. We go cyber-traveling on the Internet or we look at other Artists' websites to get ideas. Ideas come. It's up to us as to how we grab onto them, or let them go if they don't serve us personally. If we are connected to our **process**, conscious and unconscious, we certainly will be on the right path. But we are not always cognizant of the real purpose and can easily be sidetracked by the meaningless act of doing. There is so much out there it's easy to be put off, or sidetracked.

So, what if we were able to tap into this unconscious **process** and be awake during it? Wouldn't that be even more magical and success bringing? What if we ask for our biggest dreams, truly ask for them, and really tap into who we really can be? (Our highest potential.)

There is always enough. That means that whatever you want, if you truly want it, you can have. Whatever you don't want, and you focus on that, that will manifest instead, like spinning wheels. If you just follow all the opportunities and end up in a quagmire of doing and energy dispensing for no reason, then you get... TIRED.

Good news: there is always enough

If I'm tired and unmotivated about an area in my life... maybe, just maybe, I need to really listen to that as a sign that that may not be who I want to be. I don't have to live a persona just because I started off that way, or others expect me to be that way. I, and you, can change ourselves, our plans, our dreams at ANY time.

Here's the magic part about this: nothing in this business is real. It's an illusion. But this illusion is based on our own perception, our own reality, so everyone can see it and use it for their own purposes. You don't have to do this the way anyone else has. Just because one Artist goes the major record deal route, and another uses MySpace to do grass roots tour hopping and fan collecting... doesn't mean you have to follow any of that. How you work it for your benefit is up to you. Artists are imaginative. We have the great opportunity to use our gifts to come up with "out of the box" creative ways to get our messages and music heard and our

Art seen and felt.

If you want to change something, the minute you think it, the Process will change in accordance to that. Let your conscious and subconscious thoughts and mind work together to bring you success, peace and joy.

The minute you think there is not enough opportunity, creativity, people to share with, money to have, that's the moment the Process stops working for you. Believing in the "not enough" is based on fear and feeling like we have to just try and survive. Believing in "I can, and I will" is all powerful.

That being said, I can and I will go pour myself some of that nice red wine and listen to the crickets.

Blog feedback:
"Beautiful thoughts. These things go through my mind every day...and as tiring as it is, I don't think I would enjoy my life as much without the insanity that comes along with the decisions and the torture of this business. I too fell in love with the idea of being a "superstar" performing Artist, I thought about it every single day and night of my life for several years, and when I hit the reality of it...going through music school and watching several of my friend attain major record deals... I suddenly wanted to cash it in and just move somewhere completely random, some other country, live a simple life in nature and forget about the whole music thing. After moving to Los Angeles it took me almost 2 years to get the fire back...I realized the music would always be inside me....it will always will be, and I can't run from it. I envy your success and your work ethic and what you have strived so hard to achieve...this is a business that makes you feel like time is running out...even at such a young age...that you have to constantly be proving yourself to anyone and everyone, but most of all yourself. Every day I struggle with the decisions of what I'm doing, where I'm going, what do I *really* want for myself in music? Are my dreams the same as they were 10 years ago? Am I trying to keep them the same or am I just so used to going after that one thing that I haven't stopped and really re-evaluated my goals? I still haven't figured it out, and I continue, daily, to face the decisions. In the meantime I enjoy making music, creating Art, living life, and hope to inspire someone along the way."

~ *Jennifer Renee, Artist.*

36. Do not block the intersection

I was driving home last night in Sherman Oaks California and I stopped at the stop sign and began to stare at the sign:

"DO NOT BLOCK THE INTERSECTION" it said. I began to think about that.

Do not block. Block. Block what? Then I saw a car number plate with NWT. What does that mean? Naught? Nothing? No thing? Maybe, "know it" maybe "no way through"? Maybe all of the above?

I think it's time to unblock the road blocks. Being at the intersection of life, we have a road map of past travels, and so many choices to make for our future. The only way to make the right decision as to which way to go, is to let go, be open, and then the answer comes to us.

I wrote a poem about frequency while I was in Seattle. It was 5 pages long and I wrote it while connected to my higher spirit watching amazing Songsalive! Artists perform on stage... and then I gave my poem to a friend, because he needed it more than me. It was a nice gift to give. GIFTS come to us and gifts we give. It's the ebb and flow of life.

I read a little of my New York blog post and this part of a poem catches my soul right now:

"the innocence of children
reminds me that I must look at life through a child's eyes
at all times
to survive
my own ambition.
now what?
NOW. Now is WHAT.
I breathe in
I submerge to dreamland to breathe some more
and feel the blue sky beating it's heat
reminding me of life and love and California and passion surging, coursing through me.
I live an extraordinary life.
give me another slice."

I remember Seattle Washington last November. A magical place, with rain and water and orange leaves falling for the winter. Mists rising, polite traffic and creativity that hums across the city and opens my inner mind. Seattle was a really impactful weekend. The Rockgrrl conference was full on and I couldn't get enough of it. I spoke on a songwriting panel with veterans in the songwriting world, and I felt I was the lone ranger representing the new frontier of WHAT'S NEXT. It was empowering. Sue Ennis (songwriter for Heart), Wendy Waldman ("Save the Best for Last" Vanessa Williams), Harriet Schock (Helen Reddy) and Jenny Yates (writer for Garth Brooks), and then there was me. "How to write a hit song?" was the question of the day. What is a hit really? Is it the greatness of that piece of prose that touches our hearts and fills our minds with dreams and passion? Or is it how corporate conglomerates push and shake the apple tree that they grew and force consumers to like what they pay them to hear? I say the latter.

I say the music world has changed. We can no longer rest on our laurels of times forgot but be warriors, self-empowered all encompassing Artists with a vision who can be business savvy and know where the real world is... now. I was alone in thought on this subject as my cohorts rattled off their success stories. Notwithstanding, I was inspired by them and their words and I learned something: songwriting, being a songwriter, hasn't changed over the years. We are all still creative spirits channeling the higher self and wanting reaction, an audience. How to find that audience has changed now, that's all. The rest stays the same. Inspiring... Thank you wonderful women.

I went to a few workshops at Rockgrrl. One was about podcasting. I'm so inspired to embrace this new technology. I have already developed 30 podcasts. To think that each and every one of us can become a radio programmer and people can subscribe to our taste in music is just simply amazing.

One of the most beautiful gifts that I received was a Minarik Guitar. I was in the exhibition room and Bill Minarik came over and was enchanted that I was there. He had been a long time fan. He literally handed me an endorsement and asked me to choose an electric guitar. I naturally chose the most beautiful one, a honeyburst Minarik that is 1 out of only 25 special edition honeybursts in the world, (4 were left handed) and they never will be made again. Ecstatic. I've always longed to incorporate electric guitar playing into my life and my live show. I think acoustics are too cumbersome for me and I want to experiment with the melodics of an electric that I have come to know and love so well when producing in the studio. So... it's time to embrace this dream!

I had many gifts this past weekend.

Be open. Be open. Be open to the divine forces, for when you are open, many gifts come to you.

37. It doesn't matter what they Say, good or bad

In the early days of my time in Los Angeles, it was all about "showcasing" one's talents on the Sunset Strip, or anywhere close, to be heard and hopefully "picked up" by a record company, manager or agent. At the least, we all wanted good reviews by the media to stick in our media kit to help promote ourselves to record companies, managers and agents. Just when I thought I had lost hope in "being discovered", and running back to Sydney with my tail between my legs, I received an all out amazing live review of my show at Luna Park by Music Connection magazine, known to be L.A.'s best street music mag. I was so happy I cried. It changed my whole perspective on being here.

I felt like I had a chance, and I soaked up every word the review read. It wrote of my songwriting and performance style, but also about how MTV can't keep her away and if an A&R person didn't sign me within the year, "somebody has dropped the ball". I interpreted it that I was so "hot" that someone had to discover me fast, because if they don't, then they will miss out. I was so caught up in this review, that I actually believed every word of it, for better and for worse. The good part was it inspired me to stay and continue my path here in the States. I knew I had a chance. The bad part was a year went by and there was no MTV and no A&R person. I started to think, "did someone drop the ball? Or... did I?"

Having a great review can really build our self-esteem as Artists. But trying to live up to it can break you apart.

I have gone on to receive many reviews, accolades and awards. My bio and website are full of them, just in case you're curious. But I have learned, through riding the waves of criticism, adoration and the fine line in-between, that none of it is important. It doesn't matter what they say, good or bad, because all of that is part and parcel of the so-called illusion of the entertainment industry. We cannot be dependent on what someone says about us, or doesn't in order to carry on holding the Artistic torch. Ultimately, we as Artists must choose this path because *it's in our nature* not because people love us or think we are fabulous.

When we can become unattached to what people think about us, or say about us, good or bad, then we truly are living with creative success, because only you alone can give yourself the approval and the love you will need to survive this business 'till the end.

It doesn't matter what they Say, good or bad

Whatever someone says or writes about you, although flattering and seemingly true of the subject with which they write about, is not *real*. It's a pampering of your ego, that's all. It can help sometimes, because you can extract some good lines for your bio, to help shape your written story with good describing words, but it's just someone's perspective of you based on their own perception of life in general. Take the press and put it to good marketing use (for everyone else who laps up media reviews as some standard for success), but not you. You don't need a good review to be a successful Artist, or to know if you're going in the right path. So, while it's cool to post a review on your site (I do) for great marketing purposes, meanwhile don't rely on these words to keep you positive, sane, on course, etc. All THAT is up to you, and you alone. Same with bad reviews. Yes, they will come. You get the bad with the good. It's the natural law of the universe. Life can't be perfect all the time. So *knowing* that, it should make you feel even more secure and confident that you can't take these reviews personally. It's just an IS in the world of Art.

When reviews come, just understand that it's just someone's point of view based on their own lives, judgments, stories and experiences. It's *their* experience and it has no relation to who you are, how you got here, or your intention in the world. Just keep doing what you are doing, relying ONLY on your inner strength, confidence and *knowing* that you *are* the master of your own destiny – *not* a victim to circumstance, and circumstantial evidence (someone's words).

When reviews come in for my music or projects that I have created, I thank them, I appreciate it, I may even use it for marketing purposes, but I *don't* believe them or buy into them as facts. I just appreciate them for what they are, good prose.

Here's why: I'll give you an example of how my assistant reacts differently to me in these situations, and how, in the end, my reaction ultimately empowers and saves me. (Don't worry, she knows I'm mentioning this and she is always amazed at how cool I am about it all.) When a great review or letter comes in, she usually jumps up and down with joy and wants to celebrate. She calls me or e-mails me with huge exclamation marks and big smiley faces and is overly excited, that she thinks that one review is going to be my next big opportunity for some magic pie in the sky wonderland of cotton candy clouds we are all going to fall into. I, on the other hand, take the review with appreciation, but then let it go. I usually say, "Yeah, that's nice. Very thoughtful, glad they took the time to respond" or something in that vein. I remain cool, calm and collected. Don't get me wrong: I don't take reviews or praise for granted. No. I'm very appreciative of people who give their time to offer feedback. It's just, I am not so dependent, or influenced, by the feedback as to how the rest of my day will go. I don't like to be swayed either way. Because I know that the bad reviews come in also, and it's all a natural balance in how we operate as Artists.

So, when we get a bad response, review or some negative episode happened, my assistant becomes depressed and saddened, and wants to console me or be consoled. I am still fine. I am still cool, calm and collected. I have learned not to take it personally. I know that whatever happened is not about me, but about that person's own reality, perceptions, expectations and judgments, and I have learned not to buy into that drama. Instead, I take it as feedback and then, swiftly, like the warrior, I cut away and move on.

Not taking things personally is one of the hardest things to do, but it really is the only way. Whether good or bad, I let things roll off me like water on a duck's back. Mind you, I used to be *very* sensitive to criticism and what people say. I guess I'm learning as I get older to not get so caught up in it... and so is my assistant. Whether good or bad, I just keep soldiering on, no matter what, enjoying my creative process that I alone can approve of. It's no one else's right to tell me who I am or what I should be doing. This is my life. And so too, your life, your Art, is yours.

I am more able to survive the ups and downs now because I don't get attached to the ego of wanting praise, or avoiding pain. In fact, ego has left the building long ago. I've come from the school of hard knocks, and that means that through all the good and the bad, I've found the middle ground... the path of least resistance.

On an even higher note, consider this: who's to say that what you do and who you are is complete mastery and genius? How can anyone compete or criticize that when they have no credits of mastery themselves to judge you? And on what merits do we judge mastery? I suggest that we are all masters of our own Art. Art is very difficult to evaluate. I studied Art education for four years. Yep, I have a Bachelor of Education on this subject, and I still can't actually put my finger on how you can rate Art from 1 to 10. You just can't. It's not about the quick exact answer, like math or science with multiple choice. Art is all subjective: held in the eye of the observer. So, what all schools rely on, when evaluating (testing) Art for students, is the process. We try and evaluate the way students approach the process of making Art.

Your live show, your album even, may somewhat constitute an end result of some kind, but in reality, all your performances and projects are manifestations of your ongoing process, your life journey.

On what authority and expertise can a critic's voice persuade you to actually believe their review? It's only based on a brief moment in time, and you're on a perpetual journey of becoming. Take them, leave them, love them, hate them, but no matter what, when it comes to other people's opinions, don't believe them. Just believe in you.

Furthermore, what constitutes a "talent" in the eyes of these music industry execs we are so-called "showcasing" for, waiting to be discovered by them? Do we spend our Artistic lives waiting for these people to "find" us and "mold" us and tell us if we are good or bad, genius or not, deserving of some deal or no deal, or... do we just GET OUT THERE anyway and make it happen with or without them? I think you know the answer. Why wait for someone to "discover" you, when really, you've been discovering yourself for years.

"Happiness is inward, and not outward, and so it does not depend on what we have, but on what we are"
- Henry van Dyke

38. You are your own island

I recently returned from THE most beautiful place: Bermuda. If you haven't been there, I highly recommend it. I was there teaching for the Bermuda Artist and Songwriting Retreat which is sponsored by Songsalive! It's a yearly event and this was the inaugural one.

Richard, our host, picked us up at the airport and we drove along a one lane road (the main road!) from one end of the island to the other. English cut hedges juxtaposed against wild jungles and rainforests, and the ever present turquoise blue water guiding us on our path. Bermuda is still a British colony but has its own government. They have made their Bermudian dollars of equal value to the U.S. dollar, and in fact are completely identical save for the cool colors Bermudians have chosen for their cash.

I had no expectations of Bermuda except that I was going to be on a magical journey, and indeed it was. We arrived at 9 Beaches Resort, which is on the far tip of the long island (it's only 1.5 miles wide). The first thing I noticed was the array of huts (cabanas) all on stilts in the water. Was I in paradise? Apparently this Resort had once been an eco-living place. I couldn't believe the water, and the way this "village" was architecturally designed. Quite impressive. The cabana nestled perfectly on the side of the hill overlooking the water. I really felt like I was on a tropical island. Designed in white and blue cloth, with simple furniture, I ended up living in it for 6 days with peace, tranquility and joy. My view of the ocean gave me solace and inspiration.

For three days, I taught and empowered Artists at the Bermuda Artist and Songwriters Retreat, co-created with Songsalive!, which was held under a huge white tent on the grass near the water. It actually rained for the first 3 days, with the heavens opening up in torrential rain one moment, and then sun the next. Very fickle weather, but all the time it was magical. I felt like we were truly on an isolated piece of property which is so perfect for a retreat. I can't remember when I felt so tranquil as this, yet so energized at the same time.

Magic.

The grass is always greener...

We had roughly fifty participants in the retreat. My part was to work with them on Artist development, empowering the Artists to understand about the music business, marketing and taking their own steps to get out there, so to speak.

One participant, known as Blac, was a talented reggae cross hip hop Artist. He spoke very softly and showed a lot of humility. Most of the time he sat listening and enthused, soaking up everyone's presentations. In my session with the group, when asked about his goals, he meekly put up his hand and offered that he wanted to not only do well as an Artist in his country, but also in America. His dream was to make it in America. It's an interesting phenomenon that happens worldwide, you know. We all want to "make it" somewhere else, because we think it's bigger and better. Now, I understand that the U.S. has a lot that's attractive about it: big population to sell lots of records... the Hollywood glamour. Surely we all want a bit of that, no?

Most Bermudians want that too. They feel isolated because they live in such a small country, a small island in fact. The music scene there is small. But the music is amazing. They have such a cross section of people that the music is diverse and rhythmic, quite marketable for both America and Europe.

I'd have to say the same thing about Australia. I left Australia mostly because I felt that the industry was too small, and the population also, to really have a go, especially as an indie Artist, where you can't necessarily make a huge splash like the majors do, but instead build momentum over time with small markets at a time. In America you can do that with 250 million people. You can market yourself in one area, create some fans, then go to another, build your fan base, and over a few years you can have quite a solid mailing list of fans who love and follow your music.

I've met countless Artists from Australia who seem to land on my doorstep in Los Angeles (as if I'm their long lost sister who can supply them with the Holy Grail) anxious to leave their country behind and find opportunity in America. I often ask them, "What's happening back home these days?" All I get over and over again is, "Oh it's dead. There's nothing happening."

"It's too small, you can't get ahead."

"Just Australian Idols get on the radio and there aren't many radio stations so there's no hope."

I got the same answers from Bermudians. I get the same from Italian Artists, and English Artists. Any Artists from anywhere. Similar theme.

But guess what, I get the same answers from Americans! This is not just a secular phenomenon. It happens worldwide. **Many think the grass is always greener somewhere else.**

So let's get back to Blac in Bermuda. I was critiquing everyone's demos and Blac offered his up for critique. He gave me a 4 disc CD handwritten on the CD face. He did have a professionally designed CD cover though. I listened to the first track and whilst it wasn't an in-your-face hit, being slightly R&B but not quite (when you record in a certain genre you really have to nail the production to make it sound authentic, especially to American ears who invented R&B), it was still a nice song and I thought it would do well in Bermuda. He was talented. I suggested swapping out the first slow track with the second, more up tempo song which seemed to be really, really good. I told him, "good demo, a work in progress, and good luck." I left him at that. He was thankful, ready to work on his material, humbled and sat down in his seat, ready to hear the other critiques.

A bird in the hand...

Here's the hook: a week after I left Bermuda I heard that Blac won the Bermuda Music Award for best dance song. These Awards are by no means small. They are respected worldwide. He won the best award in Bermuda for that very song (the second more up tempo song on the CD that I critiqued, and... phew.. the one I liked) which also had been in high rotation on local commercial radio.

Lessons: *one*, you never know who's going to be in your vicinity (or your own workshop, that's one for me) who come across humble yet are really successful, and two, **you are your own island**.

This means that even though you may want to "make it" somewhere else, or think that somewhere else is better than where you are now, don't ignore the very real possibility that *right where you are has the most magnificent, awesome opportunities and rewards*. It's like owning your own island. Blac may have been holding onto the notion of "making it" in America, but meanwhile on his own "island" he is a star.

Think about where you are right now, soak it in and be thankful for what you have, what you have created, and what you are about to realize in your own backyard.

Be your own island.

A bird in the hand is worth two in the bush.

The silent warrior is in all of us. It's not about war, nor fight and definitely not about struggle.

It's about an inner peace and a whole lot of courage to face all fears in un-chartered waters, finding the path least traveled and at the same time, finding the path of least resistance.

I am a warrior girl and I encourage everyone to tap into their warrior within.

39. What's money got to do with it?

"What's love got to do, got to do with it..." sings Tina Turner. I just love that song. When it comes to a bad relationship, love ain't gonna fix it! You need only yourself. I see the same with money and this funny game of the music business (film business, Arts business... put your word in before 'business' and you get the same feeling).

Money doesn't fix it. You cannot buy happiness and if your dream was to just have lots of money, then what are you going to do with it? Money serves a purpose – it's supposed to come in and go out. It's a by-product of your real work, and it's a tool to create. That's it. Money will afford you luxuries but the more you spend will decrease your wealth. Wealth is what you spend, not what you make.

The language of money

This is an interesting chapter to place after discussing 'detachment'. I was sitting around the coffee table with a few Artists one day and one of them brought up an issue she was facing: her "struggle with money". She clearly spoke about the fact that she constantly faces money issues when it comes to creating and promoting her music, and it's always at the forefront of her mind. "I have a struggle with money", she proclaimed.

I immediately understood why. You see, language plays a vital role in influencing what actually happens to us. If you portray a "struggle" with something, then struggle you will have. If you see that the only relationship you have with money is one that is stressful, negative and emotionally fighting, then that is what you will attract. I have always promoted the "I AM" theory, which means that by empowering yourself through words, e.g. I AM a talented, professional Artist... it helps attract that into your life. So, in reverse, if you empower the words "I have a struggle...", then indeed you will struggle.

Perhaps a more positive statement to make would be "I am working towards having an increasing abundance of money." See how this changes it? The more you can vocalize positive, healthy statements about money, without having to lie, the less of a problem you will have with it. But even then, saying you are "working towards" something, says that's exactly what you'll get... "working towards", and not actually "having".

There is a fine line with money and language. You don't want to say you have a struggle with it, yet how do you physically get out of the struggle and be abundant? Let's get real here! We can't just all go around saying "I have money and I'm abundant" when it doesn't correlate with the bank account.

Money, wanting money, or not having enough money is the biggest question I get when I conduct an Artist Empowerment workshop. It's easy for me to respond, "well, if you change your language it will all work out", but obviously there's more to it, to actualize financial abundance.

Mindset: changing your language isn't enough. You have to be ready internally for a change. Years and years of negative build up can take a long time to change your mindset; your thought processes. You may *say* positive things about money, but inside feel the lack of it. Maybe you had a tough upbringing, always doing without, always tightening the belt.

Maybe you can't think beyond the 9 to 5 that weighs you down because you don't like the job. When you don't like the job, then you tend to not like the money you make. Negative energy transfers over to your money making skills. For example, if you worked at a bank and hated your job, and you weren't making much money by the hour, then your whole feeling about working might feel hard, and the money you make may feel like it was so hard to earn, that if you even thought for a moment that you could earn money elsewhere, you feel hardship in just the concept of doing that.

So it's about changing your attitude about money, and making money, and ultimately, get to a place where you're not thinking so hard about making the money, but just focusing on making the Art.

Focus mostly on creating

Let's look at money and your Art. What's money got to do with making Art anyway? Let's take a really good look at this. A wise person once said to me, "Gilli, all you need to focus on is creating. Create good Art. Don't worry about the money. It will come. If you focus on creating money, you'll get all the obstacles in the world trying to create your Art."

Remove money as the objective in your life, and just create. Create Art. Money comes. Easy. Right? Well, not for those who feel they need lots and lots of money to make their Art (or distribute it). So in these changing economic times, I suggest that as Artists we can think outside the box, and learn to create, produce, market and distribute with less money, or little money, rather than thinking we need a million dollars first. Let the millions come after you make the Art! This might be easy for me to write about and I totally understand the difficulty in absorbing this, with the debt collector knocking on your door, but let me put it another way:

Again, wealth is what you spend, not what you make.

So if you reduce your spending, all 'round (not just in Art making, but in all areas of your life), cut up those extra credit cards, and budget for the week (really... write a budget down), then you minimize the overheads. You may still make the same amount of money you did before, but you're spending less; hence, more savings.

There is no point spending the huge amount of Dollars, Euros or Yen on producing music these days when every Tom, Dick or Harry can create music on a Mac in their bedroom, and every Jane, Karen or Jenny are uploading their songs onto MySpace, You Tube, iTunes, with no inventory costs and quick download options. This world has become instantaneous. That means, you can make it quick, upload it quick, and sell it quick. Unfortunately, gone are the days where you spend months and a ton of money on a huge, big budget music production. So thankfully you don't need lots of money to do that.

And that goes for the rest of the music making and promoting area: distribution and marketing is taking on new forms online and for independent Artists, you can find ways to promote yourself without the big bucks.

Understandably, you do need to spend money to make money. You'll need some to invest in the *creation* of your Art (make a film, record an album) plus all the marketing and promotion that goes into that. Don't forget education along the way including the occasional research, consultations and advice. But this is ALL an investment into yourself and your product, with the prospect of a return. This is a business decision, not flippant spending. It's all part of the bigger vision. So budget yourself, do the math, and enjoy the process.

My recommendation is the do it all spend thrift; *live and create within your means*. Then, when the seed starts to grow and you gain fans, industry awareness, and people starting to believe in you, and you're making money from the different diversified talents that you have, then use that money (invest back into your business) to build upon what you started. Focus on making great music. Just get out there and plant the seeds around. All of a sudden, over time, you'll see money coming in when you least expected it, and hopefully lots of it.

That my friends, is called abundance, and even better when it becomes **passive income**. You see, *passive* income is the best income you can have. It's income you receive when you don't notice it; when you aren't counting the minutes in the hour to get that $10. It's usually from royalties, and digital distribution income, and other streams that come in, without you working the hour for it (though you did a lot of homework and ground work to set it up).

Exercise: managing your money

1. Write down 5 ways you can reduce your expenses in your life. This could be either in "extras" you buy, or eliminating credit cards, or cutting out certain luxuries you don't need.

2. Tally up the money you think you can reduce in a month. Then, open up a savings bank account which will be just for your music and Art. Put the money you didn't spend on other "extras" into your savings account.

3. At the end of 6 months, see how much money is in your savings account, that you would have spent on other areas.

All you need to focus on is creating.

Create good Art.

Don't worry about the money. It will come. If you focus on creating money, you'll get all the obstacles in the world trying to create your Art.

40. What legacy will you leave?

When I was in line behind a loud, boisterous cowboy hat clad man, who was speaking to a boy in his early twenties who just claimed he had brought a 1976 Gran Torino, I knew I was heading to the South. This was a full flight and I knew that no matter where I stood in line to board the plane, I wasn't going to escape the cowboy's hollering. I knew that I had to expect certain personalities when traveling and so I just plugged in my earphones and drowned it out with some peaceful music on my iPod.

I love going on my "music Meccas" as I call them. At least once a year if not three times, I send myself to an exciting destination that always includes music, fun, new friends and lots of adventure. This time it was Nashville, Tennessee, home of country music, and where all songwriters are either getting cuts, or giving you business cards and networking in the hope to get a cut. (A "cut" traditionally is when one of your songs is chosen for a well known Artist's record.)

I was at a barbeque the first afternoon surrounded by these songwriters, and the typical conversation was, "oh yeah, I'm just banking my first mechanical royalty check this week", or "I have five pending mechanicals", or "I'm writing with someone and we hope to get a cut". It's all about songwriting, and more specifically, making business from the songs. Any where you go, and anything you do, is aligned with writing and then meeting the right people to further your songs. No one writes just for the sake of writing. It is a business town, always has been, always will be.

I had been to Nashville before. Once in 2002 when I actually conducted my first seminar for Artists about DIY (doing it yourself) at a music convention run by David Hooper (one of the forefronts of the DIY movement, if you call it such). I also spoke that time at the Songwriters Guild of America (SGA) to songwriters about the same notion, and they were completely shocked at the time, that one could actually run their own business or publishing company. They all assumed that one needed to be signed to a publishing company to actually get any success from one's songs, rather than actually have one's own company. What a concept! What I spoke about in '02 was revolutionary because practically no one was doing it independently. The second trip was in '03 when I was flown there by Jeff Young, ex-guitarist of metal rock band, Megadeth, to record vocals on a song he wrote with well-known Brazilian Artist Badi Assad. We recorded it at Michael Wagener's studio (Alice Cooper, Janet Jackson, Queen, Ozzy Osbourne... just to name a few). Suffice to say, that I've had some cool trips to Nashville. Cut to this year and I couldn't believe it had been 6 years since I'd been to this unique music town.

This year, 2009, I was in Nashville to be honored by the non-profit women in the Arts music organization, Indiegrrl, for my contributions to the Arts and music, with a lifetime membership, and I also spoke at their conference. It was truly a great

What legacy will you leave?

10 days. I also got to speak at the new IndieConnect seminars about Artist entrepreneurship, and sang a few songs each night at songwriter rounds around town. I seemed to be the token pop Artist amongst a sea of Tim McGraw sound-alikes. No matter what, I was enamored by the notion that Nashville catered to the most important aspect in the music industry: the song. For without the song, there is no business. This whole town revolves around writing songs, writing with the right writers to write songs, and pitch to the right people who can place songs with the right Artists (thereabouts making "a cut").

A lot has happened in the 6 years since visits. Now it's standard that Artists are indie, or do it themselves (DIY) and I don't want to think I may have been a trail blazer in that department, but I can at least remarkably say, "I'M STILL HERE". It's all about the journey, really, and that's the most important thing as an Artist: to enjoy the process of living it. Then hopefully, when it all ends, that wonderful, blissful day when we all sail to the sky, Heaven, reincarnate or whatever you believe your body and/or soul does…. You can look back on your life and say: I've done something. I've left a legacy.

Legacy: The values, principles and wisdom of a well-lived life. I like that. I saw that on a website as a definition for legacy.

What will be your legacy? What will you leave behind? Will you have made an impact somehow? Will people remember you for something significant? Perhaps it will be your songs? Perhaps it will be your message? Perhaps it will be your contribution to the greater picture of the world? Who knows?

What is my legacy? I thought it was to share my songs and be a well known, talented Artist. I believe my songs are timeless and they do send a message. That's for sure. I would hope that they will live on way past me. That's why I spend so much time getting them right, in writing and in producing them. They are like babies, with their own lives, really. But more and more I feel my legacy is about being a role model for other Artists to define and master their destiny. I hope to be remembered as someone who walked their talk, who just 'got out there' and wasn't afraid to show up and DO It in life. I hope to be remembered as someone who lived her truth, lived with passion, pursued excellence and was constantly creative. I hope to inspire others by how I lived my life.

Did you know that Vincent Van Gogh only sold one painting in his lifetime? Yet he left an enormous legacy. Why? Because it wasn't about how much money he made in his life (though he probably wished he made more money, as he lived on the poverty line). His legacy was large because a) He was a prolific Artist. He painted many paintings and every day was about being creative. b) He was innately talented. You can't bluff talent. You either have it or you don't. He had it. c) He spoke his truth. He lived his pain and emotions through his Art. It was very evident in his subjects, colors, and swirling lines. His truth is what made him unique, and what we remember about him the most. In making music, or doing your Art, it is crucial to always capture your personal essence. People will talk about you, promote you, critique you, applaud you, or idolize you. But they will do that especially if you are TRUE in your Artistry. Live your Art.

When you're standing on the mountain looking back, that's when you appreciate the journey. In the meantime, just live your Art and speak your truth. Let the masses react, decide, glorify or judge. It doesn't matter. Live your truth, because this is the legacy you'll leave behind.

Exercise: my live legacy

Write down all the things you have accomplished in your life. Don't assess them based on what others would deem to be successful. Base them on your personal perspective about yourself. They may be major awards and huge accolades. Or they may be small things, like… finished writing 50 songs; or survived the music business for 10 years so far!

1.

2.

3.

4.

5.

6.

7.

8.

9.

10.

"Any situation that you find yourself in, is an outward reflection of your inner state of beingness."

-El Morya

41. Waiting for the waves

Have you ever surfed? I've body surfed since I was a kid living on the Sydney beaches. But I never actually surfed with a board, though I have often watched, for hours, those who did. Now living in California, I have gone from one surf heaven to another.

It's an interesting concept, surfing. You might be wondering why I chose the word "concept" over the word "sport". For the sake of this chapter, I'm going to call it a "concept" because the Art of surfing could almost reveal one of the secrets to life: the ability to wait.

We live in an age where we are seduced by instantaneous gratification; where we demand, and are fed, our wants and needs as simultaneous as the moment we think of them; and we are easily disappointed when we don't get what we want as instantaneously. Media, television, e-mail, and a new generation connected to it all intravenously from a young age, have created a society that has forgotten what it was like to wait for "good things to come."

But most importantly, enjoy the moment while you can. You see, if you just sit there waiting, you'll see that life will just pass you by and time goes by really fast. Life isn't always easy. There will be the ups and the downs. We'll be tried, tested and thrown into the lion's den. But we wouldn't grow or learn if we didn't have the test in life. Remember that change is constant, so knowing that, enjoy every second you have.

While you're out on that surf board, waiting for that next big wave, take a look around. Can you see the ocean? Close your eyes and visualize that moment. What do you see in your mind? How do you feel? The warm sun on your back? Your toes cold in the salty sea? Can you taste the salt on your tongue? Enjoy this moment, because it's the best damn moment you're going to have. Look back on your past, let it all go, and move into your future with excitement and joy. This is your life. Live it! Now, start kicking. Fast. Go catch that wave!

My mission from here on out, is to continue to **STAY INSPIRED** in reaching my fullest potential as a human being, and as an Artist, which includes being out in the world, no matter what happens, and pursue excellence in everything I do. It is important to me to really, fully, enjoy my journey because I know that all the "stuff", the trappings, that come with success (whilst great by-products and quick, feel good things) are not what really make me happy. The feeling of being inspired by who I am and what I want IS EVERYTHING to me.

I believe that you can be as ambitious as you want, and reach for the highest of heights. Why? Because this is what keeps you inspired. Without a goal, a dream: there is no point. I believe in seeking no one else's approval but your own, when it comes to what makes you truly happy. The Artist's life is a life long journey. You're not in it for a short time, and it doesn't matter how old you are. Being an Artist is for life. So enjoy this journey, wherever it leads you. Don't be influenced by the commercial aspects of success. If you don't get on the radio, or get a Grammy award, that doesn't mean you have failed. *There is no such thing as failure, except in your own mind.*

I believe that once you master the notion of ***living in abundance***, then abundance comes and continues to come to you your whole life.

It is very freeing once we let go of future goals having to turn out a certain way, and *start living IN THE MOMENT*.

Tapping into the journey, the day to day process, provides us with way more rewards and joy, than unrealized future dreams. Being an Artist is a lifelong journey of discovery. It's about living in the NOW and enjoying the process of creating. It's about living with passion.

Have no expectations. Define your life, your successes and your goals by your own terms, on a daily basis. Be different, unique and take risks with your creativity. Have no fear. There is nothing to be afraid of, unless we trap ourselves with unrealistic expectations and unrequited objectives.

Set yourself FREE to be the Artist you want to be. Be open, be real, be you.

42. The end of the beginning

I just got off the call from a session with one of my most enlightened Artist clients. She literally gave me the ending to my book. I was typing madly as she poured out her heart and soul about where she was at in her life. I related. It sunk in. It inspired me to write.

Here is where it's at folks:

Live your life like you are at the beginning of the road, and let go of the oars and flow...

If my only priorities were to sell CDs, make tons of money and get everyone to love me, I will make myself sick, stressed and deeply unhappy.

If my priorities are to enjoy my journey; tell a good story whether on a CD, live at a show, or in my writings; enjoy the creative process; learn and discover the world; and INSPIRE others along the way – then it's a different life, a GREAT life, a REAL life... my life. I know that I'm an Artist for life. I have much to say, and I am going to have a great time "having a go" and making it all worthwhile. The CD sales, radio play, Grammy awards and Newsweek interviews come and go. The JOURNEY of being the Warrior Artist, and the savvy successful Artist Entrepreneur LIVES ON.

- Continually step back and take a broader view of your life and your dreams.

- Have a broader mission that isn't just about you, but how you want to inspire others.

- Lead your life with dignity like a good Warrior Artist Entrepreneur does, knowing the universe will provide you all the freedom you deserve.

- Don't sweat the small stuff: let go and let it come. Allow it to unfold.

- Trust in yourself, your heart, your passion and the universe.

- Patience is key.

The end of the beginning

- ⊥ Don't take yourself so seriously. There's way more fun in laughter and it's quite entertaining.

- ⊥ Don't take it all so personally. Other people's stuff is their subjective view on reality. The less you emotionally take things personally, and listen more to your own advice, the better off you'll be.

- ⊥ Know you have to have climbed the mountain, and really feel the rocks and stones along the way, to understand what it truly feels like to succeed, and get to a place of joy. It doesn't happen overnight. It's a lifelong journey of becoming.

- ⊥ You are the actor in your play. You created your play called "your life". Enjoy it.

- ⊥ Who has the gold? You do. Be the creative explorer in your life and know you are the master of your destiny.

It's not going to be easy. It's challenging and uncomfortable. But you will feel a sense of accomplishment and satisfaction every step of the way. You will always be moving forward.

I congratulate you for reading to this page, and I wish you the utmost success, joy and creative excellence in your Artistry and life.

Thank you for stepping up to the plate to set an example for the rest.
SHINE ON!

Now,

JUST GET OUT THERE

There will come a
time when you
believe everything is
finished. That will
be the beginning.

Louis L'Amour

Flat line

I woke up and I spent the day
asleep.
Numb to my internal dreaming
I infused coffee like a drug to pump
my blood to zone.
Click click clack on the keyboard.
Hours
went by. I had died
inside.
Tick tick tock went my internal clock.
Years went by.
Letting go of vivid creativity
no more burning.
I self-medicate and watch my passion
Fry.
Until one night I saw the
light.
Surrounded by kindred talent
they spoke their work
and rapped their purpose
and knew their service
to mankind.
I woke up.
I am awake and it's
TIME to live the vision.
take it to the next level of
creation.
No more incubation.
It's not about one thing but
MANY things. Art is all
round all encompassing.
I live and breathe the floor boards
I dance
I look into the lens and let go of defense
I have the energy to
be all that I am to be.
No more flat line.
It's time. To.
Do. It.
　　　© gilli moon

Bibliography

Dyer, Dr. Wayne W. *The Power of Intention*. Hay House, 2005.

Balter, Gaylah. *Clean Your Clutter, Clear Your Life*. Learning Tree Books, 2001.

Cameron, Julia. *The Right To Write*. New York: Penguin Putnam Inc, 1998.

Carlisi, Jeff &Lipson, Dan. *JAM! Amp Your Team, Rock Your Business*. Jossey-Bass, 2009.

Clifton, Donald, O. and Newlson, Paula. *Soar With Your Strengths*. New York: Dell Publishing, 1992.

Davidson, Jeff. *The 60 Second Organizer*. Adams Media, 2008.

De Bono, Dr. Edward. *I am Right You are Wrong*. London: Penguin Books, 1991.

The Daily Guru - Higher Awareness blog. (Offer inspiring, thought-provoking self development programs to help you clearly understand how life and natural laws work, whilst enhancing intuition and creating the future you desire. For more information: www.thedailyguru.com/higherawareness.htm

Folkman, Martin. *The Musicians Atlas*. New Jersey: Music Resource Group, 2010. www.musiciansatlas.com/songsalive.asp

Fowler Wainwright International. *Circle of Personal Perspective Exercise* and *Self Discovery Exercise*. (Trains and certifies motivated individuals to provide the finest in life and business coaching through the use of its easy-to-learn, yet highly effective system of results-driven coaching.) For more information visit: www.fowlerwainright.com

Hamblin, Adrian R. "7 Tips To A Successful Independent CD Release." Ezine Articles, ezinearticles.com, 2010.

Henderson, Dean and Vestman, John. *Marketing Your Music - 10 Helpful Tips*. www.johnvestman.com, 2001.

Kennedy, Dan S. *The Ultimate Marketing Plan*. MA: Adams Media Avon, 2006.

Knopper, Steve. *Appetite for Self-Destruction*. New York, NY: Free Press/Simon & Schuster, Inc, 2009.

Mendelsohn, Ron. "Should You Sign With A Non-Exclusive Retitled Library?", *Production Music Association*. Studio City, CA: www.pmamusic.com, 2010.

O'Neil, William J. *Investor's Business Daily*. Los Angeles, CA: Investor's Business Daily, 2010.

Slessor, Kenneth. *Poems*. Sydney: Angus & Robertson, 1944.

Schneider, Bruce D. *Know Your Purpose* (audio seminar). iPEC, 2009.

Songsalive!, Articles www.songsalive.org/articles (member log in required).

Spellman, Peter and Cool, Dave. *Your Successful CD Release: Market Planning for Singer-Songwriters*. Boston: MBS Business Media, 2007.

Tolle, Eckhar. *The Power of Now: A Guide to Spiritual Enlightenment*. New World Library, 2004.

Wimble, David. *Indiebible*. Big Meteor Publishing, 2010. www.indiebible.com/sa

Wimble, David. *Indie Venue Bible*. Big Meteor Publishing, 2010. www.indievenuebible.com/songsalive

Yamada, Kitsuki. "The Way of the Warrior: Bushido". *The Last Samurai*.

Zelinski, Ernie J. *The Lazy Person's Guide to Success – How to Get What You Want Without Killing Yourself For It*. Berkeley CA: Ten Speed Press, 2002.

BE OPEN. BE OPEN. BE OPEN TO THE DIVINE FORCES, FOR WHEN YOU ARE OPEN, MANY GIFTS COME TO YOU.

Acknowledgements

I wish to thank a few people who have contributed to not only the making of this book, but the making of me, the warrior girl, who above all through the harsh world of business and conflict, she navigates with peace, love and creativity.

Jeffrey Walker, my life partner and talented writer that you are, thank you for the joy you bring, and for being my closest counsel when it comes to all things. Mum and Dad, all my life you have supported and encouraged me to be great and fly. Without that kind of parenting, it makes it rough sailing for those who want to be creative explorers. Ernie Campagna, you continue to amaze me with your calm wisdom, deep respect and faith in everything that I do. Kristi Page, thank you for always reminding me I'm human beyond being an Artist, and am loved. Karen Borger, your dedication and enthusiasm to the Arts inspires me so much. It's lovely to watch you in your element. Jennifer Julian, your ability to be the student of life is something we can all learn from. Steffen Franz, you have been indeed an inspiration since releasing "the stillness" album, and the very fact that you still believe music can be sold, (not just given away) is inspiring. We need more positive people like you in the music biz. Moses Avalon, you may not know it, but our little conversation at PF Chang's one day truly helped me understand how to value myself in the business world, and I appreciate that. Mary and Dick Schiendler, I cannot thank you enough for your constant support and love, and your wisdom in the spiritual plane coupled with the financial and business acumen has really been of great value. Ashish Kapur, whether you realize it or not, your leadership and support of who I am, has not only inspired me, but taught me a lot. I realize that what I speak about for Artists can traverse into the corporate arena, where any team or business needs that little bit of inspiration to get the job done. I love your work ethic. Thanks for showing me a world that is cutting edge and new. Deborah Bishop, thanks for coming into the Warrior Girl Music fold and rolling up your sleeves with a "can do" spirit!

Anders Jermstad, thanks for a masterful edit on this book, and for turning it around so soon. You definitely have a good 'eye'!

There are a few organizations I wish to acknowledge this book:

Fowler Wainwright International – an extraordinary professional certified coaching program that I trained with, and who have provided some useful exercises for this book, used by permission. www.fowlerwainright.com

Ariel Publicity and Ariel Hyatt: true inspirations and thanks for teaching an old dog new tricks in the marketing world of "new media".

Songsalive! – I co-founded this organization in 1997 with Roxanne Kiely. It is now the largest international non-profit organization supporting, promoting and educating songwriters and composers worldwide. I thank Dave Harvey for steering the U.S. helm, and Roxanne Kiely for her undying passion and fortitude as my partner. www.songsalive.org

Artistalive.com – my Artist community for enriching, inspiring and fostering Artist entrepreneurs , plus WarriorArtistcoaching.com. I thank all my Artist clients, for I have learned more than they realize in the coaching environment. Sometimes I wonder, who's coaching who? They amaze me for their ability to be open to new things and find new ways to approach their careers.

Also, Thanks everyone who has brightened the gilli moon flame around the world, whether it be my writings, songs, music, teachings, or just plain LOVE!

WE NEED MORE LOVE IN THIS WORLD. HUG SOMEONE RIGHT NOW. Go on, I dare ya!

About Gilli Moon

Australia's **Gilli Moon** is an Artist, Author, Motivational Speaker and Entrepreneur, with a ceaseless contribution to the creative and business communities at large.

Gilli has become a beacon for artists around the world, inspired and motivated by Gilli's story as an **Artist** herself. She is constantly creating projects for her own music and Arts passions, as well as for others.

First and foremost, Gilli Moon is an illustrious, energetic **poly-media Artist** and songwriter, with multifaceted albums and dynamic live shows that have touched music lovers worldwide, garnering high praise from the most jaded of critics. Her restless creativity and rebellious nature continually urge the Artist to push the envelope when writing a song, recording in the studio, on stage, in business and with whatever she touches. For the past 10 years she has been one of Australia's most influential and iconic Artists, forging an independent path before anyone knew what "indie" was. Gilli has produced and released 6 studio music albums of her original music, to critical acclaim, written and released hundreds of songs, winning songwriting and Artist awards and licensed to film and television shows, and has performed around the world many times.

Gilli has received **numerous press** for her courage, power and dynamic energy as an Artist and inspiration for other Artists, and has worked with other highly respected, prominent Artists including Simple Minds, Placido Domingo and Eric Idle (Monty Python). Recently she was interviewed on Australia's 60 Minutes and in the International Newsweek magazine as a pioneer and leader in the independent music business; been featured alongside Aimee Mann in discussing their mutual success in the indie music scene in Music Connection Magazine; and has had music at No. 1 on many Internet and traditional radio stations. She is constantly featured in the media, online, and radio with her music and outstanding achievements. Just Google her!

Gilli **performs and tours** around the world as an Artist and is constantly creating projects for her own music and Arts passions, as well as for others. She is the CEO of her own record company, artist development and production house, **Warrior Girl Music**, she has produced and released over 20 Artists' albums as well as music compilations., and in '07, she co-founded and co-produced the inaugural Los Angeles Women's Music Festival, featuring over 60 artists and attracting more than 3,000 on the day, raising funds for animal rescue.

Inspired to make a difference in the music industry for songwriters, Gilli co-founded **Songsalive!**, back in 1997, which is now, over ten years later, the largest internationally based non-profit 501(c)(3) songwriters' organization.

With a Bachelor of Education, and **certified as a Professional Coach**, Gilli coaches emerging and professional Artists in music and artist development. She is constantly **invited to speak** at various music conferences and workshops around the world about her story as an independent Artist, and she provides tips and tools on how independent Artists can create success in their own careers. She also delivers workshops for Actors, Dancers, and any individual interested in pursuing the Arts as a profession. Her two most successful workshops are "The Path to Artist Empowerment", and "The Successful Artist Entrepreneur", both of which are highly requested by many International Music Conferences, as well as conducting them at her own Artist Retreats, called "Artist Alive".

Complimenting this, she has written a **motivational book** for Artists of all genres called *"I AM A Professional Artist - the Key to Survival and Success in the World of the Arts"* based on her experiences in the music and general Arts businesses as an Artist and entrepreneur, and now *"Just Get Out There"*. She has written many Articles about the Music Business, Creativity & Artistry and Self-Empowerment in the Arts.

Gilli is constantly creating Artistic projects and nurturing other Artists along the way with her seminars and writings.

Visit her websites at
www.justgetoutthere.net – online updates and information about this book;
www.gillimoon.com as an artist;
www.artistalive.com artist coaching and resources member site;
www.warriorgirlmusic.com for her company pursuits;
www.artistdevelopmentcoach.com for her artist coaching;
www.warriorcreativecoaching.com for personal business coaching; and
www.songsalive.org for her Songsalive! songwriters' non-profit organization.

Follow her: www.twitter.com/artistdev www.twitter.com/gillimoon
www.facebook.com/gillimoonmusic

Join newsletter at www.warriorgirlmusic.com/enews
Contact Gilli www.warriorgirlmusic.com/contact

Also by Gilli Moon:
I AM A Professional *Artist - The Key To Survival And Success In The World Of The Arts*
The Path to Artist eMPoWeRment - Workshop on CD
The Stillness – Music CD
Skillz - Music CD (with J. Walker)
extraOrdinary life - Music CD
Woman - Music CD
Temperamental Angel - Music CD
Girl in the Moon - Music CD

www.warriorgirlmusic.com/store

About Gilli's Coaching

Warrior Girl Music
Artist Development Coaching and Creative Life Coaching

Apart from being an Artist, author and record label owner, I am an Artist development coach and life coach, who coaches Artists and individuals across all genres of creativity, including musicians, singers, songwriters, actors, dancers, writers, producers and anyone who wants to unleash their creativity. **We work together** to build your career, **achieve your goals**, develop skills, and empower your talent towards a career and life you've always imagined. ~ Gilli Moon, Coach (see back page for bio).

Coaching is conducted through **one-on-one sessions*** where the coach helps you focus on objectives, goals and processes, and achieve them faster than if you worked alone. A coach helps you to identify what you want in life and suggests strategies and tactics that will **take you from 'where you are now' to 'where you want to be'.**

My sessions are tailored around you, and where you are at in your life, **building in strategies and goals** to help you **become the person you have always wanted to be.** Whether you are a **beginner Artist, professional Artist**, or just an **individual interested in exploring your creativity**, I promise these sessions will light a fire in your heart & mind, and steer you on a positive, dynamic and action filled direction towards a higher purpose, greater passion and successful life.

* Artist Development Coaching Sessions include consultation, discussion, demo listening, creative and production guidance, artistic feedback, stage tips, personal and artistic direction, music release marketing and promotional tips, tools & resources, specially designed activities and answers to all your questions.

Creative Life Coaching Sessions are for individuals (who don't typically call themselves "Artists"), who want to learn how to think outside the box and realize their personal dreams and life goals in a creative way, tapping into their Artistic talents and passions. Includes consultation, discussion, personal direction, tools & resources, specially designed activities and answers to all your questions.

Aspects of the sessions

I've designed these sessions to really impact your career development and success by working together on your inner Artistic self (dreams, goals, visions, "who you are" and where you want to be"), combined with your outer projections (your actions, your image, marketing and promotion, career path and basically, your entire mode of being).

Together we:

- Work out your path – highest dreams fitting into a tangible direction and a plan that you can follow and achieve
- Create a monthly schedule and to-do list so you get things done, working deeply with how you manage your time, and how you balance your priorities

> Having sessions each month maximizes your career and personal Artistic development: staying accountable on your goals, building your marketing strategy together, and so much more. Consider me as your mentor, consultant, but most importantly your coach, just like a coach in a "game" - building the dream, working on the strategy and you playing the game with excellence, results and success.

- Build a plan to create the life and career you want
- Work on overcoming blocks, fears and obstacles
- Create abundance in everything you do
- Work on relationship building with establishing connections and capitalizing on who you already know
- Keep accountable your goals and visions on a monthly basis when we meet each time

part personal

- The whole person: mental, emotional, and spiritual health and synergy.
- Being the "creator" in your life: manifesting joy and enjoying the process, the journey of your life
- Improve your creativity, intelligence, and organizational abilities
- Tap into your overall sense of well-being and inner peace, as well as inner self-esteem, beating fears and creating confidence
- Create the map of your future, making tangible goals that lead you to success. Defining success on your own terms that creates personal satisfaction and a sense of fulfillment that comes with endowing success

part creative
- Musicians, singers, painters, dancers, authors, actors etc.
- Unleashing creative talents & defining your creative strengths and ambitions
- Songwriting feedback, performance development, stage presence, live performance skills, movement; confidence, awareness and being dynamic
- Stage, microphone, band work
- Work on your current audition vocal piece, role or show. All styles of music

part business
- Career building & guidance, goal making, image defining, name branding, planning and positive motivation
- Creating and projecting your 10 year plan through visualization, strategies and writing
- Marketing plans, artist branding, business direction, getting into "the biz", promotional campaigns and increasing public and industry awareness
- From creating to presenting, producing, exhibiting and promoting
- Getting deals, doing business, being out there

Notes & Journal pages

Breinigsville, PA USA
04 October 2010
246596BV00001B/8/P